Mental Retardation

ITS SOCIAL CONTEXT AND SOCIAL CONSEQUENCES

Bernard Farber

*Institute for Research on Exceptional
Children and Department of Sociology
University of Illinois*

HOUGHTON MIFFLIN COMPANY
BOSTON *New York Atlanta Geneva, Ill. Dallas Palo Alto*

PRINTED IN THE U.S.A.

EDITOR'S INTRODUCTION

While many books have been written about the mentally retarded from the viewpoints of biology, psychology, and education, few have regarded the retarded individual as presenting a social problem for study by sociologists or anthropologists.

In the past, books on mental retardation have been based on the premise that the retarded are somehow psychologically different from the rest of the population. Professor Farber, however, regards the mentally retarded as part of a surplus population and therefore a social phenomenon. Given the organization of modern industrial society, the presence of the mentally retarded in a surplus population is the logical outcome of the selection processes in its educational, political, and economic institutions. According to Professor Farber, each of these institutions requires a surplus of personnel in a constant sifting to obtain a good fit between a person and position in social organization. The label of "mentally retarded" is a means for making legitimate the designation of these people as a surplus population.

Professor Farber examines the kinds of labels applied to the retarded and the factors which account for variations in prevalence figures. He goes on to deal with the effects of the mentally retarded on social relationships. These relationships include: family life, the school, the community, and life in residential institutions.

Because of its sociological perspective, this book covers topics that have been either treated very briefly or ignored entirely in other works on mental retardation. These include a discussion of techniques for determining prevalence, social factors in prevalence, consequences of labeling persons as mentally retarded, social movements — including parent groups — and the social organization of residential institutions. In this way, Professor Farber's treatment broadens our understanding of mental retardation and its implications.

Perhaps more significant are the solutions implied by Professor Farber's analysis. Inasmuch as the problems deriving from mental retardation are based in the social structure, only a profound change in society can be effective in solving them. Professor Farber does not deny the value of educational and welfare programs in ameliorating the specific hardships of the retarded. However, since it is posited that there will always be an organizational surplus in industrial society, Professor Farber believes that these measures cannot eliminate the social basis for mental retardation. According to him, the major problems associated with mental retardation will be solved when personal growth rather than institutional efficiency is the goal of the economic and educational institutions in society. Of all the ameliorating programs, change in the value structure is probably the most difficult to attain. Farber suggests that "just how serious we are in wanting to solve social problems relating to surplus populations (and in particular the mentally retarded) will determine exactly how much effort and sacrifice we are willing to undergo in order to revise modern society." He thus sees the problems of the retarded, the poverty-stricken ethnic minorities, the untrained immigrant, and the indigent sick and aged as having a common element (that of being part of a surplus population), and he proposes that if we are to solve our national problems, our ideas about society and its social institutions must change.

Educators, psychologists, social workers, and sociologists will discover a fresh and rewarding treatment of the mentally retarded in modern society in Professor Farber's book.

SAMUEL A. KIRK

PREFACE

Visualize a world in which all of the work of educational, political, and economic enterprises is carried on by machines. Even critical decisions might be handled by computers. In such a world, almost all men would be superfluous; there would be no slots for them in these enterprises.

This book is concerned with a segment of the population that is now superfluous. Without this population, the major institutions of society would continue to operate much as they do now. Yet, this population cannot be wiped out. In one sense, the major institutions of the society need them. In industrial society, there is an attempt to maintain rationality in the selection of personnel to fit the slots in offices connected with the major educational, political, and economic institutions. This rational selection requires a surplus of personnel to carry on a constant sifting to obtain a good fit between person and slot. The mentally retarded can be regarded as a prototype of this organizational surplus.

Implications of these statements about the mentally retarded will be discussed in the various chapters of this book. Part One is concerned with the prevalence and development of mental retardation. Chapter 1 describes the mentally retarded as a surplus population in both primitive and contemporary societies. It emphasizes the role of the requirements of urbanized, industrial society in having a surplus population, with the implication that the size of this surplus will increase. The label "mentally retarded" is regarded as a means of making legitimate the inclusion of people in this superfluous segment of the population. Chapter 2 covers the relationship between definitions of mental retardation as deviance and incompetence. Chapter 3 deals with the general prevalence of mental retardation in modern societies. Chapter 4 then covers social factors in the variation of the prevalence of the retarded population. Chapter 5 discusses cultural variations as they may retard intellectual development valued in modern society. In Part Two, the emphasis of the book changes from the production of the mentally retarded as a surplus population to the treatment of the retarded in contemporary society. Chapter 6 views attempts at handling problems related to mental retardation in terms of social movements. Chapter 7 concerns itself with families with mentally retarded persons. Chapter 8 is about the social organization of residential institutions. Chapter 9 describes the role of the mentally retarded in the school and the community. Chapter 10, the final chapter, presents a recapitulation of the analysis and reviews some programs for reform.

Acknowledging assistance in preparing a book is like sending wedding invitations — invariably someone who should have been included is omitted. Persons who commented on portions of this manuscript include Ernest Q. Campbell at Vanderbilt University, Samuel A. Kirk, Michael Lewis, David L. Harvey, Robert Heiny, Jerry M. Lewis, Charles Mindel, and Mrs. Jill Quadagno, all at the University of Illinois, and my wife, Annette. Louis Schneider, now at the University of Texas, and Daniel Glaser at the University of Illinois, also influenced my ideas regarding mental retardation as a social phenomenon. The National Association for Retarded Children and Robert A. Henderson, University of Illinois, have been generous with materials pertaining to parents' associations. The Institute for Research on Exceptional Children made its resources available. I wish to express my appreciation to Mrs. Sharon Cook for excellent typing of the manuscript.

Authors and publishers have been most generous in granting me permission to quote from books covered by copyright. The copyright holders include Basic Books, Inc., Columbia University Press, Grune and Stratton, Inc., Oscar Lewis, University of Maine, and Williams and Wilkins Company. I appreciate permission granted by Dr. Roger F. Tredgold and Macmillan and Company, Ltd., to quote material from an article by Dr. A. F. Tredgold in *Archives of Neurology*.

BERNARD FARBER

Urbana, Illinois

CONTENTS

PART TWO

Treatment of the Retarded in Contemporary Society

MENTAL RETARDATION

Its Social Context and Social Consequences

PART ONE

Mental Retardation as a Social Product

I. ❧

The Mentally Retarded
as a Surplus Population

Most people can indicate intuitively what they mean by the mentally retarded: dull-witted, deficient in vocabulary, slow to understand, unable to follow an argument logically, inattentive, poor in memory, and unable to manipulate symbols readily. For many, the image of the mentally retarded includes clumsiness, irresponsibility, sloppiness, carelessness, nervousness, timidity, reticence, and abnormality.[1] These impressions are often false and contradictory; however, in the absence of systematic investigation by social and behavioral scientists, one must rely on personal impressions based on limited experience.

Until recently, social scientists have generally ignored mental retardation. They have regarded the mentally retarded as inconsequential in influencing the major social, political, and economic institutions in modern society and have left the study of mental retardation to psychologists and educators. This book attempts to remedy this neglect (a) by indicating how the retarded play an important role in maintaining the social structure, (b) by presenting an analysis of previous social research on mental retardation, and (c) by suggesting avenues for future investigation. Chapter 1 is intended as an orientation to the remainder of the book. First it presents a preliminary statement regarding the use of terminology and the assumptions made in reference to etiology. The discussion then shifts to an exposition of the perspective of mental retardation as a social phenomenon.

3

Preliminary Statement

Prior to discussing the social aspects of mental retardation, the position this book takes in regard to terminology and etiology will be clarified. These statements are necessary to preclude misinterpretations of assertions in later chapters.

TERMINOLOGY

Fads in the use of terms denoting intellectual incompetence have appeared in rapid succession since 1900. The World Health Organization proposed in 1954 that the term "mental subnormality" be applied to the general condition, with two subdivisions reflecting etiology— "mental deficiency" for biologically determined cases and "mental retardation" for socially determined cases. However, this usage has been largely ignored in the literature.[2] Depending upon the context, mildly retarded persons have been referred to as marginally independent, high-grade defective, debile, moron, feebleminded, educable retarded, and familial or "garden-variety" mental defective. More severely retarded persons have been called semidependent, imbecile, trainable retarded, mentally deficient, organically-impaired retarded, and low-grade mental defective. The very severely retarded have been designated as totally dependent, severely defective, and idiot. Although the terms "mildly or educable retarded" and "severely retarded" will ordinarily be used in this book, other designations will be employed when they are utilized in specific writings cited.[3]

Some of these terms have a long history; others are of recent origin. References to idiots as people who are grossly deficient intellectually appeared in English literature about the year 1300. Chaucer used it in this sense in the *Canterbury Tales*. In 1648, John Milton pointed out that "By the civil laws a foole or Idiot born shall lose the lands whereto he is born because he is not able to use them aright." Traditionally, "idiot" has referred to persons who are incapable of ordinary reasoning or rational conduct.

In contrast, "imbecile" in its historical usage has denoted a personal weakness. Early references to imbeciles (around 1550) did not connote a mental deficiency but rather a physical one. By 1750, however, the word "imbecility" applied to both physical and mental weakness, and about a century later it seems to have become restricted to weakness of mind. Yet imbecility apparently has not been used as a synonym for feeblemindedness. The term "feebleminded" was early applied to persons of normal intelligence who were unable to perform intellectual chores or moral acts adequately. For example, the essayist Macaulay wrote in 1859, "Rigid principles often do for feeble minds what stays do for feeble bodies." Thus, historically, feeblemindedness has denoted a higher degree of intelligence than imbecility[4] and has been equated instead with the word "moron," derived by Henry H. Goddard from the Greek "stupid" or "dull."[5]

The traditional terms that have emerged in everyday experience do not contain implications for treatment. In fact, many past behavioral scientists who regarded mental retardation as innate and hereditary have used these concepts in their writings. However, evidence has been accumulating for over a century that nongenetic factors may be involved in mental retardation. For example, in 1862 the British obstetrician Little wrote several papers "clearly relating poor neurologic outcome in the child (cerebral palsy and mental retardation) to certain pregnancy factors, particularly trauma and hypoxia during delivery."[6] Yet the idea of instituting procedures for remediation of intellectual deficits did not become popular until the mid-twentieth century. As Chapter 6, "Mental Retardation: A Problem in Social Reform," will indicate, mental retardation was redefined as illness at that time, when parents' associations were active as pressure groups and publicists in the reconceptualization of mental retardation. With this redefinition, the medical perspective has been permeating special education, residential institutions, and social welfare agencies.

In the light of the shifting emphasis to remediation, the revised terminology reflects the kind of treatment indicated. Clinicians and researchers today try to determine the impediments that *retard* intellectual development. Accordingly, the term "mental deficiency" has given way to "mental retardation." In special education, the words "feebleminded," "moron," and "high-grade defective" have been replaced by "educable mildly retarded,"[7] and "imbecile" by "trainable severely retarded." In medical, social welfare, and rehabilitation institutions, marginally independent retarded persons are comparable to the educable, semidependent persons to the trainable, and totally dependent persons to the very severely retarded.[8] However, by the middle nineteen-sixties, the noun "rétard" was being used as an expression of opprobrium, so presumably the retardation terminology will be replaced eventually.

ETIOLOGY

The causes of mental retardation can be classified as follows: (a) heredity; (b) prenatal, perinatal and postnatal trauma; and (c) social-cultural factors. Each of these categories includes numerous conditions. There is a tendency in attributing etiology either to reify these categories and to attribute "causation" to them or to consider the conditions in one category as responsible for most mental retardation. Since the position taken with regard to causation implies certain ideas about society, it is important to indicate the perspective on etiology assumed in this book.

Undoubtedly a relationship exists between political belief and theories of mental retardation. The nature-nurture controversy about the causation of mental retardation was considered an important issue in scientific and political circles in the first part of the twentieth century. Nicholas Pastore examined the views of twenty-four prominent scientists and related these views to their positions in the nature-nurture controversy. His hypothesis was that since there is insufficient evidence to conclude that either nature or nurture is more important in the development of intelligence, the positions taken resulted from an attempt to integrate political and scientific beliefs. Pastore based his classification of scientists as conservative or liberal (including radical) on the basis of their attitudes toward the potentialities of the common man and democracy, their views on the need for social reconstruction, and their opinions regarding the origin of social ills. Scientists who were pessimistic regarding the innate possibilities of the average man or critical of attempts to broaden the participation of the citizenry in governmental affairs were considered conservative; while those classified as liberal approved of the necessity for change as well as of attempts at achieving greater democracy in government, and also believed in the dignity of man.

Pastore selected for study scientists who had worked in the years 1900–1940 and who had written about both their stands in the nature-nurture controversy and their political beliefs. With two exceptions, all of those who held a hereditarian position were classified as conservative, while those who took a liberal stand were classified as liberals or radicals. The hereditarians included, among others, Francis Galton, Henry H. Goddard, Leta S. Hollingsworth, William Mc-Dougall, Karl Pearson, Paul Popenoe, Lewis Terman, and Edward Thorndike. However, there is some question whether Karl Pearson should be classified as a conservative; he did attempt to integrate

Darwinian doctrine with socialistic views regarding reconstruction of society, and there are contradictions in his writings. The environmentalists included Franz Boas, James Cattell, Charles H. Cooley, Frank Freeman, J. B. S. Haldane, Lancelot Hogben, Herbert Jennings, Hermann Muller, George Stoddard, Lester F. Ward, and John Watson. The two exceptions to the generalization were Watson and Terman.[9]

The problem of interpreting data on factors on mental retardation suggests that we should admit the lack of knowledge and make decisions regarding social reform or amelioration without regard to the "cause" of mental retardation. This strategy seems appropriate since, for most mentally retarded persons, the physiological and social influences are unknown.[10]

Traditionally, mental retardation has been viewed as a result of heredity, physiological factors, or social and cultural factors. From these perspectives, mental deficiency is classified as endogenous and exogenous, primary amentia and secondary amentia, neurological and social, or hereditary and environmental.[11]

The etiology of mental retardation, however, is much more complicated than a simple division into organic and nonorganic factors. Given ordinary environments, there are only a few types of mental retardation that are clearly attributable to genetic factors. These include phenylketonuria (due to a congenital faulty metabolism); Down's Syndrome (mongolism); a class of familial idiocy known as sphingolipidoses (such as Tay-Sachs); and other rare conditions. These, however are of more interest for their potentiality in providing information about genetic processes than for research on mental retardation as such.[12]

For the most part, the contributions of social and somatic environments to intellectual development are unknown in any specific case. Even in monozygotic (identical) twins, there is no assurance that, when the first cell divides, the cytoplasmic matter of the two daughter cells is identical. In fact, according to Roger J. Williams, there is evidence to show that the division is not equal, quantitatively or qualitatively. If genetic identity cannot be assumed in monozygotic twins, how much similarity exists in the genetic makeup of parents and children?

The genetic uniqueness of individuals raises serious doubt about classifying the origins of mental retardation as either exclusively hereditary or exclusively environmental. In fact, similar environments operating on genetically different organisms may produce great variations in the development of these organisms. Conversely, different environments operating on these organisms may sometimes produce similar development in them.[13]

The relationship between genetic and environmental factors is complicated further by the phenomenon of a phenocopy.[14] The term "phenocopy" denotes a trait, ordinarily ascribed to a particular genetic component, which develops in some special instance through environmental factors different from those normally operating. The same intellectual condition may be attributed in one instance to distinct genetic characteristics and in another to a peculiar environment. The existence of phenocopies implies that even in cases such as mongolism or phenylketonuria there can be no certainty of a hereditary basis. And in so-called familial mental retardation, chances are even greater that social, physiological, and genetic factors are substitutable.

Regardless of the imputed cause, environment is a crucial factor in maximizing the intellectual development of the individual. Under these circumstances, it is imperative to know which environmental factors reduce mental retardation in most individuals, and to determine how much the individual's life is affected by his intellectual incompetence and by being labeled as mentally retarded.

In this book "intelligence" or "intellectual ability" will refer to the level of functioning an individual has attained. The discussion will be based on the assumption that this level of functioning is a result of the interaction between genetic, somatic, social, and cultural factors. There is no implication intended regarding the potential intellectual attainment if the environment were changed. Undoubtedly, a change in social and cultural environment or the introduction of appropriate physiological treatment would increase the intellectual functioning of all human beings. In the distant future there may be certain drugs or chemicals that will give normal intelligence to a child with Down's Syndrome (mongolism), or as-yet-undiscovered teaching techniques may compensate for stultifying social environments. At present, however, all that can be done is to regard the level of intelligence as the result of the complex interaction of a set of genetic, physiological, and social-cultural variables, and to focus on the consequences for society.

Mental Retardation as a Social Phenomenon

Our first task is to indicate how the rights and obligations of the mentally retarded are related to social structure. This chapter will first suggest that the mentally retarded comprise a surplus population whose societal position varies with major value systems. Second, it will present in broad outline some of the general consequences of the individual's being labeled as mentally retarded or incompetent. And finally, it will introduce the assertion that "mental retardation" is itself insufficient to explain the life chances of intellectually incompetent persons in modern society. The remainder of the book will elaborate upon the implications of this assertion.

The Concept of Surplus Populations

Individuals who are identified as mentally retarded can be viewed as constituting one kind of surplus population. This section deals with the definition of surplus population, its composition in the United States, and its role in modern society.

WHAT IS A SURPLUS POPULATION?

The concept of a surplus population has stimulated much investigation in social science. However, the term "surplus population" has been used in two different ways — one referring to the ecological surplus, the second involving an organizational surplus. This book will focus on the mentally retarded as an organizational surplus population.

Briefly, the ecological view of a surplus population is concerned with matters of consumption; at its base is the Darwinian concept of the struggle for existence through competition for scarce goods. It relates the size of the population and its subsistence needs to spatial, economic and food resources. The ecological surplus population refers to that portion of the population which exceeds the number that the subsistence base will support at a given standard of living. The Malthusian concern with the tendency of the population to grow faster than economic resources provides one definition of a population surplus.

The organizational view of a surplus population pertains to matters of production and division of labor in regard to the scarcity or surplus of personnel to fill the slots or offices in a social organization. (These offices refer to duties associated with any role in carrying out the tasks of the organization.) According to this view, a group will try to establish a division of labor to maximize its output (or maximize gains resulting from output) of economic goods, power over others, or other product relevant to the particular institution (for example, transmission of knowledge in a university). The attempt at maximization sets an upper limit on the number of offices in a productive unit. Aron suggests that "men of no use to production have of necessity almost always existed."[15] There is a greater elasticity in the organization of offices in some productive units than others. Take, for instance, the family. Each family can have as many children as it likes, but there is generally a relatively fixed number of slots for mothers and fathers. Most social structures seem to have relatively inelastic tables of organization.

In any society, there are always persons who cannot be used to fill slots in tables of organization. Frequently, this inability to fill an organizational slot results from the incompetence of the individuals. (On the other hand, Marx indicated that capitalist society requires a surplus labor market in order to minimize costs of production.) Some slots will go unfilled because there are few individuals who are specifically trained for them. There will also be persons who are incapable of, unwilling to, or prevented from filling any of the existing slots, and they constitute a surplus population.

The organizational view of a surplus population implies that there is an optimal size and composition of people to utilize a given machinery of social organization. That is, instead of starting with a population and adjusting the social organization to suit it, we begin with the existing social structure and then ask about the population required to operate the roles and statuses connected with it.

The position that the slots in social organization are more or less fixed assumes further that there are powerful groups in the society, both economically and numerically, whose interests lie in restricting the expansion of slots. Evidence for this restriction exists in many places in the United States. First, major industrial organizations, such as automobile manufacturers, do not attempt to maximize output; instead, they regulate output to maximize long-range profits. Since both output and cost per manufactured unit are involved in profit prediction, industrial organizations are cautious about creating additional slots. A second restricting factor is the automation of industrial, commercial, and government enterprises; a third is the inclination of segments of the population to restrict governmental services, especially in regard to health and welfare. The limitation on membership in guild-like organizations, such as trade unions, which prevents surplus populations from gaining skills or access to jobs, is a fourth factor. In other areas of life, competition operates to inhibit the expansion of desirable slots. In marriage, there is a scarcity of highly desirable mates. In education, costs and the scarcity of talent restrain the expansion of academic institutions.

Haldane takes the position that mental defect is more a social than a biological problem and suggests that in a society offering employment for all individuals slots would be found for many, if not most, people now considered feebleminded. He indicates that any increase in the number of "feebleminded" persons may result from greater difficulties in finding appropriate employment rather than from a decline in general intelligence.[16]

Who Are Surplus?

The composition of the surplus population is complex, and many of its members can be classified as being in more than one segment of it. The so-called culturally disadvantaged are included in the surplus population, but the surplus population is by no means restricted to them. Many persons who are surplus from an organizational viewpoint have become so through old age, genetic factors, chronic illness, or personal misfortune. Harrington includes in "the other America" the human rejects in skid row, the victims of technological unemployment, the property-owning poor in rural areas, Mexican and Anglo migratory workers, unskilled Negro and hillbilly migrants to the city, the aged, and the physically and emotionally disabled.[17] Frost and Hawkes consider the following as disadvantaged children: slum dwellers, the rural poor, migrant children, Indian children, the school dropout, the delinquent, and the mentally and educationally retarded.[18] Although not all of the children described by Frost and Hawkes qualify as members of the organizational surplus population, there is a high probability that eventually a large proportion in each category will be classified as such. At any rate, a large segment of the American population (perhaps 20 to 25 percent) may be organizationally surplus or in the process of becoming part of the surplus population.[19]

The surplus population need not be poverty-stricken. Nineteenth-century Russian literature dealt with the "superfluous man," who was generally a member of the aristocracy. The superfluous man was reduced to incompetency, dependency, and ennui because he did not fill a meaningful slot in the social structure. He did not manage his properties; his familial obligations were minimal; he was not motivated to participate in intellectual activities; and his indolence made him powerless vis-à-vis those who managed his household, his properties, and his personal life. The aristocratic superfluous man included Pushkin's Eugene Onegin, Turgenev's Rudin, and Goncharov's Oblomov.

The character Oblomov in Goncharov's novel was regarded in the mid-nineteenth century as the model of the superfluous man. The literary critic Dobrolyubov regarded "Oblomovshchina" as the "key to the riddle of many of the phenomena of Russian life." Oblomov was apathetic toward everything that went on in the world. According to Dobrolyubov, "in fact there is no need for him to do anything. Why should he trouble? Has he not people to fetch things for him and do everything he needs? . . . that is why he will never tire himself with work, whatever people may tell him about work being a necessity and a sacred duty: from his earliest years he sees that all the domestic work in his home is performed by flunkies and house maids, and all that Papa and Mama do is give orders and scold the servants if they don't carry out the orders properly. And so, the first conception forms in his mind — that it is more honorable to sit with folded arms than to fuss around with work." Oblomov's demands become unreasonable in the novel as he "soon loses the power to keep his wishes within the bounds of the possible and practical, loses all ability to make means conform with aims," and is baffled by any obstacle that requires his own efforts for its removal. Yet, with all his nominal power, Oblomov's complete dependency leaves him at the mercy of those who do his bidding. Oblomov loses the power to love, since a love relationship requires mutual respect and mutual obligation. He cannot sustain a stable personal relationship with others. Incapable of self-sacrifice, Oblomov has a sense of isolation, and he views his environment as hostile. Above all, Oblomov feels powerless to change his life. He is resigned to his existence as a superfluous man.[20]

Undoubtedly, there are American counterparts to the superfluous man of Russian literature. The separation of corporate management from ownership and the existence of "jet sets" suggest the presence of superfluous men in the uper strata of contemporary society. Their style of life obviously differs from that of the superfluous poor, but in many ways their role in society is similar.

As part of the surplus population, the mentally retarded join others who are incapable of filling slots in social organization. Like the infirm, the illiterate, and the aged, mentally retarded persons are marginal in the work force. Along with neurotics, sexual deviants, and bohemians, the mentally retarded have difficulty maintaining marital relationships. And, like recent migrants, the blind, the deaf, the emotionally disturbed, and the unmotivated, mentally retarded children cannot find a slot in the ordinary school room. But it is not just because they have been labeled as mentally retarded that they fail to fill slots in social organization. In addition, they are also generally illiterate, sometimes infirm, often emotionally disturbed, and frequently poverty-stricken. Thus they join an amorphous group that exists but has no integral role in the social organization of the society, which could easily continue to function without this surplus population. Instead, society must divert much of its energy to the maintenance of a population that is unproductive in the institutions of the economy, the family, the arts, the sciences, and the political arena. In all important respects, this amorphous population is surplus; and part of this surplus population is mentally retarded.

ROLE OF SURPLUS POPULATIONS IN MODERN SOCIETY

Although ostensibly modern society could continue to exist without surplus populations, the presence of the latter contributes to maintaining the existing social structure in at least three ways: first, they generate a series of special institutions; second, they make possible the effective operation of the basic social institutions of the society; and third, they aid in the perpetuation of the social classes.

Institutional Contribution. Organizationally surplus populations make an indirect contribution to social structure through the particular problems they create for the society. By their very incompetence and deviance, these populations require, for remediation and control, a series of institutions to meet the legal, welfare, health, and educational difficulties involved. As technological advances create additional segments of surplus populations, the agencies founded to meet their problems expand in size and diversity. The number of persons presently engaged in handling problems related to surplus populations in the United States is large enough so that there would be serious economic dislocations if all organizationally superfluous individuals were to be removed from society.

Contributions to Efficiency. In one sense, organizationally surplus populations are necessary in modern society as it is now constituted. The efficient use of human beings in the economic, political, family, and educational institutions of modern society depends upon a good fit between the abilities of persons and the slots they fill in organizations. In order to achieve this fit, there must be a surplus in the population so that appropriate persons will be selected for any given slot, since a surplus permits a constant rearranging of persons to maximize efficiency. Rationalization of economic institutions requires a population in excess of the number of persons that can be employed at any one time. In much the same way, political democracy needs a large segment of people who are not interested in major issues so that complete disagreement will not rend the society apart; and, with personal satisfaction as the primary criterion for successful marriage, a surplus of men and women is necessary for effective assortive mating. Finally, academic standards themselves imply that a segment of the population cannot perform adequately in educational institutions. In all of these instances, there is a residual population in modern society that cannot maintain activity at levels demanded for participation. By virtue of their general incompetence, the mentally retarded tend to be included in this surplus.[21]

Persistence of Social Classes. The concept of an organizational population surplus is related to that of *life chances.* The concept of life chances has been used in many contexts in sociological literature to describe the persistence of social classes. Ordinarily, it means the probability of any individual attaining a successful social and economic position in the society, although the meaning of "a successful position" varies with the particular social structure. In a society that values military competence, the successful individual would hold an esteemed position among the most powerful military men; in one that honors its wealthy, life chances would refer to the likelihood of attaining riches; and in a society that glorifies political power, success is measured in terms of the position held in determining the decisions of the society.[22]

The very idea of an organizationally surplus population suggests that life chances of the people in this group are minimal. Without participating in the major institutions of the society, the surplus population has no hope of attaining high social status. In an industrial society, where the major administrative power is held by those who can think in terms of abstract principles and are highly articulate, the mentally retarded obviously have little chance to achieve success.

If individual ability and accomplishment were the sole criteria for slots in social organization, there would still be social classes as long as a complex division of labor existed. The perpetuation of social classes occurs, however, through the inheritance of privilege and wealth for the elite (and of general subjugation and poverty on the part of the surplus populations). As a result, membership in surplus populations, regardless of the basis for this membership, tends to be inherited from one generation to the next; thus the effects of mental retardation on life chances are not confined to the individual retardates but extend to their descendants as well.

Labeling and Incompetence

The presence of organizationally surplus populations creates the necessity (a) to justify classifying particular population segments as "surplus" and (b) to develop procedures for identifying these segments. In a society that values individual competence in complex political, economic, and educational activities, intellectual ability provides one basis for labeling population segments as "surplus." Goslin indicates that "as the skills required for most jobs in modern industrial society become increasingly complex, it becomes correspondingly more important that individuals are given responsibilities according to their abilities and aptitudes."[23] Educational and industrial institutions, military establishments, and other bureaucratic organizations have placed much emphasis upon aptitude testing as a means of identifying the incompetent.

Two widely divergent positions have been promulgated in discussing the consequences of mental retardation for the life chances of an individual. One is that the vicissitudes in the life of the mentally retarded individual result primarily from the status and role assigned to him by virtue of the label. The second point of view is that the poor life chances of the retarded person result from his own incompetence. Differences in the approach to the study of mental retardation stemming from these divergent viewpoints will be discussed below, and then the position taken in this book will be described.

LABELING AND LIFE CHANCES

Social scientists who place a great deal of emphasis upon the consequences of labeling the mentally retarded are concerned with deviant behavior. According to Goffman, the label imposes a stigma upon the individual which marks him for special kinds of interaction and tends to segregate him from those without this stigma.[24] That is, the label rather than the disability defines the individual's function in society.

In some societies the mentally retarded are perceived as mystical or evil. For example, Murphy and Leighton found that the St. Lawrence Eskimos traditionally regard the mentally retarded as "the hand-maidens of sorcerers." The workers of black magic use the retarded to run their errands and coerce them into "collecting nail parings or scraps of hair from the victim against whom evil [is] to be worked."[25] Among the Ojibwa the mentally deficient are considered to be possessed by devils and are accordingly killed by shooting or strangling, and then their bodies are burned. In the Ojibwa view of life, disability is believed to be inherited, and sinning parents pass it down to their children or grandchildren.[26]

The social scientists who regard labeling as crucial in affecting life chances assume that this label may refer to role failure in some institutions, notably the school, since it implies a value judgment about the person whose behavior is regarded as deviant. However, an individual who is considered mentally retarded by school authorities may not be so regarded by his friends and family. The label may then affect the child's school career but not his neighborhood and family relationships. Consequently, when the individual is out of school, being labeled mentally retarded will no longer be appropriate and, except for special training in school or a derogatory self-concept, his life will no longer be influenced by this label.

Dexter considers the labeling a "self-fulfilling prophecy." By labeling an individual, the authorities define a particular life career for that individual. If they had not labeled him, presumably his life would not be perceptibly affected. According to Dexter, just as we discriminate against dope addicts, alcoholics, the mentally ill, and Negroes as outsiders, so do we discriminate against the mentally retarded by labeling them as such.[27] Dexter suggests that "there is also the experience which may be observed over and over again of the denial of employment, of legal rights, of a fair hearing, of an opportunity, to the stupid (e.g., have a low IQ or show poor academic performance), *and not because the stupidity is relevant to the task, or claim, or situation.*"[28]

To be sure, Dexter realizes that the severely retarded would be limited in their life chances regardless of labeling. His major concern is that the degradation of stupidity is not essential to the workings of modern society. He writes, "It seems probable that the attitude and response toward stupidity, characteristic of our society, is a function of the common school and of two interrelated ideologies which affect that school. These ideologies are: (1) the post-Renaissance emphasis upon achievement in certain lines of activity as a justification of one's righteousness, the Protestant Ethic, and (2) the radical aspect of democratic thought, identified particularly with the French Revolution and, later, with Jacksonian democracy, with its emphasis on the rights and obligations of equality."[29]

Dexter believes that because of the great heterogeneity of modern society, there are sufficient roles available which can be fulfilled by *anyone*. He calls for a simplification of role expectations. In a community where a large proportion of the population is "feeble-minded," certain legal and social inventions would have to be developed to protect this group. Compulsory education or even compulsory literacy would have to be abandoned. Voting privileges, the right to borrow and lend on credit, and perhaps other rights and obligations would have to be curtailed. Yet Dexter ignores the fact that once the mentally retarded are singled out for differential treatment legally, the labeling would make them second-class citizens. As second-class citizens, the mentally retarded would still be excluded from certain privileges and opportunities accorded the rest of the society.

INCOMPETENCE AND LIFE CHANCES

The second point of view expressed in the treatment of the mentally retarded is that life chances are affected not so much by the labeling process as by the incompetence of the individuals themselves. This position is prevalent among educators and rehabilitation workers, who seek to increase the life chances of the retarded by minimizing areas of incompetence. According to this viewpoint, the low valuation of stupidity or mental retardation is necessary and proper. If the ability to adapt to new situations and to solve problems is considered "good," then the inability to do so (which is stupidity) must be considered "bad." In modern society, it is inevitable that the mentally retarded will be affected in their quest for success in occupations and in family life.

The assumption made by educators, vocational rehabilitation experts, and researchers who emphasize competence is that if all the retarded could be improved to a point of adequate performance, there would be statuses available for all individuals. In their view, the problem is not one of having a *surplus* population but one of finding the appropriate slots and then adjusting or improving the individuals to fit these slots. Those who view incompetence as the major factor in affecting life chances focus upon minimal criteria for adequate performance in different areas of social life. They then seek the bases for deficiency in psychological, social, and physiological-medical factors.

Surplus Population and Life Chances

This book takes the position that neither labeling nor incompetence is sufficient to explain the consequences of mental retardation for the life chances of that segment of the population defined as mentally retarded. We shall consider the mental retardation label and condition only as contributing factors to the life chances of the mentally retarded population.

The relative influence of intellectual functioning upon the life chances seems to vary with the level of intelligence. It is possible that extremely gifted individuals can overcome almost any environmental handicap in becoming successful (however the society chooses to define success). On the other hand, the severely retarded can rarely, if ever, be successful in occupation or family life regardless of social situation.[30] Between these two extremes, however, the social environment may play a large role in determining life chances. In a society that has severe labor shortages, the bright person in a poverty-stricken situation may not have greater life chances than a stupid individual born into a middle-class family. However, the mildly retarded person in a middle-class home is the exception rather than the rule; the general tendency is for mildly retarded individuals to come from poor and often unstable homes.[31]

The life chances of individuals in modern society depends upon many labels (such as race, religion, occupation, deviant or conventional identity, age and sex attributes) as well as upon perceived intellectual competence. With increasing multiplicity of statuses and social situations, mental retardation alone (except in the extreme case) cannot be the primary determinant of life chances. The diversity of status positions and biological characteristics in any modern society raises the question as to which combinations offer the greatest life chances.

It does not seem accidental that the mildly retarded tend to be found in situations of poverty and family instability. Actually, this situation probably emerges from the "need" for a labor surplus in a production system based on rational placement of personnel. This surplus is especially apparent at the unskilled, semiskilled, and service occupational levels, which are sensitive to fluctuations in demands in production. For these slots, there are always more candidates in the population than there are slots available. This surplus was present in the early stages in industrialization and, with the growth of automation, is possibly even more prevalent today.[32]

This book suggests that mental retardation tends to occur in connection with other characteristics whose combination may operate to prevent the incorporation of the mentally retarded person into the stream of social life of the society. Perhaps, if the individual were not mentally retarded, he might possibly compensate for some of his other handicaps (such as "cultural deprivation," being a Negro or a Puerto Rican, having an unstable family background). However, the combination of mental retardation *and* other social handicaps may affect his life chances appreciably. For these reasons, this book regards the mentally retarded as a surplus population rather than as a group solely affected either by labeling or by their own incompetence.

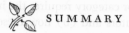 SUMMARY

This chapter has depicted the mentally retarded as a surplus population, which is that segment of the total population exceeding the number of individuals needed to fill the slots in a social organization. Modern society requires a surplus of persons to maximize the fit between persons and positions in the rational selection of personnel in economic, educational, political, and marital institutions. The surplus population consists of various segments that lack certain social and technical characteristics considered desirable in these institutions. Often these population segments combine a number of undesirable attributes that limit their life chances. But, in spite of their superfluous position in modern society, the organizationally surplus population contributes to the maintenance of the existing social structure. First, the organizationally surplus generate a series of special welfare and legal institutions; second, they make possible the effective operation of the basic social institutions of the society; third, they aid in the perpetuation of the social classes.

This book regards the mentally retarded as constituting a segment of the organizationally surplus population both by being labeled as deviants and by their incompetence. As deviants, they are stigmatized and treated differently from others; as incompetents, they generally fail to perform roles adequately in the basic institutions of the society. Moreover, especially in mild mental retardation, other attributes inhibiting life chances are also present, and the combination of these life-chance inhibiters insures the continued existence of retarded persons in the organizationally surplus population.

GENERAL DISCUSSION

The view of the mentally retarded as a surplus population has various consequences for developing an adequate understanding of problems pertaining to mental retardation and, therefore, for instituting remediation programs. Insofar as mental retardation operates to limit the life chances of persons, it must be regarded as a member of a class of life-chance-inhibitors. These life-chance-inhibitors do not appear at random in a population but, instead, tend to be concentrated among certain segments of it. An adequate understanding of phenomena in the life-chance-inhibitor category requires the investigation of (a) the attributes of the inhibitors and (b) how these inhibitors interact to place individuals in organizationally surplus segments of the populalation. Accordingly, the first part of this book will describe mental retardation as a social phenomenon—its prevalence, its nonrandom distribution, and its cultural aspects. The second part of the book will suggest how mental retardation is related to other social characteristics in affecting the participation of retardates in social institutions. It will deal with social movements, the family, residential institutions, and the community. The remediation implicit in the discussion is that, in order to be effective, amelioration techniques must deal simultaneously with many phenomena in the life-chance-inhibitor category — not with each inhibitor separately.

NOTES

[1] Samuel Guskin, "Social Psychologies of Mental Deficiency," in Norman R. Ellis, ed., *Handbook of Mental Deficiency* (New York: McGraw-Hill, 1963), pp. 334–335.

[2] A notable exception is Richard L. Masland, Seymour B. Sarason, and Thomas Gladwin, *Mental Subnormality* (New York: Basic Books, 1958).

[3] See analysis of concepts referring to mental retardation in Joel R. Davitz, Lois J. Davitz, and Irving Lorge, *Terminology and Concepts in Mental Retardation* (New York: Bureau of Publications, Teachers College, Columbia University, 1964). See also Rick Heber, ed., "A Manual on Terminology and Classification in Mental Retardation," *American Journal of Mental Deficiency* (Monograph Supplement), 64 (1959), pp. 3–111; and Rick Heber, "Modifications in the Manual on Terminology and Classification in

Mental Retardation," *American Journal of Mental Deficiency,* 65 (1961), pp. 499–500.

4 Discussion of historical usage of "idiot," "imbecile," and "feebleminded" based on *Oxford English Dictionary* (New York: Oxford University Press, 1933).

5 See Eugene E. Doll, "A Historical Survey of Research and Management of Mental Retardation in the United States," in E. Philip Trapp and Philip Himelstein, eds., *Readings on the Exceptional Child* (New York: Appleton-Century-Crofts, 1962), p. 33.

6 Janet B. Hardy, "Perinatal Factors and Intelligence," in Sonia F. Osler and Robert E. Cooke, eds., *The Biosocial Basis of Mental Retardation* (Baltimore: Johns Hopkins Press, 1965), p. 41.

7 In England, the equivalent term is "educationally subnormal." See S. S. Segal, "Dull and Backward Children: Postwar Theory and Practice," *Educational Research,* 3 (June, 1961), pp. 177–194.

8 See Gunnar Dybwad, *Challenges in Mental Retardation* (New York: Columbia University Press, 1964), p. 4 and pp. 200–201.

9 Nicholas Pastore, *The Nature-Nurture Controversy* (New York: King's Crown Press, 1949).

10 Eckland has provided an excellent summary of literature relevant to behavior genetics and intelligence. Bruce K. Eckland, "Genetics and Sociology: A Reconsideration," *American Sociological Review,* 32 (April, 1967), pp. 173–194. See also Richard L. Masland, Seymour B. Sarason, and Thomas Gladwin, *op. cit.,* with regard to the complexity of biological and social circumstances surrounding the development of mental retardation.

11 See Samuel A. Kirk, *Educating Exceptional Children* (Boston: Houghton Mifflin, 1962), pp. 92–93.

12 See Arthur L. Drew, "The Clinical Neurology of Mental Retardation," in Irving Philips, ed., *Prevention and Treatment of Mental Retardation* (New York: Basic Books, 1966), pp. 33–34; and Peter Cohen, "Medical Treatment of the Mentally Retarded," *ibid.,* pp. 201–220.

13 See Roger J. Williams, "Why Human Genetics?" *Journal of Heredity,* 51 (March–April, 1960), pp. 91–98; and Jerry Hirsch, unpublished manuscript.

14 J. Fuller and W. Thompson, *Behavior Genetics* (New York: Wiley, 1960), pp. 36–37.

15 Raymond Aron, *Peace and War* (Garden City, New York: Doubleday, 1966), p. 236.

16 J. B. S. Haldane, *Heredity and Politics* (London: George Allen and Unwin, 1938), pp. 100–101.

17 Michael Harrington, *The Other America* (New York: Macmillan, 1962).

18 Joe L. Frost and Glenn R. Hawkes, "The Disadvantaged Child: Overview and Recommendations," in J. L. Frost and G. R. Hawkes, eds., *The Disadvantaged Child* (Boston: Houghton Mifflin, 1966), pp. 1–12.

19 See Harrington, *op. cit.,* pp. 175–191.

20 N. A. Dobrolyubov, *Selected Philosophical Essays* (Moscow: Foreign Languages Publishing House, 1956), pp. 174–217 ("What is Oblomovshchina?"). *See also* Marc Slonim, *Modern Russian Literature from Chekhov to the Present* (New York: Oxford University Press, 1953), pp. 64–65.

21 In Max Weber's conception of social structure, the organizational surplus constitutes an outcast or proletarian class. See Max Weber, *The Theory of Social and Economic Organization* (New York: Oxford University Press, 1947), pp. 425–426.

22   *Mental Retardation as a Social Product*

[22] H. H. Gerth and C. Wright Mills, *From Max Weber: Essays in Sociology* (New York: Oxford University Press, 1964), pp. 181–183.

[23] David A. Goslin, *The Search for Ability* (New York: Russell Sage Foundation, 1963), p. 189.

[24] Erving Goffman, *Stigma: Notes on the Management of Spoiled Identity* (Englewood Cliffs, New Jersey: Spectrum Books, 1963).

[25] Jane M. Murphy and Alexander H. Leighton, "Native Conceptions of Psychiatric Disorder," in Jane M. Murphy and Alexander H. Leighton, eds., *Approaches to Cross-Cultural Psychiatry* (Ithaca, New York: Cornell University Press, 1965), pp. 84–85.

[26] Joseph B. Casagrande, "John Mink, Ojibwa Informant," in John B. Casagrande, ed., *In the Company of Man* (New York: Harper, 1960), pp. 467–488.

[27] Lewis A. Dexter, "The Sociology of the Exceptional Person," *Indian Journal of Social Research*, 4 (January, 1963), pp. 31–36. See also Jane R. Mercer, "Social System Perspective and Clinical Perspective: Frames of Reference for Understanding Career Patterns of Persons Labeled as Mentally Retarded," *Social Problems*, 13 (Summer, 1965), pp. 18–34.

[28] Lewis Dexter, "On the Politics of Sociology of Stupidity in our Society," *Social Problems*, 9 (Winter, 1962), p. 224.

[29] *Ibid.*, p. 225.

[30] Cf. Cyril Burt, "The Gifted Child," *British Journal of Statistical Psychology*, 14 (November, 1961), pp. 123–129.

[31] See Chapter 7, "The Family."

[32] In 1962, about 6 percent of the civilian labor force in the United States was unemployed. Those persons out of work were concentrated at low socioeconomic level jobs. Twelve percent of the nonfarm laborers, 6.4 percent of the service workers, and 7.5 percent semiskilled operatives were unemployed. On the average, unemployment rates during the 1960s have been higher than those during the previous decade. Moreover, as time elapses, the American economy may require proportionately fewer males in the labor force. In 1890, about 84 percent of all males aged fourteen or over were in the labor force; by 1940, the percentage had dropped to 79 percent; and in 1960 it fell below 78 percent. Although the proportion of women in the labor force has risen markedly in the past seven decades, the occupations of women tend to be in clerical, sales, and semiskilled operative categories. Hence the position of the organizationally surplus population in the United States economy is becoming increasingly precarious. See Murray Glendell and Hans L. Zetterberg, *A Sociological Almanac for the United States* (Second Edition) (New York: Scribner, 1964), pp. 65–66.

2. 🌿

Deviance Versus Incompetence

The mentally retarded are sometimes labeled as deviant and sometimes as incompetent. The concept of deviance focuses upon the qualitative differences between mentally retarded and intellectually normal populations; that of incompetence concentrates on the quantitative differences. Deviance implies a social problem, a threat to established social relationships; it suggests that a proportion of the population is using inappropriate means or goals. On the other hand, incompetence refers to the inability of a few to attain the level of conduct necessary for the continuation of an existing social organization. Incompetent individuals are not considered a threat to social structure. In fact, Goode suggests that the very presence of ineptness in an organization adds to the participants' sense of security, since they know that failure to perform their duties with maximum efficiency will not result in elimination from the group. Also, the ineptness of a small number of individuals may actually serve to increase the efficiency of the organization.[1]

Deviance is distinguished from incompetence in yet another way. Deviance implies a motivation, conscious or unconscious, to act in a manner that is contrary to the norms and values of the organization. The alcoholic, the bandit, the drug addict, the hoodlum, the homosexual, and other deviants are regarded as motivated to behavior that

23

is antithetical to the cultural norms. On the other hand, incompetent individuals are viewed as trying to conform to the accepted standards of conduct but unable to do so because of some impediment. Whether physiological or social in origin, this obstacle does not threaten the structure of norms and values in society.

Perhaps the most significant distinction between deviance and incompetence concerns the use of labels. Deviance as a social phenomenon implies that an attribute has been labeled and that, as a result of this label, the individual is expected to play an abnormal role in his relationships with others. "One does not play the role of the deviant until he has been so identified by others or by himself."[2] Incompetence, on the other hand, does not imply a different set of prescriptions for behavior. The incompetent person is expected to continue to try to play the role normally expected.[3]

One of the basic presuppositions of social relationships in the United States is that individuals are competent to perform almost any social role. This presupposition is implicit in the tradition of universal suffrage, in the spoils system in politics, and in the system of standardized school curricula. In law, an individual must be demonstrably incompetent mentally before his civil rights are denied him. One is presumed responsible in criminal cases unless it can be shown clearly that he is mentally incompetent. In the economic sphere, any adult is considered capable of being an entrepreneur. Conversely, in special education, an individual must be "certified" as incompetent before he can join a class for the mentally handicapped.

Logically, it would be just as reasonable for individuals to have to prove their competence in order to secure civil privileges, entrepreneurship, or attendance in regular classes. It could easily be assumed that one is incompetent until he proves otherwise. The age-grading ceremonies in many primitive societies are aimed at demonstrating ability to occupy adult status. And in the United States, in an effort to achieve a high competence in technical matters, the supposition of incompetence is being increasingly applied in selection procedures for personnel who will eventually become the intellectual and professional leaders in the society. Ability testing is being used almost universally for college entrance and special classes for "highly gifted" students. Goslin[4] has suggested that performance on standardized tests of ability may have profound consequences for the individual's educational motivation, his self-concept, his family relationships, and his relationships with others who have been tested in the same way.

In ordinary relationships, however, the presupposition is that an individual is competent to perform social roles. The criteria for selection are much less rigorous than those for highly technical and professional roles. Given this presupposition of competence, what happens when an individual fails to perform his social roles competently? This question suggests a variety of problems to research. One point of interest is how much relationship exists between the presupposition of competence and the definition of mental retardation as a form of deviance. The studies by Fred Davis on families of polio victims and on the interaction between healthy and physically disabled persons suggest, by analogy, that people try to ignore the effects of incompetence on interaction and tend to attribute role failures to situational factors.[5] In effect, persons interacting with an incompetent individual apparently attempt to maintain the system of relationships as if there had been no role failure. At a certain point, however, this disavowal of problems becomes impossible. One problem for possible investigation is finding the point at which failure in the performance of roles is no longer ignored, given different kinds of social situations. Labeling this role failure as deviance rather than incompetence would determine the kind of action taken.

The presupposition of competence may pervade social and educational agencies dealing with the retarded. If so, this pervasion would influence the application of the "retarded" label by professionals associated with these agencies. One problem that might be researched is how much medical and educational institutions differ from welfare agencies in their labeling of mental retardation. Presumably, the medical and educational institutions focus more upon incompetence, while social agencies deal to a greater extent with deviance.

This chapter will describe the historical traditions associated with the views of mental retardation as deviance and as incompetence. It will indicate how ideas regarding mental retardation as either deviance or incompetence may originate as justifications for reform but are eventually taken over to support the status quo.

Mental Retardation as Deviance

New perspectives on mental retardation have tended to emerge as efforts at social reform. Then, later, the same views have been used to support existing social conditions. One of these conceptions, the theory of degeneracy, seems to have dominated nineteenth-century treatment of mental retardation.

The theory of degeneracy was described by Benedict Morel in a book published in 1857, just two years before Darwin's *Origin of the Species.* Morel had reached the conclusion that all varieties of mental disease, such as insanity and mental deficiency, are related. He regarded these disorders as hereditary and hypothesized that they become more profound with each succeeding generation. He indicated that "degenerations are deviations from the normal human type, which are transmissable by heredity and which deteriorate progressively toward extinction."[6] This deterioration, said Morel, is also reflected in the fact that there is an association between sterility and mental disorder. (Few idiots, for example, are capable of conception.) The progression as seen by Morel was a continual loss of "vital energy" from one generation to the next until the state of idiocy was reached. The causes of this degeneracy were to be found in diseases, alcoholism, and the social environment. Morel focused upon these causes and sought to show that more adequate housing, food, and working conditions would prevent this genetic deterioration.

The juxtaposition of Darwin's work upon Morel's seems to have led to the conclusion that individuals living under poor social conditions were already degenerate and unfit members of the human species. Then publication of Richard L. Dugdale's study of the "Jukes" family in 1875, which came at a time when social Darwinism was reaching its zenith, popularized the familial aspects of degeneracy.

Social Darwinism in the nineteenth century seems to have resulted in confounding two conceptions of mental retardation. One concept was that the races of mankind had evolved at different rates. The most progressive societies technologically were expressions of the most advanced human races, while primitive societies demonstrated a slower intellectual development. The second concept pertained to the theory of degeneration; that is, the degenerating races of mankind had been subjected to environmental and social conditions which reduced their fitness to survive and prosper. These two conceptions were bound together by a vague notion of vitalism. The higher races were supposed to display greater vitality and the lower races lesser vital energy; this vitality was in some mystical way believed to be related to level of intelligence.[7]

Two kinds of evidence were presented to support the theory of degeneracy and racial differences. One consisted of demographic data, the other was based on systematic investigation.

DEMOGRAPHIC EVIDENCE

During most of the nineteenth century, investigators sought evidence for racial degeneracy and/or primitiveness in the U.S. Census reports and other vital statistics. This reliance on federal agencies for prevalence data continued through 1890, after which the practice was discontinued, apparently because the procedures were unreliable.

The Report of the 1840 U.S. Census, which showed that there were 17,456 "insane and idiots" in the United States, was used to indicate innate Negro-white differences in intellectual functioning. There was little difference reported in the rate of insanity or idiocy between northern and southern whites. The northern ratio was one per 995, while the southern ratio for whites was one per 945.3. For the Negroes, however, there was a considerable discrepancy between the northern and southern ratios. The ratio for Negroes in the North was one per 144.5 persons, while in the South it was one per 1,558. As might be expected, the proponents of slavery used this report to indicate how the protective environment of slavery prevented the constitution of the Negroes from manifesting itself in insanity and idiocy. Although there was an immediate reaction to this interpretation by some abolitionists at the time, the impact of the census figures remained.[8] While later analysis of slave inventory and appraisement records by Postell revealed that the southern Negro ratio should have been one per 85.8, the inaccuracy of the reports is irrelevant in terms of the historical significance of the published census data. The 1840 census data upheld the degeneracy and "lower" race conceptions of mental defects at a time when this support was needed.

The degeneracy theory was bolstered by vital statistics on the foreign born. Dublin reported in 1921 that "in both sexes, the death rates of the foreign born and of their native-born offspring are considerably in excess of those for the native born of native parents after the period of middle life is reached . . . the foreign-born enter the United States, for the most part, as adults: they have lower vitality than the native stock and their addition to the population can have only one effect, namely, to increase the death rate at the middle ages of life and at the older ages."[9] In the same publication, Laughlin described the nativity of the institutional population of the United States. His findings with respect to the feeble-minded were as follows:

In the case of the feeble-minded, we find that the *native born, both parents native born,* contributed 88.08 per cent of their quota, whereas the native born, *one parent native born, one parent foreign born,* 174.63 per cent; the *foreign born* only 32.72 per cent. This means of course, that our recent immigration sieve has been fairly effective in preventing the admission of feeble-minded persons to the United States, but that the stock from which our immigrants of the past generation came, was of a highly degenerate nature, as shown by the relatively high numbers of their offspring which are today found in institutions for the feeble-minded.[10]

Here also, the empirical evidence (in this case demographic analysis) lends weight to the vitalistic conception of intelligence, which in turn provides a rationale for restraining the rise of the lower socioeconomic classes politically, economically, and in education.

Those who sought it found further evidence for the degeneration position on mental deficiency in the United States census toward the end of the nineteenth century. For example, in the years 1880 and 1890 an attempt was made to determine the extent to which mental deficiency was congenital. Of the total of 76,895 individuals reported as idiots in the 1880 census of population, 46,874 or 74.2 percent were considered as retarded from birth. These were then classified as congenital idiots. Another 21.0 percent became "idiots" before the age of ten, and the age of onset for the remaining 5 percent was between ten and twenty. Of the children born in the decade preceding the 1890 census, 64,962 were reported as mentally deficient. Of these, 42,805 or 65.9 percent were considered as congenital idiots. The fact that many of these children were not retarded from birth did not imply to the adherents of vitalistic doctrines that these cases were produced by environmental factors alone. The prevalent vitalistic conceptions of race and ability indicated that "neuropaths" were prone to mental aberration under unfavorable conditions. The 1880 census report actually states that, although an accident or disease may produce onset of mental deficiency at a later time, the defects reported as occurring later may reflect prenatal predispositions.

There was also an attempt in the 1880 and 1890 census reports to indicate the extent to which mental deficiency, as compared with deafness and blindness, could be considered congenital. According to the 1880 census report, prenatal influences are most likely to have their fullest effect in the production of the mentally retarded (74.2

percent); next on the deaf (54.1 percent); and least on the blind (12.8 percent). In 1890, an attempt was made to determine whether those individuals who were reported as feebleminded, deaf, or blind had relatives who were also afflicted. Of the 44,033 feebleminded individuals in the 1890 census for whom data were available, 28,844 or 56.4 percent had at least one relative who was insane or feebleminded. On the other hand, of the 48,458 deaf or blind individuals for whom information was available, only 2,077 or 4.3 percent had deaf or blind relatives. Here again, given the vitalistic conception of intelligence, the available evidence supported the existing hereditary theories.[11]

EVIDENCE FROM SYSTEMATIC INVESTIGATIONS

In the early twentieth century, the theory of degeneracy was still in vogue. As mental tests were introduced into prisons, it was found that a large proportion of prisoners could be classified as "feebleminded." In addition, authorities regarded mentally retarded women as being sexually promiscuous and as producing many illegitimate children. Estimates among the criminal population and unmarried mothers were that as many as 40 to 45 percent were mentally retarded. Moreover, the feebleminded were seen as being unable to sustain regular employment and hence to become hardened criminals and paupers. In addition, they were considered a general menace and a danger to the community and to the "race." Hence the only solutions seemed to be segregation and sterilization.[12]

The view expressed by Tredgold and others was: the less adequate the physiological makeup of the individual (especially the brain), the greater would be the effect of the stresses of life upon his ability to adapt and to learn. Idiots and imbeciles had the poorest genetic composition, while those who were feebleminded were more affected than normal individuals by environmental "degeneracy."

Histological bases for mental deficiency were found. Bolton reported the "depth of the pyramidal layer of nerve-cells . . . varied inversely with the degree of amentia or of dementia present in each case."[13] Tredgold found various other anatomical characteristics of the mentally deficient. He noted that the skull is thicker and denser than the normal skull, and that the convolutions of the brain may be less complex. "The cells composing the gray matter of the cerebral cortex are decidedly fewer than in the normal brain. . . . Irregularity in the arrangement of the nerve-cells of the cerebral cortex is far more commonly met with in the brains of the mentally defective than in those of normal intelligence," and there is an imperfect development of the nerve-cells.[14]

The significance that Tredgold attached to these pathological characteristics is indicated in his discussion of the etiology of mental deficiency. Tredgold regarded "not only idiocy and imbecility, but also insanity, epilepsy, and a large number of neuroses [as being], in the majority of instances, the results of ancestral defects."[15] He conceded that some individuals with a lesser degree of mental retardation could be taught various kinds of handicraft and become partially self-supporting. But he warned that "it cannot be too clearly understood that those patients are defective from the very beginning, and that no process of education or training will supply such defects and enable them to take a place in the world and compete with normally developed persons. In the present day [1903] it is even questionable if such methods of so-called education are not carried a little too far, the training of imbeciles is in danger of becoming a popular fad, and there is a tendency to allow it to run in lines which are altogether unsuited to the requirements and capabilities of these patients."[16]

For Tredgold, social "degeneracy" influenced heredity:

There are certain diseases and morbid influences which bring about a profound change in many, if not all, of the organs and tissues of the body, either, it may be, by a direct poisonous action, or by causing pronounced alterations of nutrition. Among this class are consumption, syphilis, and alcoholism. Whether the action of such factors is directly toxic in nature, or whether they interfere with the general nutrition of the body, is of no great matter; daily clinical experience and *post-mortem* examination amply show that there is present a great and almost universal pathological change. *Is it conceivable that amid all this change the germinal plasm should remain entirely unaffected? . . .*[17] Idiocy, then, is the final expression of a neuropathic tendency, the earliest manifestations of which are hysteria, chronic neuralgia, and the minor forms of epilepsy; in the next stage appear more severe epilepsy (usually dating from an earlier period of life), insanity, and the tendency to early dementia; and last of all idiocy, with obvious evidences of physical degeneracy and very often extinction of the family. The most reasonable view would seem to be that the germinal plasm shares in the general bodily deterioration which results from the harmful conditions mentioned above, and that, therefore, the offspring to which it gives rise is rendered unstable and of diminished vital energy in which the most delicate and newly acquired portion of its complex organization — the nervous system — in other words, a neuropath has been created; should such a person marry another of similar neuropathic tendencies an aggravation of the condition will be the result in the next generation, and epilepsy and actual insanity will probably be present.[18]

Tredgold related this view of the development of mental deficiency to the conception of society in terms of a competitive system. According to Tredgold, "it is indeed more than likely that many of the conditions of life at the present day, the struggle for place or for mere existence, with its accompanying wear and tear and nervous strain, and often insufficiency of food and fresh air, contribute largely not only to the deterioration of our manners but also of our nervous system, and tend to initiate that neuropathic diathesis, that slight departure from the nervous normal, which, if unchecked, will pass on to epilepsy, to insanity, and finally to idiocy."[19]

Under Henry H. Goddard, director of the research laboratory at the training school at Vineland, New Jersey, the work of Binet and Simon was translated into English and published in the United States. It is noteworthy that Goddard was a firm believer in the idea that mental deficiency was primarily a hereditary condition related to central nervous system functioning.

Goddard published *The Kallikak Family* in 1912 as substantiation of the hypothesis that feeblemindedness is hereditary. In a genealogy of one of the Vineland patients, Goddard indicated how the patient's great-great grandmother was responsible for 143 proven feebleminded individuals out of 480 descendants. About three-fourths of the descendants were considered as degenerates of one kind or another. On the other hand, tracing the descendants of the patient's great-great-grandfather, who had then married a woman of normal intelligence, Goddard found the 496 direct descendants in this line considered to be responsible persons and normal in intelligence. Goddard concluded that his finding supported Mendelian expectations.

The concept of vitalism played a significant role in defining mental retardation as deviance in the nineteenth and early twentieth centuries. The tropics were thought to sap vitality in human beings; therefore races that had developed in tropical climates were considered inferior. On the other hand, constant exposure to cold and mental and physical strain also undermined the strength of people and prevented their dominance in the evolutionary process. Through the concept of vitalism, various forms of "degeneracy" could be scaled.

McDougall reported that there was evidence that "superior intelligence is positively correlated with general superiority in vigor and in good moral disposition. "[20] He indicated:

> Seven separate researches made in different parts of England and America by independent experts, using different methods of gauging intelligence and social standing and using a variety of statistical methods, concur in a well-marked positive correlation between superior native intelligence (or innate intellectual capacity) and superior social status. The conclusion that such correlation is a general fact (in England and America at least) is very strongly indicated.[21]

The vitalistic position has not yet been discarded; instead it is sustained by findings in recent research. For example, Kagan, Sontag, Baker, and Nelson report that IQ tends to increase over time among aggressive children, whereas those who decrease in IQ tend to be more passive.[22] Similarly, studies of the social relationships of gifted children indicated that in comparison with normal and dull children they are more active, healthier, better in athletics, and interact more. On the other hand, retarded children have been found to be less agile than their normal peers.[23]

Even more significant for current support of the theory of degeneracy are findings on the age of parents and the birth of handicapped children. For various kinds of handicaps associated with mental deficiency, especially mongolism, the age of the mother is a significant variable; the risk of mental deficiency tends to increase with maternal age. The explanation given is that all of the eggs to be discharged during the woman's entire reproductive life are present from puberty; as time goes on, the probability of mutation increases through decomposition or recomposition of genetic material. The father's age is also related to the incidence of birth defects, although its effect is somewhat less than that of the mother. Newcombe and Tavendale, through a study of linkage between birth records and the registry of congenitally handicapped children in British Columbia, found malformations of the nervous system, "mental deficiency," and mongolism all to be more prevalent among children of older fathers. Although much of the paternal influence disappeared when the effect of the mother's age was removed statistically, a small paternal-age effect nevertheless remained.[24] These findings on parental age can be interpreted as indicating that as the parent approaches middle age, his vital processes decline. This decline affects his genetic material, and the quality of his offspring decreases.

In summary, the history of mental retardation as deviance represents an attempt to integrate a variety of social problems. The theory of degeneracy tried to explain a connection between retardation and poverty, alcoholism, crime, and other forms of deviance. This theory, as well as related concepts (such as vitalism), arose in response to the recognition that often there is a convergence of mental retardation and other stigma. It attributed the persistence of the "degeneracy" to the "neuropathic constitution" and focused on the mental condition rather than on the combinations of attributes.

This section has discussed mental retardation as deviance from an historical perspective. The traditional emphasis has been on biological determinants of retardation. Later, in Chapter 9, "Community Relationships," the focus will be upon deviant social roles.

Mental Retardation as Incompetence

Like the nineteenth-century view of mental retardation as deviance, the concept of retardation as psychological and social incompetence emerged as an effort at social reform, when, with the democratization of education, psychological testing was developed to screen out those children who were unable to function in ordinary classrooms. The emphasis in the incompetence theory of retardation is upon areas of deficiency rather than upon etiology. Interest in etiology appears to be a medical concern—the medical treatment is to remove the physiological or social "cause" of the disability. The educational focus is upon the disability itself; regardless of basis, all mental retardation represents an inability to learn. The conception of retardation as incompetence, therefore, stresses the learning process and the development of teaching techniques.

In the early nineteenth century, ideas concerning mental retardation were influenced by such men as Saint-Simon. In emphasizing the interdependence of all members of society, Saint-Simon utilized an organic analogy:

> Society is not at all a simple conglomeration of living beings whose actions have no other cause but the arbitrariness of individual wills, nor other results than ephemeral or unimportant accidents. On the contrary, society is above all a veritable organized machine, all of

whose parts contribute in a different way to the movement of the whole. The gathering of men constitutes a veritable being whose existence is more or less certain or precarious according to whether its organs acquit themselves more or less regularly of the functions entrusted to them.[25]

A second important characteristic of Saint-Simon's views was his attempt to develop a positivistic conception of society through a science of sociology. Saint-Simon proposed that "politics will become a science of observation, and political questions handled by those who would have studied the positive science of man by the same method and in the same way that today one treats those relating to other phenomena."[26] With the moralistic and epistemological preconceptions brushed aside, Saint-Simon then proposed that all phenemena could be viewed objectively, which would, of course, have resulted in defining mental retardation as incompetence rather than deviance.

Saint-Simon's major significance for the study of mental retardation lies in the fact that one of his followers, Edouard Seguin, was a pioneer in the education of the mentally retarded. Seguin regarded the mentally handicapped as one of the most neglected populations. As a disciple of Saint-Simon, Seguin focused upon the rehabilitation of the retarded; he viewed them in a "positivistic" manner. Seguin regarded mental deficiency as isolation of an individual's mental life and personality because of an infirmity of the nervous system. This infirmity was said to make impotent "the faculties of the child from under the control of the will, giving him up to the dominion of instinct."[27]

Through sensory-motor training, Seguin hoped to arouse and develop the central nervous system, thereby enabling the child to control his will and become united with the outside world. Through this unity, the individual could become integrated into the organic whole of society. In 1864, Seguin published *The Moral Treatment, Hygiene, and Education of Idiots and Other Backward Children.* In 1837, he had founded a school for the mentally retarded in Paris. The principles developed by Seguin received wide recognition, and schools based on his work were opened in Switzerland, Berlin, and Boston.

Seguin's contribution to educating the mentally retarded lay in his physiological program for educating idiots. His motor training was aimed at compensating for deficiencies in the nervous and muscular apparatus. The training of the senses consisted of stimulation, first by gross stimuli, and then by refined cues.

Seguin (and, indirectly, Saint-Simon) influenced succeeding generations of educators and psychologists profoundly. Definitions of mental deficiency developed in the latter part of the nineteenth century followed Seguin's view. Refinements were introduced, but sensory-motor characteristics predominated. For example, in the description by Bourneville, the concept of age was introduced so that mentally deficient children could be compared with others of their own age.

A second important step in the definition of mental deficiency as incompetence also occurred in France. Seguin's sensory-motor definition of mental deficiency was insufficient for the administration of educational programs for masses of children in the French educational system. At the beginning of the twentieth century, a commission was formed to study measures to be taken "showing the benefits of instruction for defective children." The work of the commission resulted in the development of the Binet-Simon Intelligence Test, developed by Alfred Binet and Theodore Simon, which was influenced by Bourneville but focused upon mental rather than sensory-motor processes.[28]

Binet was commissioned by the French government to develop a test that would determine when a child who was suspected of retardation should be transferred to a special class. The child was to be certified as mentally deficient when the state of his intelligence was such that he was unable to profit from regular class instruction. With this focus upon socialization and the educating process, Binet and Simon constructed a test based upon age grading according to intellectual abilities. Binet, who distinguished between native and acquired intelligence, regarded his immediate task as the measurement of native intelligence. The classes for the mentally retarded organized by Binet dealt with "mental orthopedics" — with training in memory, reasoning, perception, problem-solving, and attention — rather than with sensory-motor activities. Binet regarded the blocking of these processes as a native, central nervous system deficiency rather than a result of sensory-motor defects that denied the individual access to major social institutions.[29]

Although Binet and Simon were commissioned to prepare a test to screen potential school failures, they emphasized the ability of the children to exercise judgment. They wanted to measure a fundamental aspect of intelligence:

> The alteration or the lack of which is of the utmost importance for practical life. This faculty is judgment, otherwise called good sense, practical sense, initiative, the faculty of adapting one's self to cir-

cumstances. To judge well, to comprehend well, to reason well, these are the essential activities of intelligence. A person may be a moron or an imbecile if he is lacking judgment; but with good judgment he can never be either. Indeed, the rest of the intellectual faculties seem of little importance in comparison with judgment. What does it matter, for example, whether the organs of sense function normally? Of what import that certain ones are hyperesthetic, or that others are anesthetic or are weakened? Laura Bridgman, Helen Keller and their fellow-unfortunates were blind as well as deaf, but this did not prevent them from being very intelligent. Certainly this is demonstrative proof that the total or even partial integrity of the senses does not form a mental factor equal to judgment. We may measure the acuteness of the sensibility of subjects; nothing could be easier. But we should do this, not so much to find out the state of their sensibility as to learn the exactitude of their judgment. . . . As a result of all this investigation, in the scale which we present, we accord the first place to judgment; that which is of importance to us is not certain errors which the subject commits, but absurd errors, which prove that he lacks judgment.[30]

Lewis Terman revised the Binet-Simon scale and adapted it to American children.[31] Whereas the Binet-Simon scale measured intelligence merely by mental age, Terman introduced the intelligence quotient, which was based on the ratio of a child's mental age to his chronological age. Moreover, the intelligence quotient provided a quantitative criterion for mental retardation. And, more than that, it made it possible to describe mental retardation in statistical terms of probability. The statistical concept of mental retardation has persisted in psychological and educational definitions of mental deficiency.

Since World War II, parents organizations, special community schools and classes, and welfare agencies have promoted ideas regarding the incorporation of the mentally retarded into the community. Within this movement, the Binet-Simon-Terman definition of mental retardation in terms of intelligence quotients or mental age has met with much opposition.[32] Sarason and Gladwin in 1958 suggested that "a more comprehensive theoretical formulation of intellectual functioning than we now have" will be required for intelligence testing to provide valid conclusions in research and diagnosis.[33] An example of the kinds of tests now being developed is the Illinois Test of Psycholinguistic Abilities. This test focuses upon encoding, association, and decoding processes in communication. It stresses the sensory-motor elements in the development of intelligence and is aimed specifically at remediation of specific intellectual defects. With this emphasis upon both remediation and sensory-motor factors in intelligence, the test of psycholinguistics is closer to the ideas of Seguin than to those of Binet or Terman.[34]

Greater attention is also being given to a spectrum of "adaptive behavior," which Heber has defined as "a composite of many aspects of behavior and a function of a wide range of specific abilities and disabilities. Intellectual, affective, motivational, social, sensory, and motor factors all contribute to, and are a part of, total adaptation to the environment."[35]

Several observers have defined mental retardation as including *social* incompetence. This view represents a difference in emphasis, but not in quality, from educational and psychological definitions. For example, Doll (while at the Vineland Training School) published the definition of mental deficiency as "(1) social incompetence, (2) due to mental subnormality, (3) which has been developmentally arrested, (4) which obtained at maturity, (5) is of constitutional origin and (6) is essentially incurable."[36] Doll has indicated that "a serious limitation of the social criterion is its variability in time and place and according to the relative complexity of the social structure."[37] McCulloch, however, has indicated that although norms of competence vary, gross social incompetence would be apparent in almost any community.[38]

According to Jastak and his associates, the ultimate criterion of mental deficiency is the social one. "Biological and psychological criteria are only as good as their ability to predict social competence by multiple measures of achievement."[39] Moreover, if a medical criterion is applied and the social development then exceeds the estimate of retardation, Jastak continues, the medical criterion has only limited validity.

Although Jastak considers the criterion of social adjustment crucially important in the assessment of mental retardation, he also regards it as difficult to define and to assay. Social adjustment may suffer not only through lack of intelligence but also because of social pressures or personality problems. The "idea of competence" must be qualified by other considerations: sex, age, type of work, level of skills, area of residence, and opportunity for education. Psychological and biological criteria are relevant only insofar as they affect the competence of the individual with respect to the expectations based on age and sex categories, type of work and educational level. Thus Jastak, like Heber, does not rely exclusively on social criteria in defining mental retardation but seeks also psychological and biological bases.

To summarize, the view of mental retardation as incompetence represents an attempt to isolate retardation from other social problems. The emphasis of amelioration from this viewpoint has been upon educational practices, mental testing, and adaptive behavior of retarded individuals. From the perspective of incompetence, the association between mental retardation and other social problems is considered irrelevant to the assessment and treatment of the retarded.

SUMMARY

Mental retardation has been defined by some as deviant behavior and by others as incompetence. Deviant behavior involves an aberrant role and set of values associated with a stigmatized label. Those who regard the retarded population as deviants have attempted to connect retardation with other deviant behavior. Those who consider the retarded population as incompetent have treated mental retardation in terms of the unique problems it evokes. Two historical traditions have developed in mental retardation — deviance and incompetence.

The observation that there tends to be a correlation between intellectual and social deficits has stimulated various explanations. Social Darwinism was associated with the speculation that the multiple deficiencies were the result of either an evolutionary obstacle or the degeneracy of genetic matter. The theory of degeneracy was formulated as a basis for social reform but was eventually used to justify the repression of segments of society. The continued growth of the surplus population through the late nineteenth and early twentieth centuries created a threat to the stability of the existing social structure and resulted in an attempt to interpret mental retardation as deviance. Demographic data and the findings of systematic investigations were construed as supporting the evolutionary and degeneracy hypotheses. Mystical concepts, such as vitalism, were employed in relating diverse sets of research results; some contemporary studies continue to make vitalistic interpretations.

The definition of mental retardation as incompetence emerged with the democratization of education and the accompanying development of special classes for the retarded. Seguin, in attempting to implement the ideas of Saint-Simon, tried to develop the integration of the retarded with society through sensory-motor training. Then, as a screening device for special classes, Binet and Simon devised an intelligence test which emphasized an individual's judgment. This test has served as a point of departure for subsequent procedures for assessing intelligence. Since World War II, there has been much pressure to broaden the criteria to include language facility and adaptive behavior of various kinds. Greater attention is being given to social incompetence as a criterion for retardation.

 GENERAL DISCUSSION

Much of the material in subsequent chapters will pertain to the different consequences which emanate from viewing retardation as deviance rather than incompetence. This discussion will therefore be confined to two more specialized topics: adaptive behavior and the retarded as an organizationally surplus population, and the effects of labeling.

Adaptive Behavior and Surplus Populations. A distinction can be drawn between the view (advanced by Heber, Jastak, Doll, McCulloch and others) that mental retardation implies deficiency in adaptive behavior and the position that the retarded are organizationally surplus. If mental retardation is mainly a matter of adaptation, treatment involves either personal remediation of the retarded or simplifying the social environment. The adaptive behavior perspective evokes essentially the traditional educational and psychological approaches to deviance (but without the genetic overtones) and to incompetence. The view of the retarded as a surplus population, however, implies that the social structure itself must be included as a significant factor in determining the nature and prevalence of mental retardation. Hence effective remedial measures would necessarily involve major reforms of the structure of society. This point will be elaborated upon in the epilogue (Chapter 10).

Effects of Labeling. The implications of labeling, as distinct from incompetence, for the individual's life chances have not been investigated systematically. Such study would require classification of individuals in at least four categories as shown in Table 1. Until now, studies of the social life of the retarded have assumed that the retarded fall into a single cell. In prevalence studies, the investigators generally regard all individuals as previously unlabeled retarded. In some social-organization investigations, the researchers treat all individuals as mislabeled retarded and explain the organization as a consequence of labeling. Investigation, especially of the mislabeled normal and unlabeled retarded children, is needed. Ethical questions might be raised about officially mislabeling children of normal intelligence as retarded or about denying special education services to children diagnosed as retarded. However, there are situations where normal children are inadvertently labeled officially as retarded or retarded children receive no publicized label. The effects of these errors on the life chances of the children can then be observed in conjunction with their other social attributes.

TABLE 1

The Label of Mental Retardation and Actual Level of Intelligence

Label	Actual Level of Intelligence	
	Normal	Retarded
Normal	Normal	Unlabeled retarded
Retarded	Mislabeled as retarded	Retarded

NOTES

1 William J. Goode, "The Protection of the Inept," *American Sociological Review,* 32 (February, 1967), pp. 5–19.

2 Eliot Freidson, "Disability as Social Deviance," in Marvin B. Sussman, ed., *Sociology and Rehabilitation* (Washington, D.C.: American Sociological Association, ND), p. 82.

3 Freidson makes distinctions between types of deviance on the basis of the individual's responsibility for the deviant behavior on the one hand and the curability of the deviance on the other. (*Ibid.,* pp. 74–80.) His typology suggests that there is always a set of deviant roles to accommodate individuals who do not conform to the dominant norms. The discrepancy between his formulation and that presented here (deviance versus incompetence) suggests various problems for research. For example, under what circumstances do deviant roles emerge when individuals are not competent to conform to accepted standards? The deviant and the incompetent may represent two distinct subpopulations of the mildly mentally retarded.

4 See David A. Goslin, *The Search for Ability* (New York: Russell Sage Foundation, 1963).

5 Fred Davis, *Passage Through Crisis: Polio Victims and Their Families* (New York: Bobbs-Merrill, 1963); and Fred Davis, "Deviance Disavowal: The Management of Strained Interaction by the Visibly Handicapped," *Social Problems,* 9 (1961), pp. 120–132.

6 Benedict A. Morel, *Traité des Dégénérescences Physiques, Intellectuelles et Morales de l'espèce Humaine* (Paris: Bailliére, 1857). Cited in Erwin H. Ackerknecht, *A Short History of Psychiatry* (New York: Hafner, 1959), p. 48.

7 See Richard Hofstadter, *Social Darwinism in American Thought* (Boston: Beacon Press, 1955), pp. 186–192.

8 For example, Edward Jarvis, "Insanity among the Colored Population of the Free State," *American Journal of Medical Science*, 7 (1884), p. 74. Cited in William Dositt Postell, "Mental Health among the Slave Population on Southern Plantations," *American Journal of Psychiatry*, 110 (1953), pp. 52–54.

9 Louis I. Dublin, "The Mortality of Foreign Race Stocks," *Eugenics in Race and State*, Vol. II, Scientific Papers of the Second International Congress of Eugenics (Baltimore: Williams and Wilkins, 1923), pp. 79–80.

10 Harry H. Laughlin, "Nativity of Institutional Inmates," *Eugenics in Race and State, op. cit.*, pp. 404.

11 Information on tables 183 and 184, pp. 412 and 413. Information for 1880 census figures:

U.S. Department of the Interior, Census Office, *Report of the Defective, Dependent, and Delinquent Classes of the Population of the United States as Returned at the Tenth Census (June 1, 1880)*, Vol. 21, Publications of the Tenth Census (publication date, 1888).

Information on 1890 census:

U.S. Department of the Interior, Census Office, *Report on the Insane, Feeble-minded, Deaf and Dumb, and Blind in the United States at the Eleventh Census, 1890.*

12 See *Eugenics in Race and State, op. cit., passim.*

13 Joseph Shaw Bolton, "The Histological Basis of Amentia and Dementia," *Archives of Neurology from the Pathological Laboratory of the London County Asylums*, Vol. 2, 1903, p. 424.

14 A. F. Tredgold, "Amentia (Idiocy and Imbecility)," *Archives of Neurology from the Pathology Laboratory of the London County Asylums*, 2 (1903), p. 391. Dr. Tredgold's views regarding mental retardation were modified considerably during the subsequent fifty years of his life.

15 *Ibid.*, p. 372.

16 *Ibid.*, p. 373.

17 *Ibid.*, pp. 363–364.

18 *Ibid.*, pp. 365–366.

19 *Ibid.*, p. 366.

20 William McDougall, "The Correlation between Native Ability and Social Status," *Eugenics in Race and State, op. cit.*, pp. 373–376.

21 *Ibid.*, pp. 375–376.

22 J. Kagan, L. W. Sontag, C. T. Baker, and Virginia Nelson, "Personality and I.Q. Change," *Journal of Abnormal and Social Psychology*, 56 (1958), pp. 261–266.

23 See Clifford E. Howe, "A Comparison of Motor Skills of Mentally Retarded and Normal Children," *Exceptional Children*, 25 (1959), pp. 352–354; and studies cited in G. Orville Johnson and Rudolph J. Capobianco, "Physical Condition and its Effect upon Learning in Trainable Mentally Retarded Children," *Exceptional Children*, 26 (1959), pp. 3–5 and 11. However, Laycock and Caylor suggest that physical differences between children by level of intelligence may derive from socioeconomic factors instead. "Physiques of Gifted Children and Their Less Gifted Siblings," *Child Development*, 35 (1964), pp. 63–74.

24 Howard B. Newcombe and Olwyn G. Tavendale, "Effects of Father's Age on the Risk of Child Handicap or Death," *American Journal of Human Genetics,* 17 (March, 1965), pp. 163–178.

25 Quoted from *Physiologie sociale,* X, 177, in Emile Durkheim, *Socialism* (New York: Collier Books, 1962), pp. 136–137.

26 Quoted from *Science de l'homme* in Durkheim, *Socialism, op. cit.,* p. 137.

27 Quoted from Martin Barr, *Mental Defectives,* 1904, p. 69 in Davies, *op. cit.,* p. 17.

28 See S. Davies, *The Mentally Retarded in Society* (New York: Columbia University Press, 1959) and Herbert Goldstein, "Social Aspects of Mental Deficiency," doctoral dissertation, University of Illinois, 1957.

29 Reported in Samuel A. Kirk, "The Challenge of Individual Differences," paper prepared for Conference on Quality and Equality in Education, Princeton University, December 2–4, 1964. See also N. O'Connor and J. Tizard, *The Social Problem of Mental Deficiency* (New York: Pergamon Press, 1956).

30 A. Binet and T. Simon, *The Development of Intelligence in Children* (Baltimore: Williams and Wilkins, 1916). Cited in Clemens E. Benda, *Developmental Disorders of Mentation and Cerebral Palsies* (New York: Grune and Stratton, 1952), p. 6. Quoted by permission of Dr. Benda, Grune and Stratton, and Williams and Wilkins.

31 Actually, Cattell had introduced a mental test into the United States in the late nineteenth century. However, Goddard, who popularized intelligence testing in America, preferred the Binet-Simon test. See G. Wilson Shaffer, "The Nature of Intelligence," in Sonia F. Osler and Robert E. Cooke, eds., *The Biosocial Basis of Mental Retardation* (Baltimore: Johns Hopkins Press, 1965), pp. 23–24.

32 Actually, the Binet-Simon test had met with harsh criticism from its inception. See Eugene E. Doll, "A Historical Survey of Research and Management of Mental Retardation in the United States," in E. Philip Trapp and Philip Himelstein, eds., *Readings on the Exceptional Child* (New York: Appleton-Century-Crofts, 1962), pp. 33–35.

33 Seymour B. Sarason and Thomas Gladwin, "Psychological and Cultural Problems in Mental Subnormality," in Richard L. Masland, Seymour B. Sarason, and Thomas Gladwin, *Mental Subnormality* (New York: Basic Books, 1958), p. 160.

34 Samuel A. Kirk, "Amelioration of Mental Disabilities Through Psychodiagnostic and Remedial Procedures," in George A. Jervis, ed., *Mental Retardation* (Springfield, Ill.: Charles C Thomas, 1967), Chapter 13.

35 Rick Heber, "Mental Retardation: Concept and Classification," in Trapp and Himelstein, *op. cit.,* p. 76.

36 Edgar A. Doll, "The Essentials of an Inclusive Concept of Mental Deficiency," *American Journal of Mental Deficiency,* 46 (October, 1941), pp. 214–219.

37 Edgar A. Doll, *Clinical Studies in Feeblemindedness* (Boston: Badger, 1917), p. 26.

38 T. L. McCulloch, "Reformulation of the Problem of Mental Deficiency," *American Journal of Mental Deficiency,* 52 (October, 1947), p. 134.

39 Joseph F. Jastak, Halsey M. MacPhee, and Martin Whiteman, *Mental Retardation, Its Nature and Incidence* (Newark, Delaware: University of Delaware Press, 1963), pp. 11.

3.

General Prevalence of Mental Retardation

Systematic study of the prevalence of mental retardation began with the growth of special educational services and residential facilities and the popularity of social Darwinism. Before that time, it made little difference whether those classified as mentally retarded constituted one per hundred or one per thousand of the general population; the suffering and indignities inflicted upon them were inhuman regardless of the number involved. Dorothea Dix wrote that there were:

> More than 9,000 idiots, epileptics, and insane in the U.S. destitute of the appropriate care and protection, bound with galling chains, bowed beneath fetters and heavy iron balls attached to drag chains, lacerated with ropes, scourged with rods and terrified beneath storms of excrement and cruel blows; now subject to jibes and scorn and torturing tricks; now abandoned to the most outrageous violations.[1]

With universal education, decisions had to be made about the schooling of the mentally retarded. Their numbers had to be ascertained, and criteria for classifying individuals as mentally retarded had to be established. This chapter deals with (a) the problems of classification and case-finding in surveys for estimating the prevalence of mental retardation, (b) findings in prevalence studies, and (c) the implications of these findings.

43

Estimating the Prevalence of Mental Retardation

The problems of estimating rates of mental retardation are similar to those of establishing delinquency rates. Delinquents are violators of the law; the mentally retarded fall within the province of educational, medical, and welfare agencies. Just as the police, courts, and prisons become the contact points for identifying delinquents, the mentally retarded are labeled by their contact with educational and welfare agencies. Furthermore, persons judged as delinquent by the courts and police agencies under-represent the actual number of persons engaged in the crime; and the records of educational, medical, and welfare organizations may underestimate the number and kinds of mentally retarded people in the population. Because of the possible under-representation of the true number in official records, various attempts have been made to determine empirically the proportion of persons who are mentally retarded.

Early estimates of the prevalence of mental retardation were associated with alarming statements about feeblemindedness being largely hereditary and about the feebleminded tending to have a higher birthrate than others in the population. These estimates were used to justify nativistic ideologies and antagonism to lower-class populations. According to A. F. Tredgold, "the number of children born of feeble-minded women throughout the country [England] must be very considerable, and when we remember how strongly hereditary this condition is, and how exceedingly probable it is that these children will grow up, if not actually mentally defective, at any rate, paupers, prostitutes, criminals, or ne'er-do-wells we see how serious must be the consequences of this propagation upon the future of the nation . . . the birthrate of the country is steadily declining; but this decline is not general, it is selective and unfortunately, the selection is in the wrong direction."[2] The association between feeblemindedness and "degeneracy" of the lower socioeconomic groups was inherent in Tredgold's concept of the inheritance of a "neuropathic" constitution. Neuropaths were regarded as responsible for not only feeblemindedness but also crime and degradation in society.

In the early part of the twentieth century numerous estimates were made of the proportion of criminals, paupers, and alcoholics who were mentally retarded. At Sing Sing Prison, Dr. Bernard Glueck studied about 600 consecutive admissions. About 28 percent were classified as intellectually defective.[3] A 1917 study of unmarried mothers reported that 40 to 45 percent were "almost without question so low-grade mentally as to make life under institutional care the only happy one for themselves and the most economical and the only safe arrangement for society."[4] The mentally retarded were regarded as a threat to the continuity of the society, and it was important to determine the size of this deviant segment of the population.

The major early prevalence studies of mental retardation were European. Estimates made in France by Binet and Simon in 1907 were 1.0 percent for boys and 0.9 percent for girls of school age. The English Royal Commission in 1906 provided an estimate of 4.6 per thousand. About 1915 to 1920 various investigations were undertaken in the United States, but they were generally poorly conceived and ineptly carried out. The Wood Report done in England in 1929 by E. O. Lewis, which will be discussed later, provided the most comprehensive study to date. In summarizing earlier studies, the Wood Report indicated that it is "so difficult to compare the conditions and standards of these investigations . . . that it would be an unprofitable task to attempt a detailed discussion of these various estimates." The several early estimates presented in Table 2 are far lower than those found in later investigations.

TABLE 2

Investigations of the Prevalence of Mental Retardation
in the Early Twentieth Century[1]

Year	Investigation	Estimated Number of Mentally Deficient per 1000 Population
1906	Royal Commission (England)	4.61
1915	New York State Commission	4.13
1915	W. E. Fernald (Massachusetts)	4.00
1915	Porter County (Indiana)	7.35
1916	Newcastle County (Delaware)	3.82
1916	C. H. Strong's investigation of New York charities	3.40
1916	Nassau County (New York)	5.44

[1] From the Wood Report, presented in N. O'Connor and J. Tizard, *The Social Problem of Mental Deficiency* (New York: Pergamon Press, 1956), p. 19.

The first significant American investigation of the prevalence of mental retardation was undertaken by Lemkau, Tietze, and Cooper in the 1930s in Baltimore, Maryland. The investigators searched the records of all community and state agencies concerned with mentally deviant individuals. Included were mental and general hospitals, state schools for both mentally retarded and delinquent children, clinics, social agencies, special education classes, and court records. These records were linked with those of a special census of Baltimore, and the information was collated. The investigators did not administer intelligence tests but instead obtained test scores from records. As a result, IQ scores from different kinds of tests were included. Children who were found to have an IQ below 70 on these tests were classified as mentally retarded. The investigators categorized the retarded population by IQ ranges of 69–50, 49–25, and 24–0. A fourth group of retarded persons, consisting mainly of adults with an official history of mental deficiency, was classified as "untested." The findings of the Baltimore study showed a prevalence of 12.2 per thousand population. The tabulation by age is shown in Table 3, which indicates an increasing prevalence to the period of young adolescence and then a steady decline.

TABLE 3

Prevalence of Mental Retardation by Age, per 1,000 Population, in Baltimore[1]

Age in Years	Retardates per 1000 Population
0– 4	.7
5– 9	11.8
10–14	43.6
15–19	30.2
20–29	7.6
30–39	8.2
40–49	7.4
50–59	4.5
60 and over	2.2
All age groups	12.2

[1] P. Lemkau, C. Tietze, and M. Cooper, "Mental Hygiene Problems in an Urban District," *Mental Hygiene*, 26 (1942), pp. 275–288.

Moreover, more boys than girls were found to be retarded, and the proportion of high-grade mental retardates was approximately ten times the proportion falling into the 49 and below IQ categories. These tendencies have been found in almost every succeeding investigation of prevalence.

In the years following World War II, prevalence studies were undertaken again. However, this time the motivation for the studies was not the impending threat to the survival of the society. Instead, the impetus came from the development of special education and welfare facilities. The surveys were needed to determine the amount of service that would be required in school systems, social agencies, and medical facilities.

The use of survey methods to estimate prevalence is generally costly and inefficient; yet few governments require the registration of mentally retarded children at the time of diagnosis. Under provisions of continuous care (as provided by national health programs in the Scandinavian countries and Great Britain), estimates of incidence from records are feasible. Without a registration procedure, however, the incidence of new cases per year cannot be ascertained. As a consequence of this situation, surveys have been undertaken in the United States to indicate the prevalence of mental retardation. This section will discuss first the procedures used for gauging mental retardation in these surveys and then the methods applied in case-finding. The investigations listed include only those which illustrate different procedures that can be applied. There are numerous other prevalence studies that are too limited in scope, too carelessly performed, or which almost duplicate the techniques described below.

MEASUREMENT OF PREVALENCE OF MENTAL RETARDATION

Difficulties encountered in estimates of the prevalence of mental retardation include both (a) developing procedures to estimate intelligence and (b) defining cutting points in the range of intelligence at which children are to be characterized as mentally retarded. Listed below are cutting points and procedures used in prevalence surveys which should indicate the comparability of the studies.

1. Maine Survey in 1957. Principals and head-teachers of children in the regular grades were asked to do the following:

> Please list below all mentally retarded children in your school and also those out-of-school in your school's territory except those

enrolled in special classes or programs for retarded children. A child is to be counted as retarded if he has received an IQ below 75 on an individual mental test which is believed to be valid by the tester. He is also to be counted if you believe his mental ability is below 75 per cent of average mental ability for his age. Please estimate the mental ability of the children for whom you cannot give individual IQ's of the sort named. But note that it is per cent of *average* ability that is wanted, not per cent of superior ability. Usually when a child has average ability and is placed in the proper grade for his age, he can do C work in school (though he may not actually be doing C work). But when a child has mental ability below 75 per cent of average, he will either be found in a grade two or three years below his age-level, or he will be doing work far below C quality. In any case, it is mental *ability* that is to be estimated, not school ranking. Please do not list children who are behind in school, but whom you do not believe to be mentally retarded. But include mentally retarded children who are severely enough physically handicapped or emotionally disturbed to constitute an additional educational handicap, and specify the additional handicap.[5]

2. New York State Censuses.   In the census of severely retarded children, school superintendents were requested to report all children "whose I.Q. score was known to be below 50 and to include all children without an I.Q. record whose behavior and physical characteristics, as judged by a responsible official, would place them in the category of severely retarded."[6] The criteria used in the Onondaga County study of all mentally retarded were even more ambiguous. The investigators considered "The specific signs and symptoms included under the rubric 'retardation' . . . [to be] heterogeneous, confused, and confusing because retardation is a word conveying a variety of symptom manifestations which reflect many patterns of troublesome development."[7] They decided to include questionable cases in the retarded category:

> In order to be as inclusive as possible, responsible child-care agencies were requested to report all children under 18 years of age, and residents of Onondaga County on March 1, 1953, identified as definitely mentally retarded, or suspected of mental retardation on the basis of developmental history, poor academic performance, IQ score, or social adaptation when contrasted with their age peers.[8]

3. Illinois Census of Exceptional Children in 1958.   The criterion applied in Illinois was only vaguely defined. However, the instructions were elaborate:

The Educable Mentally Handicapped (EMH) child does not have the intellectual ability to succeed in the regular program. But he can develop independence and self control in work and school relationships. He may not be able to read better than 2nd or 4th grade level.

The Trainable Mentally Handicapped (TMH) child is not able to be self-dependent. He cannot succeed in academic work but he can develop in self-care and social adjustment.

It will help in selecting possible mentally handicapped to keep the following in mind. The most proficient can be checked as Slow-Learners; the very lowest as T.M.H.; and the middle group as E.M.H.

a. Primary — (Grades, 1, 2, 3, CA 6–8)

(1) Appears to be socially immature; lacking in self help skills; noticeably inept in social participation; has difficulty in getting to and from school on his own; speech may be very infantile; may not seem to understand "sharing concept," does not adjust to new situations.

(2) May appear to be physically immature; noticeably different or retarded in manipulative skills; drawing with pencil may be at a very low level; may have difficulty in tying shoes and putting on outer clothing.

(3) Intellectual Immaturity: low level of information about self such as age, address, family names and occupation; low level of general information such as dates, time, and community information; has difficulty in understanding and following directions; has poor planning ability; always waits for new directions or acts very impulsively; has very narrow range of interests with little intellectual curiosity.

(4) Academic Immaturity: may not know colors; may not know how many pennies in a nickel, nickels in a dime, etc.; reading level (with understanding) two or three years below what one would expect from chronological age; may be able to count but has no functional understanding of addition or subtraction; has difficulty in re-telling stories.

(None of the above are complete lists — just examples.)

b. Above Chronological Age of Nine.

(1) Demonstrates very little constructive initiative in self direction. Needs constant direction.

(2) Academic retardation of two or three years in comparison with chronological age.

(3) Group intelligence test scores are generally below 80.
(If group intelligence tests are available.)

(4) Much of behavior and/or verbal responses seem irrelevant to the situation.

(5) May prefer to play with younger children.

(6) Has a great deal of difficulty in adapting to structured games or activities wherein complex rules must be observed.

(7) Has difficulty in applying what has been learned from one situation to a similar situation.

(8) Does not seem to realize what is required from him in social situations.

(9) Seems little concerned about frequent errors in academic work.

(Again — just examples.)[9]

4. Middle-sized City, California Survey.   In this study, persons were defined as mentally retarded when they scored low on a social-developmental questionnaire as well as on a standard intelligence test. The composition of the social development test differed for various ages. The test for children under the age of five included a modification of the Vineland Scale, Gesell items, the respondent's spontaneous report of the child's behavior, and the interviewer's rating of the child's intellectual level. Failure on any of these screening devices was considered as a failure for the social developmental scale. For children of school age, another criterion was added — that of falling behind two or more years below the grade level expected for that age. For adults, the criteria for success in social development were different: college attendance or completion of a high school course in a college preparatory curriculum, an occupation rated above the first decile of the Duncan Socioeconomic Index, the respondent's and the interviewer's ratings of the intellectual level of the person, and finally a modification of the Vineland Scale. If the adult failed both the occupational and educational criteria, he was considered a failure in the social-developmental scale. Intelligence was indicated by IQ. When an IQ test score was not available in school or social agency records, Stanford-Binet tests were given to older children and adults; the Kuhlmann test was used for younger children.[10]

5. Delaware Survey.   Jastak's study in Delaware utilized four criteria to indicate mental retardation: (a) The first was a psychometric average based on a test battery including vocabulary, similarities, arithmetic, reproduction of drawings, auditory digit span, the Raven Matrices Scale (sections), recall of vocabulary, picture anomalies, coding of symbols, form boards, a pegboard test, picture reasoning, oral reading, recollection of the content of the picture anomalies series, and social concepts portraying some action capable of being apprehended under a generalization such as help, reassurance, hostility, or punishment. (b) In addition to the psychometric average, the psychometric altitude in these tests was also used as a criterion. Thus, if an individual was very high on one or more tests, this would be taken into account. (c) The third criterion was an index of the number of years of school completed. (d) And the fourth index was occupational achievement. For an individual to be classified as retarded, he had to score low on all four indices. Three levels of retardation were utilized as cut-off points on the four indices — 25 percent, the 9 percent, and the 2 percent levels.[11]

6. *Wyoming Mental Ability Survey in 1957–1958.* The California Test of Mental Maturity, short-form, was used as a screening test. Most children with low IQs on the California Test of Mental Maturity were then given individual examinations (revised Stanford-Binet Scale). Those children with an IQ of 80 or lower on the California test were classified as mentally retarded.[12]

The implications of using different criteria for designating individuals as mentally retarded will be discussed at the end of this chapter. Whatever variations in prevalence have been found in these surveys may be a consequence of the disparate criteria of retardation applied.[13]

CASE-FINDING

Both the measure of intelligence and the manner in which population is screened to uncover cases of mental retardation are important factors in determining prevalence. This section will describe the procedures for case-finding in the surveys discussed above. First, however, the results of investigations pertaining to case-finding methodology will be presented.

Wishik investigated the prevalence of handicapped children in two Georgia counties. He compared two techniques — a voluntary reporting procedure and a canvassing of households. In the first technique, for a three-week period all inhabitants were asked to report to the local health department children whom they suspected of having a handicapping condition. Copies of the questionnaires were distributed in churches, stores, newspapers, and other public places. School personnel, parents, physicians, nurses, and friends and neighbors were asked to report on children within and outside their families. The second technique was a sample canvass on the basis of selecting every tenth household for questioning. Fifty-three women from church groups were trained as volunteer interviewers.

The two techniques in the Wishik study were compared in the following way: All voluntary and canvass reports were edited by a pediatrician, and a presumptive diagnosis was made on the basis of reported symptoms. Then a sample of persons was drawn from each diagnostic category for invitation to clinics. The canvass diagnostic reports were found to be slightly more accurate. In terms of coverage, the canvass missed 7.6 percent of the cases, while the number reported through the voluntary procedure would have overlooked about 10 percent of the mentally retarded children found on the basis of the canvass.[14] Hence, in terms of accurate case-finding, the sample canvass seems somewhat more efficient than voluntary reporting.

Although the Wishik study indicated that household interviews on the basis of a probability sample provide better estimates than voluntary reporting, Trussell and his associates reported that respondents in household interviews fail to reveal known conditions or may even be ignorant of them. In a sample of approximately 850 respondents, household interviews revealed only 46 persons with mental, psychoneurotic, and personality disorders; however, medical examination of this sample indicated 153 affected individuals.[15]

In addition to the problem of under-reporting of mentally retarded persons, estimates of prevalence may also suffer from biases against participating either in interview studies or in psychological examinations. A sizable part of every community opposes attempts to assess a population in terms of psychiatric problems or mental retardation. Presumably, these are the individuals who view behavioral scientists with suspicion and distrust. This opposition has taken the form of burning answer sheets to socio-psychometric measures, linking the investigation to socialism or communism, and creating public sentiment against research on mental health.[16]

Aware of the opposition engendered by mental health research, Mercer, Dingman, and Tarjan attempted to obtain active cooperation by agencies in one community to be studied. They wished ultimately to sample about 450 children and adults who had been screened in a first interview and administered intelligence tests in a second one. In order to find cases of mental retardation, they contacted approximately 2,600 households. The investigators tried, first, to involve local officials, newspapers, and school personnel in the project.

Second, the community leaders were kept constantly informed of current problems faced by the staff. An advisory group made up of consultants from community social agencies and prominent social scientists was formed. In addition, the project staff addressed school personnel and parents' groups. And third, the investigators provided data, especially census data and case-reporting of the mentally retarded, to the schools. They sent introductory letters to parents, and newspaper articles informed the public. In this study, screening interviews were held in 2,659 households, with a completion rate of 91 percent.[17]

The cost of undertaking a project of the kind described by Mercer, Dingman, and Tarjan must be weighed against the results obtained through less efficient methods. Possibly, to obtain minimum estimates, voluntary reporting or interviews obtained through probability sampling may suffice. The variety of case-finding procedures used in prevalence studies of mental retardation is illustrated below.

1. Maine Survey.   "In the second week of May, 1957, questionnaires were mailed to all known Maine schools and child-serving residential institutions, requesting the reporting as of May, 1957, of all children known or believed to be retarded whether in the school or institution, or out-of-school among the clientele of the particular school. Reporting of the fact that a particular school had no retarded children enrolled or out of school was also requested. For each child the following facts were asked: name, birth date, placement in school or special program, presence and nature of any additional handicap of educational significance and IQ; whether this IQ was a test score or an estimate; and, if it was a test score, the identity and the data of the test and the qualification of the tester. For each school, the identity of the person filling out the forms and the total enrollment of the school were also requested."[18]

2. New York State Surveys.   The procedure in New York State was somewhat similar to that in Maine. In the severely retarded child survey, blanks and instruction sheets were mailed to all school superintendents with a request that all children in their district with an IQ known or believed to be below 50 be reported. It was suggested that the superintendent obtain the cooperation of all local agencies having knowledge of these children. A few of the superintendents in small cities and villages failed to report. Records in the state department of education and the New York City child guidance clinics, and state institutions and hospitals were also canvassed. The Onondaga survey included schools in its canvassing, as well.

3. *Illinois Survey.* The 1958 survey in Illinois involved the colleclection of data by the teachers and local school administrators. The collation was performed by the county superintendent and forwarded to the State Office of Public Instruction. This survey made the county superintendent responsible for collecting data from public schools, private schools, social agencies, public health nurses, and courts. The forms were prepared by the State Office. The instructions to the teachers (or other enumerators) requested that *all* children in the classroom be listed on the basic form so that each child would be considered in reporting exceptionalities. This task, however, produced complaints from the enumerators and may have impeded cooperation in the collection of data. In two sparsely settled counties, the county superintendents submitted reports only after they were threatened with the withdrawal of state funds; the validity of these reports is questionable. Because of the reluctance of several county superintendents to cooperate in the processing of data, later surveys were based on direct submission of raw data to the State Office for processing.

4. *Middle-sized City, California Survey.* This survey, considered a pilot study, was based on a 1 percent probability sample of a community of approximately 60,000 persons. All household members were covered by the questionnaire. A second sample was used in addition to the area probability sample; to increase the number of retardates in the study, thirty households with children in special education classes in public schools of the community were selected at random.

5. *Delaware Survey.* The cases were found through an extensive survey based on an area probability sample. About 1,000 households were surveyed initially. Contacts with the families chosen for the study consisted of first a screening interview and then an intensive examination. In the screening interviews, the sample was divided into two provisional groups, the retarded and the nonretarded, on the basis of three Wechsler-Bellevue tests. All families with one or more individuals classified as retarded were scheduled for an

intensive examination consisting of the administration of fifteen psychological tests and seven interview schedules relating to education, occupation, marital history, health, social participation, and residential situations. About 450 families were included in the intensive examination stage.

6. *Wyoming Survey.* The California Test of Mental Maturity was made available to all schools in the state, including parochial and private schools. Habitual absentees were probably missed. Of the 70,000 children enrolled in public school classes, approximately 65,000 were tested. It was estimated that about 92 percent of the children enrolled in public schools and 87 percent enrolled in non-public schools were tested.

In summary, the techniques for case-finding vary widely in surveys undertaken to determine the prevalence of mental retardation. Some enumerations have relied heavily on standardized tests, while others have utilized observations by teachers and other professionals. Several surveys have applied systematic sampling of city or state populations, with the investigators collecting the data. For the most part, however, the surveys have been based on reports by school and welfare agencies whose professional staff acted as enumerators. Obviously, where the investigator must rely on reports of observers or staffs of schools and agencies for case-finding, he has little control over data collection.

Findings on Prevalence of Mental Retardation in the United States

Interest during the 1950s in problems associated with mental defects stimulated investigations throughout the United States to determine the extent of mental retardation among the American population. Significantly, these investigations occurred simultaneously with the growth of the parent-group movements, the striving for full employment of the working population, the marked expansion of enrollment in the American educational system, and the development of movements for promoting research and care in all areas of illness.

The findings of the major investigations are presented in Table 4. The characteristics of the communities and areas studied differed widely. Some of the studies took place in large cities, others in rural-dominated countries and sparsely settled areas, still others in states with much industry and widely differentiated economic areas. In addition, the studies covered a wide variety of ethnic and racial groups; for example, the ethnic and racial composition of Hawaii differs markedly from that of Philadelphia or Illinois. Similarly, wide ranges in climate and geological character provided the settings for these surveys. Yet Table 4 reveals a marked similarity in the prevalence rates produced by these investigations. The lowest rate was 1.52 percent in New Jersey, and the highest rates were 3.7 percent in the Georgia study and 5.0 percent in Wyoming. The similarity among rates is remarkable not only because of the different populations sampled but also because of the wide variety of case-finding procedures and measurement techniques applied. The significance of this similarity will be discussed later in this chapter.

European Prevalence Studies

Generally, European countries are more homogeneous ethnically than the United States. Except for the major turmoil during and after World War II, the countries of Europe have been settled for centuries by relatively stable populations. Although there has been much internal migration in these countries, symbols of nationalism still segregate these populations from one another.

Because of their smaller size and greater homogeneity, European countries permit greater latitude in the kinds of investigations of the incidence and prevalence of mental retardation than does the United States. Akesson describes four techniques for estimating the number of mentally retarded individuals in a population: the genealogical random-test method, the birth register method, the period method, and the census method.

The genealogical random-test method involves random sampling of a number of normal individuals to test relatives (usually siblings and parents) for possible mental retardation. The error usually made with this technique is using convenient, easily obtained samples. Such "judgment" samples weaken the generalizability of results; the groups' marriage rates, fertility rates, and migration patterns influence the accuracy of estimates made in this way.[19]

The birth register technique involves random sampling from the birth register of a political unit. While it provides a complete sampling list, this method depends upon the accuracy of the vital statistics and the residential stability of persons born in that area. In his study of individuals born between 1883 and 1887 on the Danish island of Bornholm, Fremming traced 92 percent of the persons appearing in the register. In a highly mobile population, the percentage located would undoubtedly have been smaller.

The period method of estimating the number of mentally retarded individuals involves everyone born or living in a specified area during a certain period of time. This type of investigation is generally feasible in rural areas with low migration rates. For example, Larsson and Sjogren investigated thirteen parishes on islands off the coast of Sweden for a period from 1900 to 1944. The total population was approximately 25,000. Because of the length of investigation, Larsson and Sjogren found 320 individuals of low-grade mental deficiency (estimated IQ below 55). The period method permits the investigators to observe the population through various time periods. Thus cyclical conditions, long-term trends, personal disabilities with gradual onset, and variations in mortality and fertility are taken into account. Like the birth register method, the period method suffers from inaccuracies of vital records and the effects of large-scale migration.

The census method is the most widely used means for estimating the prevalence of mental deficiency. It is independent of rates of migration, fertility, and mortality, but it usually results in underestimations of the rates of mental deficiency in the community. The usual procedure is to contact persons and institutions where the probability of finding mentally retarded individuals is high. For example, Akesson canvassed institutions, hospitals, and clinics who might have contact with the retarded; he consulted district physicians and perused the parish registers for persons listed as mentally deficient. Finally, he consulted with local informants, including ministers, teachers, district nurses, representatives for social organizations, superintendents of homes for the aged and for children, and persons knowledgeable of local conditions. Akesson then examined referred individuals by (a) an interview, (b) a short screening test, (c) the revised Stanford-Binet test (Swedish version), (d) objective data concerning the individual's accomplishments and social environment, and finally (e) a medical examination. He regarded those persons with an IQ of less than 68 on the Stanford-Binet test as mentally deficient. About 90 percent of the individuals referred

TABLE 4

Prevalence Studies of Mentally Retarded Children in the United States, with Year, Location of Study, Age Range, and Prevalence Estimate per 1000 Population

Year	Location	Report	Age Range	Estimate of Prevalence (per 1000)
1953	New Jersey	Howard[1]	school age	15.2
1953	Onondaga, N.Y.	Goodman[2]	under 18	35.2
1954	Philadelphia	Ferguson[3]	preschool	32.2
			school age	33.9
			adulthood	19.2
			all ages	23.2
1954	Georgia	Wishik[4]	0–20	37.0
1956	Hawaii	Weiner[5]	Grades K–12	23.6
1956	Delaware	Jastak[6]	All ages (through adult)	
			– at 25% cut-off pts.	83.3
			– at 9% cut-off pts.	20.3
			– at 2% cut-off pts.	3.8
1957	Maine	Levinson[7]	5–20	29.9
1958	Illinois	Farber[8]	6–15	18.8
1957–8	Wyoming	———[9]	6–21	50.2
1962	Middle-sized City, California	Mercer[10]	All ages (through adult)	36.1

[1] John W. Howard, ed., *Found, A Report of the Committee to Study the Education of Handicapped Children* (Trenton: New Jersey Department of Education, 1954.)

[2] Melvin B. Goodman, Ernest M. Gruenberg, Joseph Downing, and Eugene Rogot, "A Prevalence Study of Mental Retardation in a Metropolitan Area," *American Journal of Public Health*, 46 (June, 1956), pp. 702–707.

[3] Robert G. Ferguson, "A Study of the Problem of Mental Retardation in a Large Urban Community," *American Journal of Orthopsychiatry*, 27 (1957), pp. 490–501.

[4] Samuel M. Wishik, "Handicapped Children in Georgia, A Study of Prevalence, Needs, and Resources," *American Journal of Public Health*, 46 (February, 1956), pp. 195–203.

[5] Samuel A. Kirk and Bluma B. Weiner, "The Onondaga Census — Fact or Artifact," *Exceptional Children*, 25 (January, 1959), pp. 226–228, 230–231.

[6] Joseph F. Jastak, Halsey M. McPhee, and Martin Whiteman, *Mental*

were tested. Akesson found 1.8 percent of the total population to be mentally deficient. Like other investigators, Akesson found that the age group from ten to fourteen had the highest prevalence and that more males than females were mentally deficient.

In summary, despite the alternatives for estimating the prevalence of mental deficiency available to the European investigators, the census method predominates. Findings of European investigators are shown in Table 5. The rates in this table vary from about 1.3 percent in northern Sweden to 5.6 percent in northern Norway. The findings are thus generally comparable to those in the United States.

The investigation by Dr. E. O. Lewis in 1925–1928 has served as a model and base-line for later studies of prevalence. Prior to the Lewis survey, estimates of retardation were based on hunches, educated guesses, and personal prejudices. Lewis was commissioned by the Mental Deficiency Committee of Great Britain to undertake a survey of the prevalence of mental retardation in six areas in England and Wales, each with a population of about 100,000 persons. The areas were chosen to provide a broad representation geographically, industrially, occupationally, ethnically, and in housing conditions.

Instead of testing all children, Lewis tested only those in high-risk segments of the population. The head teacher at each school was asked to list the 15 percent of children over the age of nine who seemed to be "most backward." When too many boys were listed, additional names of backward girls were requested. Other children were added to the list: the 6 percent of the children who were most backward in the "infants" departments of schools, children with paralysis and epilepsy, and children who were designated as "abnormal temperamentally." Names of children excluded from school, children who had left school at later ages, and preschool

Retardation, Its Nature and Incidence (Newark, Delaware: University of Delaware Press, 1963).

[7] Elizabeth J. Levinson, *Retarded Children in Maine, A Survey and Analysis* (Orono, Maine: University of Maine Press, 1962).

[8] Bernard Farber, *Prevalence of Exceptional Children in Illinois in 1958* (Springfield: Illinois Superintendent of Public Instruction, 1959), Circular — Census IA.

[9] *Wyoming Mental Ability Survey, 1957–1958* (Cheyenne: State Department of Education, May 10, 1959).

[10] Computed from data in Jane R. Mercer, Edgar W. Butler, and Harvey F. Dingman, "The Relationship between Social Developmental Performance and Mental Ability," *American Journal of Mental Deficiency,* 69 (September, 1964), pp. 195–205.

TABLE 5

European Investigations of the Prevalence of Mental Retardation

Country	Year	Investigators	Tests — Criterion	Prevalence (per 1,000 Population)
England (urban and rural)	1925–1928	Lewis[1]	Census	29
England (rural community)	1934	Matthews Newlyn and Penrose[2]	All ages; Otis: two std. dev. below mean; for adults, relied on clinical statements	16
Denmark (island)	1883–7 through 1939	Fremming[3]	Birth registry method; biographies	30
Norway (throughout country)	1933	Lofthus, Rasmussen, and Ribsskog[4]	Group test; IQ below 75; children aged seven	38
Norway (North; small community)	1939–1944	Bremer[5]	Clinical statements; ages: 10 and over	55.6
Sweden (North; rural)	1949	Böök[6]	"roughly equivalent to . . . upper IQ limit of 60–70"; ages: 10 and over	12.8
Sweden (South; rural)	1961	Akesson[7]	Stanford-Binet: two std. dev. below mean; clinical statements; ages: 10 and over	17.9
Germany (villages)	1950	Schade[8]	Clinical statements; all ages	30

[1] E. O. Lewis, *Report of the Mental Deficiency Committee* (Wood Report) (London: His Majesty's Stationary Office, 1929).

[2] M. V. Matthews, D. A. Newlyn, and L. S. Penrose, "A Survey of Mental Ability in a Rural Community," *Sociological Review,* 29 (January, 1937), pp. 20–40.

[3] Kurt H. Fremming, *Morbid Risk of Mental Disease and Other Mental Abnormalities in an Average Danish Population* (Sygdomsrisikoen for Sindslidelser og andre sjaelelige Abnormtilstande i den danske Gennemsnitsbefolkning) (Copenhagen: Ejnar Munksgaard, 1947), p. 253.

children were obtained from schools, child welfare officers, and public health nurses. Lewis regarded case-finding among children out of school as the least adequate section of the survey.

There were two criteria by which the children were judged as mentally deficient. The first was social inadequacy, and the second was lack of both school and intelligence-test abilities. The children who were regarded as backward by their teachers were administered a group test; and the low scorers on the group test (from 2 to 7 percent of all children in a school) were given individual tests that had been standardized by Cyril Burt on English children. Generally, children with IQs below 70 were classified as mentally deficient. However, the criterion of social inadequacy caused some children with a history of poor school records or of other signs of "degeneracy" to be judged as mentally deficient. On the other hand, some children who had IQs below 70 but were getting along in school were not so classified.

Lewis found about 2.9 percent of all school-age children between the ages of seven and fourteen to be mentally deficient. Of these, 2.42 percent were feeble-minded (mildly retarded), 0.38 percent imbeciles, and 0.10 percent idiots (very severely retarded). He found a somewhat higher prevalence in rural areas than in urban centers (3.97 percent versus 2.09 percent).[20]

Lewis also attempted to estimate the prevalence of adult retardates. He contacted a large number of agencies dealing directly or indirectly with the mentally retarded. These included the local authority under the mental deficiency act, the local educational authority, the poor law authority, health and school medical officers, special mental deficiency medical officers, general practitioners and district nurses, certified institutions and hospitals, charitable homes and organizations, and the police and prison authorities. Home visits were paid, and as much information as possible was sought from

---

[4] Cited in Johan Bremer, "A Social Psychiatric Investigation of a Small Community in Northern Norway," *Acta Psychiatrica et Neurologica* (Copenhagen: Ejnar Munksgaard, 1951) (Supplement 62), pp. 76–84.

[5] *Ibid.*

[6] J. A. Böök, "A Genetic and Neuropsychiatric Investigation of a North-Swedish Population," *Acta Genetica et Statistica Medica,* 5 (1953), pp. 345–414.

[7] Hans Olof Akesson, *Epidemiology and Genetics of Mental Deficiency in a Southern Swedish Population* (Uppsala: Institute for Medical Genetics of the University of Uppsala, 1961).

[8] Cited in Bremer, *op. cit.*

clergymen, doctors, and social workers. All borderline cases were examined closely. Lewis regarded the ascertainment of adult retardates as more thorough in rural than in urban areas. On the basis of his findings, he estimated that there were 5.21 retardates per one thousand population over age sixteen in England and Wales.

About thirty-five years after the Lewis survey, Goodman and Tizard undertook a prevalence investigation of the children in Middlesex and London counties and compared their findings with his. The counties maintain central files in which all cases of mental subnormality that have been brought to notice are registered. Although Goodman and Tizard attempted to use criteria that were comparable to the Lewis study, they had to make modifications. A different test was used, and, while Lewis distinguished between the feebleminded and imbeciles on criteria other than test data for those children falling in the range of 45 to 50 IQ, Goodman and Tizard placed the cut-off point arbitrarily at 50 IQ. Moreover, since Lewis used social inadequacy as a criterion, he may have included some children with a physical handicap who were actually only borderline retarded. Finally, there has been an increase in facilities for training, and this may be responsible for differences in findings.

In spite of the central registry, there was still much variation in the rate of mental retardation by age groups. Although Goodman and Tizard found overall rates of 2.53 per thousand for imbeciles and idiots, the rate was lowest among preschool children and it rose to 3.61 per thousand among children between the ages of ten and fourteen.

Several differences were apparent between the findings of the Lewis study and the Goodman-Tizard investigation. For children aged seven to fourteen, the Lewis study provided a prevalence rate of 4.55 idiots and imbeciles per thousand children; but the Goodman and Tizard study showed for Middlesex County a prevalence of only 3.45 per thousand. On the other hand, when the prevalence of mongolism was examined, the Goodman-Tizard report for Middlesex showed higher prevalence among all age groups than did the Lewis report. In children under fourteen, the Lewis study found only 0.17 Mongoloids per thousand, while Goodman and Tizard reported 0.82.

Goodman and Tizard recognized several possible alternative interpretations of their findings but suggested that the findings could be best understood as reflecting an improvement in maternal and child health. With the dramatic change in prenatal and postnatal care and medical attention since the advent of national health insurance programs, the Mongoloid children could be expected to survive more readily; and there might be a general decline in obstetric abnormalities and low birth weight.[21] Fairweather and Illsley in England and Pasamanick and his associates in the United States have shown a consistent relationship between the presence of obstetric abnormalities, low birth weight, and the presence of mental retardation.[22] The findings of the Goodman-Tizard study indicate that repeated surveys over an extended period of time may be of value as epidemiological research.

 SUMMARY

Investigations into the prevalence of mental retardation began when educational institutions were democratized. With universal education, decisions had to be made regarding the schooling of the mentally retarded. Early estimates of mental retardation were based on studies that were poorly conceived and ineptly carried out. The rates estimated were lower than those of more recent studies.

With the expansion in special education services after World War II, numerous surveys were again undertaken to provide data on prevalence. Much attention was given to measurement procedures and case-finding techniques in these investigations. The methods used in major surveys were reviewed in this chapter. The characteristics of communities and areas studied varied widely. Despite the differences in measurement and case-finding procedures, there was considerable consistency among ten surveys reviewed in their prevalence estimates of generally 2 to 3 percent.

Inasmuch as European countries are more homogeneous ethnically and smaller in population and area than the United States, they permit more latitude in the kinds of procedures that can be applied in prevalence estimates. Four techniques have been used to appraise the number of mentally retarded in a population: the genealogical random-test method, the birth register method, the period method, and the census method. The census method is the most widely used. The findings of European studies are generally comparable to estimates of prevalence of mental retardation in the United States.

The investigation by E. O. Lewis has served as a model and baseline for later studies of prevalence. Its epidemiological value was demonstrated in a resurvey of areas of England included in the Lewis study. The resurvey indicated that the general prevalence of severe mental retardation had declined, but that mongolism had increased in frequency. The interpretation was that the marked improvement of medical services in Great Britain over the thirty-five-year period between surveys was responsible for a decline in obstetrical abnormalities and prematurity. This advance in medical services increased the life span of Mongoloid as well as other children.

GENERAL DISCUSSION

One question elicited by the review of studies pertaining to the prevalence of mental retardation is: Why is there general agreement in these studies that 2 or 3 percent of the total population of a society is mentally retarded? (The Wyoming study differs markedly from the others in the criterion of mental retardation and, consequently, in findings.) Since mental retardation is not a specific disease entity, the explanation must be sought elsewhere. The criterion for mental retardation is arbitrary; the cutting point could just as easily be 10 percent or 25 percent.

A partial answer to the question is that the persistence of social structure requires a given level of intelligence. According to Piaget, certain intellectual operations in judgment frequently are not found among the mentally retarded. Especially important is the development in normal persons of the facility for propositional or formal operations at about eleven to fifteen years of age. This stage in development is marked by an ability to reason by hypothesis, an operation that permits the individual to classify and order things in ways that allow him to organize his thoughts into a structured whole. He learns the possibility of "accepting any sort of data as purely hypothetical, and reasoning correctly from them." The process permits the individual to start from theory and to verify propositions. Moreover, one learns to construct mentally the range of combinations that are possible outcomes and to make deductions regarding these outcomes.[23]

Why are these operations necessary for the persistence of social structure? One of the features of social structure is that, in order to participate in meaningful and predictive ways, each individual must develop a conceptual map of the society. Where kinship groups predominate, the person must learn how he is related to all individuals he calls by a particular terminology and he must also learn how relatives with certain kin terms are related to one another. Without this conceptual map, he cannot organize his world, and without this organization the social structure could not persist. Indeed, one of the basic propositions regarding a culture is that, at least to a minimal degree, it must "work."[24]

For example, the Murngin aboriginal Australian tribe studied by Warner is very primitive technologically but has a highly complex kinship organization, which recognizes seventy-one kinds of relatives. In this system, there are seven lines of descent and five generations in each lineage. The seven descent lines include the individual's own patrilineal group, three lines of descent on his father's side, and three on his mother's side. Moreover, men cannot marry into the particular lineages into which their sisters marry; on the other hand, the sisters cannot marry into the lineages into which their brothers are required to marry. The choice of marital partners is highly restricted; a man must marry his real or classificatory mother's brother's daughter. In order for this system to operate, every member of the society must carry in his mind a conceptual map of the kinship organization. He must be able to recognize the persons and roles associated with each of the seventy-one kinship terms, and he must be cognizant of the sanctions for violating his obligations to these kin.[25]

A major criticism of modern society is that its organization requires an understanding beyond the capacity of many people. Elton Mayo in his critique of industrial organization pointed out that a worker's lack of motivation to apply himself fully in his work was partly due to an inability to conceptualize the entire process of manufacturing and marketing to which he was contributing. The concept of anomie describes the normlessness occurring when an individual cannot define changes in his position in the social structure.[26] Durkheim suggested that many suicides take place, during both economic depressions and periods of prosperity, because of substantial changes in status. The cognitive map of the operation of social relationships is no longer considered valid by individuals, and they are not aware of norms to guide them in their altered positions in the social structure. For example, the nouveau riche do not know the norms connected with their new position and they are no longer in a situation where their old norms apply. Under these conditions, traditional cognitive maps of social structure do not "work," and the social structure is then in danger of collapsing. The situations described by Durkheim and by Mayo pertain to dislocations of individuals in the social structure.[27] However, a comparable loss of identity and situations of normlessness would occur where the individuals did not have the intellectual equipment to develop and utilize cognitive maps of the social structure.

Although the level of culture may be dependent upon the ability of the most intelligent members of the society to solve a number of problems (in collaboration with those of lesser intelligence), its persistence as a "working culture" depends on a minimum level of competence among the general population. This minimal level includes the cognitive mapping through ability to handle organizing principles and, in making judgments, to develop and test hypotheses.

This speculation suggests that a society *cannot* tolerate a considerable amount of intellectual incompetence and still survive. The increase in American prevalence rates in mental retardation at mid-century over those in the early twentieth century, as reported in this chapter, may represent not only technical improvements in conducting surveys but also the greater degree of intellectual competence required to comprehend the workings of contemporary society. With broad diffusion of automation, the proportion of the population classified as mentally retarded may increase still further. (Similarly, European studies of isolated rural populations generally reveal lower prevalence rates than do surveys in cities or urbanized areas.) The 2 or 3 percent prevalence rate of the mentally retarded in contemporary urbanized society may indicate a necessity for highly complex conceptual mapping by the population.

The above speculation on the intellectual prerequisites for society is based in part on a content analysis of the kinds of items in IQ tests which educable mentally retarded adolescents and adults would fail. The discussion does not imply that virtually all persons classified as retarded in the surveys described in this chapter are actually retarded or that either genetic or environmental factors are the primary causes. Problems of test reliability and of etiology are not at issue here.[28] Rather, this speculation bears upon the question of the general similarity of prevalence estimates despite the different criteria of mental retardation applied and the diverse case-finding procedures used in surveys.

NOTES

[1] Dorothea L. Dix, *Memorial to the Legislation of Massachusetts*, 1843, Old South Leaflets, Vol. 6, No. 148, Boston, 1904.

[2] *Contemporary Review* (June, 1910), pp. 720–721.

[3] "Concerning Prisoners," *Mental Hygiene*, Vol. 2, pp. 177–218.

[4] Jean Weidensall, *Mentality of the Unmarried Mother*, National Conference of Social Work, Pittsburgh, 1917. Quoted in Stanley P. Davies, *The Mentally Retarded in Society* (New York: Columbia University Press, 1959), p. 47.

[5] Elizabeth J. Levinson, *Retarded Children in Maine: A Survey and Analysis* (Orono, Maine: University of Maine Press, 1962), Appendix 1.

[6] Theodore Bienenstock and Warren W. Cox, *Census of Severely Retarded Children in New York State* (Albany: Interdepartmental Health Resources Board, 1956), pp. 12–13.

[7] New York State Department of Mental Hygiene, *Technical Report of the Mental Health Research Unit, Syracuse* (New York: Syracuse University Press, July 1, 1955), p. 86.

[8] *Ibid.*, p. 87.

[9] Illinois Census of Exceptional Children, *Information and Directions, Circular — Census I* (Springfield: Superintendent of Public Instruction, 1958), pp. 14–15.

[10] Jane R. Mercer, Edgar W. Butler, and Harvey F. Dingman, "The Relationship between Social Developmental Performance and Mental Ability." *American Journal of Mental Deficiency*, 69 (September, 1964), pp. 195–205.

[11] Joseph J. Jastak, Halsey M. MacPhee, and Martin Whiteman, *Mental Retardation: Its Nature and Incidence* (Newark, Delaware: University of Delaware Press, 1963).

[12] *Wyoming Mental Ability Survey, 1957–1958*. Report issued by Superintendent of State Department of Education, May 10, 1959.

[13] See Samuel A. Kirk and Bluma B. Weiner, "The Onondaga Census — Fact or Artifact," *Exceptional Children*, 25 (January, 1959), pp. 226–228, 230–231.

[14] Samuel M. Wishik, "Handicapped Children in Georgia: A Study of Prevalence, Disability, Needs, and Resources," *American Journal of Public Health*, 46 (February, 1956), pp. 195–203.

[15] Ray E. Trussell, Jack Elinson, and Morton L. Levin, "Comparisons of Various Methods of Estimating the Prevalence of Chronic Disease in a Community — The Hunterdon County Study," *American Journal of Public Health*, 46 (February, 1956), pp. 173–182.

[16] See Leonard D. Eron and Leopold Walters, *American Psychologist*, 16 (May, 1961), p. 237; Gwynn Nettler, *American Psychologist*, 14 (November, 1959), p. 682; and J. Cummings and Elaine Cummings, *Closed Ranks* (Cambridge: Harvard University Press, 1957).

[17] Jane R. Mercer, Harvey F. Dingman, and George Tarjan, "Involvement, Feedback, and Mutuality: Principles for Conducting Mental Health Research in the Community," *American Journal of Psychiatry*, 121 (September, 1964), pp. 228–237.

[18] Levinson, *op. cit.*, p. 57.

[19] Hans Olof Akesson, *Epidemiology and Genetics of Mental Deficiency in a Southern Swedish Population* (Uppsala, Sweden: Institute for Medical Genetics, University of Uppsala, 1961). Unless otherwise indicated, the studies in this section have been described by Akesson and by N. O'Connor

and J. Tizard, *The Social Problem of Mental Deficiency* (New York: Pergamon Press, 1956).

20 Board of Education and Board of Control, *Report of the Mental Deficiency Committee* (Wood Report) (London: His Majesty's Stationary Office, 1929).

21 N. Goodman and J. Tizard, "Prevalence of Imbecility and Idiocy Among Children," *British Medical Journal*, 1 (January 27, 1962), pp. 216–219.

22 D. V. I. Fairweather and R. Illsey, "Obstetric and Social Origins of Mentally Handicapped Children," *British Journal of Preventive Social Medicine*, 14 (1960), pp. 149–159. Benjamin Pasamanick and A. M. Lilienfeld, "The Association of Maternal and Fetal Factors with the Development of Mental Deficiency: II. Relationship to Maternal Age, Birth Order, Previous Reproductive Loss and Degree of Mental Deficiency," *American Journal of Mental Deficiency*, 60 (1956), pp. 557–569. See also Benjamin Pasamanick and Abraham M. Lilienfeld, "Association of Maternal and Fetal Factors with Development of Mental Deficiency: I. Abnormalities in the Prenatal and Paranatal Periods," *Journal of the American Medical Association*, 159 (September 17, 1955), pp. 1–6; and D. J. P. Barker, "Low Intelligence: Its Relation to Length of Gestation and Rate of Foetal Growth," *British Journal of Preventive and Social Medicine*, 20 (1966), pp. 58–66.

23 Jean Piaget, *Logic and Psychology* (New York: Basic Books, 1957).

24 A. R. Radcliffe-Brown, *Structure and Function in Primitive Society* (Glencoe, Ill.: Free Press, 1952), p. 62. Edgerton points out that mildly retarded adults who are incompetent in handling concepts and numbers pertaining to time and space cannot "pass" as normal in sustained social interaction. Time and space are fundamental dimensions of social relations in modern society. (Robert B. Edgerton, *The Cloak of Competence* [Berkeley and Los Angeles: University of California Press, 1967], pp. 215–217.)

25 W. Lloyd Warner, *A Black Civilization: A Study of an Australian Tribe* (New York: Harper, 1937).

26 Elton Mayo, *The Human Problems of an Industrial Civilization* (New York: Viking Press, 1960) (initially published in 1933).

27 Emile Durkheim, *Suicide* (Glencoe, Ill.: Free Press, 1951).

28 The reliability of IQ tests in predicting future performance seems to vary by IQ range. In their fourteen-year follow-up of the intellectual development of cerebral palsied children, Klapper and Birch found that IQ scores under 75 were generally more stable than higher scores. The most unstable scores were in the 75–90 range. On the basis of analogs of intellectual development (derived from London data collected by Burt), Farber arrived at the same conclusion. See Zelda S. Klapper and Herbert G. Birch, "A Fourteen-Year Follow-Up Study of Cerebral Palsy: Intellectual Stability and Change," *American Journal of Orthopsychiatry*, 37 (April, 1967), pp. 540–547; and Bernard Farber, "Social Class and Intelligence," *Social Forces*, 44 (December, 1965), pp. 215–225. See also discussion of stability of IQ in Halbert B. Robinson and Nancy M. Robinson, *The Mentally Retarded Child* (New York: McGraw-Hill, 1695), pp. 391–394; and Benjamin Bloom, *Stability and Change in Human Characteristics* (New York: Wiley, 1964).

4.

Variations in the Prevalence of Mental Retardation

The previous chapter dealt with the general prevalence of the mentally retarded in society. But the mentally retarded are not distributed at random throughout the population; instead, certain social characteristics are associated with variations in the prevalence of retardation. This chapter will describe the relationship between population characteristics and mental retardation.

For several generations the controversy over hereditary versus environmental influences on mental retardation has remained alive in academic circles. Although data on the relationship between mental retardation and social characteristics of the population cannot resolve this controversy, they may provide leads that will ultimately prove fruitful. Factors to be examined in this chapter include age and sex of the retarded, community differences, social class variations and intelligence, differential fertility, and differential death rates.

Age and the Prevalence of Mental Retardation

Age is a crucial factor in prevalence studies of mental retardation, since one of the major problems in these studies is case-finding. Those periods in an individual's life when he has most contact with the official agencies gauging his intellectual competence must also be those in which case-finding is most accurate. Table 6 describes age variations in prevalence based on two studies. It is apparent here that prevalence is highest in the early adolescent years. Prior to early adolescence, the divergence in intellectual attainment between moderately or minimally mentally retarded and normal children is not readily apparent. With the development of the more abstract competencies at adolescence, the discrepancy between the normal and the mentally retarded seems to be greater, and identification of the retarded is easier. As adolescents leave school, they tend to be lost to the official case-finding agencies, and, since intellectual competence is no longer of official concern, mentally retarded adults become harder to find.

TABLE 6

Age Specific Estimates of Prevalence of Mental Retardation in the Maine and Illinois Studies (in Percentages)

Age (in years)	Estimate of Prevalence	
	Maine[1]	Illinois[2]
5	0.7	
6	1.1	
7	1.7	
8	2.3	2.7
9	2.8	2.7
10	3.5	2.8
11	3.7	2.7
12	4.3	2.8
13	3.9	3.1
14	4.25	3.4
15	3.6	3.8
16	2.6	2.9
17	1.8	2.0
18	1.7	
19	1.0	
20	0.6	

[1] Elizabeth J. Levinson, *Retarded Children in Maine: A Survey and Analysis* (Orono: University of Maine Press, 1962).
[2] Bernard Farber, *Prevalence of Exceptional Children in Illinois in 1958* (Springfield: Superintendent of Public Instruction, 1959), Circular — Census IA.

TABLE 7

Estimates of Prevalence of Mental Retardation of Children Aged 10–14 Based on Studies in the United States (Estimate in Rate per 1,000 Population)

Year	Location of Study	Investigators	IQ Range	Criterion of Retardation	Estimate of Prevalence
1936	Baltimore	Lemkau	0–69	Various tests	43.6
1953	Onondaga County, N.Y.	—	0–74	(Estimated by Levinson[1])	29
1954	Georgia County	Wishik	0–69	Stanford-Binet	32
1957	Maine	Levinson	0–75	Various tests	39.3
1956	Delaware	Jastak	Bottom 9% on four criteria	Four tests and classifications	42 (ages 10–12)
1958	Illinois	Farber	Undefined	Various tests and estimates	30
1964	Middle-sized city, California	Mercer	0–85 and low Social-Developmental Index Scores	Stanford-Binet and Kuhlmann	62.5 (ages 10–15)

[1] See Tables 2 and 3 for bibliographical references to sources.

Because the estimates of prevalence in the various studies are based on different age ranges, Table 7 presents estimates of mental retardation based on children aged ten to fourteen. This is the period of life by which perhaps 90 percent of the intellectual capacity has been attained, and when the official agencies of government are directly concerned with educability. For these reasons, the estimates in the ten to fourteen age range are probably the most reliable. The estimates in Table 7 for studies in the 1950s vary from about 3.0 percent to 4.2 percent, and the 1964 investigation shows a prevalence of 6.25 percent. The differences in cutting points of intelligence tests, kinds of intelligence tests applied, cultural conditions, and case-finding methods account for at least part of the variation in findings. But despite these confounding influences, there is still a narrow range in the estimates of the prevalence of mental retardation.

The diversity in case-finding techniques cannot explain entirely why the rates rise rapidly from about five years of age to about ten or twelve and then reach a plateau until about fourteen or fifteen years of age. At these ages certain developments generally occur in the child's thinking. The tasks required of children in tests of intelligence change at about age seven or eight. At this mental age level, children are asked to:

1. Identify essential similarities between concepts.
2. Produce connected and appropriate language in order to solve problems.
3. Answer verbal absurdities that require them to reconstruct mentally the total situation to indicate the irrelevancies.
4. Define such words as "haste," "lecture," and "skill."[1]

Piaget calls this the "concrete level stage." "At the level of concrete operations the subject tries to structure reality as completely as possible but he remains close to reality in its raw form — *i.e.*, as it appears without isolation of variables. When the subject classifies, orders, formulates, correspondences, etc., he registers the facts directly without adopting a critical attitude toward the empirical world or adopting systematic methodological precautions."[2] If the individual never develops to this stage, very likely he will be classified as a trainable retarded individual and will score below 50 in IQ.

The next stage in thinking develops from about eleven or twelve to about fourteen or fifteen years of age. This is the stage of formalization in logical thinking discussed in the previous chapter. According to Inhelder and Piaget:

Thinking becomes formal as soon as it undertakes the coordination of concrete groupings into a single system (of the second degree) because it deals with possible combinations and no longer with objects directly. However hesitating, however incomplete the first trials of formal thinking . . . we can nevertheless see a tendency toward a new form of equilibrium which is characterized by a new type of structural integration deriving from both the lattice and the group of inversions and reciprocities.[3]

Formal thinking is characterized by the use of propositions rather than classifications. Those children who do not achieve the level of propositional logic are nevertheless educable and tend to perform on tests in the IQ range of about 50 to 75.

The basis for the development of formal thinking, according to Inhelder and Piaget, lies in the interaction between the individual and his environment.

We wonder whether the individual manifestations of formal thinking are not simply imposed by the social groups as a result of home and school education. But the psychological facts allow us to reject this hypothesis of complete social determinism. Society does not act on growing individuals simply by external pressure, and the individual is not, in relation to the social any more than to the physical environment, a simple *tabula rasa* on which social constraints imprint ready-made knowledge. For, if the social milieu is really to influence individual brains, they have to be in a state of readiness to assimilate its contributions. So we come back to the need for some degree of maturation of individual cerebral mechanisms.[4]

Thus, according to the views of Inhelder and Piaget, the failure to develop past the educable stage could result from either a defective brain, a defective environment, or inadequate interaction between brain and environment. In addition, some failure by lower-socio-economic-status adolescents on IQ tests can probably be attributed to test unreliability.

Sex Differences in the Prevalence of Mental Retardation

Prevalence studies find more mentally retarded boys than girls. This finding occurs regardless of time or place. In the English study by Lewis, for children under sixteen, the overall prevalence rate for males was 17 percent higher than that for females. The differential rate was related to the level of intelligence. At the low level of intelligence, the male rate was 30 percent higher, but at the high level it was only 14 percent higher.[5] In the Onondaga County Survey, the percentage of male retardates was also related to IQ level. In the IQ range of 50 to 74, 64.3 percent of the retardates were male; among the trainable children (IQ 25 to 49), 50 percent of the retardates were male; for the totally dependent retardates (IQ 0 to 25), 45.6 percent were male.[6] In the Maine survey, the males constituted the majority of retardates at all IQ levels. As in the Onondaga survey, the proportion of males was higher among the educable than among the trainables or "custodials." Findings in other studies, such as the Hawaii survey by Weiner, are comparable.[7]

Levinson interprets the preponderance of males among the higher-level retardates as resulting from social factors in mental retardation. At low intellectual levels, retardates are often characterized by observable physical deformities and diagnosed brain damage. These disabilities are frequently the result of recessive genetic tendencies in males. The greater probability for recessive genotypes in males affects both brain development directly and susceptibility to diseases (which in turn might influence development). Recessive genotypes tend to be lethal, and many retardates do not survive to school age. The educable mentally retarded, however, do not ordinarily present physiological and anatomical peculiarities. Levinson believes that socioeconomic influences on the inhibition of intellectual development are more profound for males than for females. If that is the case, environmental differences in the home for male and female children may be greater than investigators have suspected previously. Perhaps the greater amount of street life of slum boys is reflected in these prevalence rates.[8]

Sarason and Gladwin have offered a different interpretation. They suggest that in the normal range intelligence tests do not find large differences between boys and girls because the test developers have generally removed those items on which males and females perform differently. The rationale for removing these items is that genetically there should be no sex difference, and, since boys and girls are raised in the same families, their general fund of knowledge and experience should be similar. Sarason and Gladwin, however, point out the continual differentiation in sex role in modern society, and they contend that there are definite cultural differences for males and females in modern society. They claim that one reason more males than females are classified as retarded is that, as Lemkau *et al.* have suggested, boys have more problems in communication skills and are more aggressive. This greater aggressiveness often leads to problems in deportment and to academic failure. Since most case-finding is based on reports of known cases of retardation rather than probability samples, estimates may exaggerate the extent of mental retardation among males.[9]

Few studies of the prevalence of mental retardation have applied probability sampling in data collection. Jastak, MacPhee, and Whiteman used a random sampling procedure in their investigation of the prevalence of mental retardation in the state of Delaware. For those persons who were diagnosed as retarded by being in the lowest 9 percent on four criteria, the prevalence for males was 23.5 per thousand, whereas the prevalence for females was 14.8 per thousand. For those falling in the lowest 25 percent of scores for criteria, the results were less extreme, with the prevalence for males being 89.6 per thousand and for females 72.0 per thousand.

The differences between rates for males and females in the Jastak, MacPhee, and Whiteman investigation are smaller than other estimates. In this respect, the findings suggest that to some extent boys are often over-represented in estimates of retardation because of case-finding procedures. On the other hand, the difference in rates by sex does not disappear; hence the results are also generally consistent with Levinson's interpretation.[10]

Community Differences in the Prevalence of the Mentally Retarded

The findings on the effects of community differences, especially urban versus rural residence, are complicated by differential cooperation and resources in case-finding. For example, in the Maine survey, the rate is higher for urban school systems, while rural school systems show a greater tendency to report more "doubtfuls." In reporting the Maine survey, Levinson points out that "the fact of unusually high male excess, especially in the rural areas, coupled with a great excess in numbers at ages 10–14, suggests that some of the boys reported at these ages may be considered retarded partly as a result of cultural and social pressures, while some girls go undetected because of the greater social acceptance of intellectual incompetence in girls."[11]

The Illinois survey reported by Farber indicates a similarity in prevalence between mental retardation and other handicapping conditions. He reports an inverse relationship between prevalence rates and population size of counties in Illinois for physical handicaps, hearing impairment, vision handicap, trainable and severe mental retardation, and slow learners. In contrast, the prevalence of speech handicaps, social maladjustment or emotional disturbance, educable mental retardation, and multiple handicapping conditions does not show a linear relationship to the size of the population in the county.[12] However, a relatively high rate of educable children appeared in counties with fewer than 30,000 children enrolled in school.

The findings in the Illinois survey suggest that, in the smaller school systems, biologically handicapped individuals are more visible and the application of testing is less frequent. As a result, teachers tend to perceive a greater degree of handicapping than in large school systems which rely to a greater extent on formal case-finding procedures. In some areas, the "doubtfuls" in intellectual ability are probably treated by teachers and other adults as mentally retarded, since there are no formal special education services to provide differential handling. Formal testing procedures and criteria for special education services would undoubtedly screen out many of the children considered as possibly mentally retarded.

Factors other than case-finding affect urban-rural differences in the prevalence of mental retardation. Hans Olof Akesson presents the hypothesis that community differences in the distribution of mental defectives are mainly due to selective migration. He proposes that people who migrate to industrial communities tend to be more intelligent than the residual rural population. He cites studies showing that men in the National Service who enlisted in a place other than their birthplace generally had higher scores in intelligence than those who enlisted at their place of birth. He also refers to a study in which the mean intelligence of children in rural areas was correlated with the percentage population change from 1931 to 1951. In Akesson's own investigation, the regions with the greatest rates of "dull" and "backward" children also show the greatest net losses in population through emigration. Akesson sees no reason to suspect regional differences in the frequency of mutation, tendencies toward genetic drift, or genetic selection. He concludes that migration differences remain as the most plausible explanation.[13]

To provide a rough test of the Akesson hypothesis of retardation in residual populations, the prevalence rates of educable and trainable mentally retarded children for the 102 counties in Illinois are compared below with the net migration rates for these counties. The relationship between the prevalence of mentally retarded children in 1958 and net migration is shown in Table 8. Because the prevalence data are probably unreliable for counties of population under 10,000, Spearman rank correlations have been computed for three groups of counties — over 50,000 population, between 10,000 and 50,000, and under 10,000 population. Inasmuch as the state census on exceptional children was taken in 1958, the period used for net migration is 1950–1960 as reported in the 1960 U.S. Census.[14] It may be significant that all counties with population less than 10,000 lost population through migration in the period covered.

TABLE 8

Rank Correlations Between Prevalence of Mentally Retarded Children and Net In-migration for Illinois Counties, 1958[1]

Characteristics of Counties	Number of Counties	Spearman Rho	
		Educable Mentally Retarded	Trainable Mentally Retarded
Over 50,000 population	23	−.38	−.20
10,000–49,999 population	65	−.15	−.29
Under 10,000 population	14[2]	−.04	+.17
Counties with special education services	(38)	−.34	——[3]

[1] Prevalence data from Bernard Farber, *Prevalence of Exceptional Children in Illinois in 1958* (Springfield: Superintendent of Public Instruction, 1959), Circular — Census IA. Data on net migration, 1955–1960, from U.S. Bureau of the Census, *County and City Data Book*, 1962 (A Statistical Abstract Supplement) (Washington: Government Printing Office, 1962).

[2] All counties with fewer than 10,000 inhabitants lost population through migration in 1955–1960.

[3] The number of counties with special education services for trainable mentally retarded children in 1958 is unknown.

The rank correlations for both the educable and trainable mentally retarded are in the expected direction for all counties of over 10,000 population. Although the correlation coefficients are not very high, they confirm the selective migration hypothesis for urbanized counties. Because counties with special education services are likely to be the ones with the most efficient means for securing estimates of prevalence, a separate rank correlation was computed for them. Thirty-eight counties in Illinois had special education provisions for the educable mentally retarded in 1958. The rank correlation coefficient was −.34 for these counties, and this correlation too is consistent with the hypothesis. The size of the rank correlation coefficients suggests that selective migration is responsible for a small portion of the variation in prevalence rates of mentally retarded children in different urbanized communities.

The general tendency for mental retardation to be more prevalent in rural than in urban areas may reflect the results of mass migration whereby intellectually retarded people tend to remain as residual population. Rural families are often poverty-stricken surplus populations. In 1962, farm and nonfarm rural families contributed far more than their share (22 percent) to the proportion of families having a total income below $3,000. In fact, the median income in 1959 of husband-wife farm families with two children under age eighteen was $3,779. For nonwhite farmers, the median was only $1,323.[15] Thus residual families display many attributes of an organizationally surplus population.

Selective migration may influence not only urban-rural differences but also the prevalence of mental retardation within different areas of the city. Fairbank compared persons of normal and subnormal intelligence seventeen years after they had first been evaluated in Baltimore. The normal persons had moved to other parts of the city in greater numbers than the subnormal group.[16] Similarly, a study by Baller, which compared mentally retarded adults with persons of normal intelligence, showed that a larger percentage of normal natives of Lincoln, Nebraska, migrated to other states than did retarded natives. The mentally retarded persons moved more often from one part of a given neighborhood to another in Lincoln, but they were inclined to confine their mobility to restricted areas of the city.[17]

The selective movement of retarded persons in urban areas influences the prevalence of mental retardation of school-age children in different areas of cities. Using the data presented by Mullen and Nee in their article on the comparative spatial distribution in Chicago of trainable and educable mentally retarded children,[18] Farber correlated the rankings for seventy-four community areas in the city (excluding the Loop) on rates of educable and trainable retardates with the socioeconomic ranks of these areas. The Spearman rank correlation coefficient between socioeconomic rank of the community area and the proportion of educable mentally handicapped children was −.60, while the correlation between socioeconomic rank and rate of trainable children was −.34. Thus, generally, the higher the rank on the socioeconomic scale, the lower the proportion of both trainables and educables to the total number of public school children in the community area. The prevalence of educable mentally retarded children seems to be more highly associated with socioeconomic rank than does the prevalence of the trainable retardates. These patterns are of course influenced by the tendency of some ethnic groups to remain in a given section of the city over several generations, while others are more prone to disperse eventually.[19]

The Heredity and Environment Controversy as Related to Social Class Variations in Intelligence

Intelligence is said to play an important role in social mobility and social differentiation. Svalastoga points out that numerous studies of various societies have shown a relationship between social mobility and intelligence test scores.[20] There is a similar association between intelligence test scores and occupation.[21] Honzik found a high correlation ($r = .5$) between men's intelligence-test scores at the age of thirty and their fathers' incomes reported about twenty-eight years previously.[22]

There seems to be little doubt that tested intelligence is related to social differentiation.[23] However, the process by which intelligence affects social differentiation is open to numerous interpretations. Some observers believe that genetic factors account for most of the difference between social classes; others adhere to the interpretation that environmental factors predominate. The discussion below will present some of the major arguments from both viewpoints.

THE HEREDITY POSITION

Those who favor the hereditarian point of view find support in research findings on intergenerational regression toward the population mean in IQ, the intergenerational constancy of IQ scores, and twin and family correlation studies. Some of these investigations will be described below.

Intergenerational Regression Toward the Population IQ Mean. Those observers who prefer the hereditarian view describe the distribution of intelligence test scores by social class as consistent with the expected distribution under conditions of polygenic inheritance. In accordance with these expectations, Burt has found that:

> (i) The mean intelligence of the children belonging to each occupational class deviates far less than the mean of the parents from the average for the population as a whole, and (ii) the intelligence of the individual children within any one class varies over a far wider range than that of their parents.[24]

This regression toward the mean and the greater variation of children's intelligence over that of their parents contrasts with expectations drawn from an environmental interpretation. If environment were the main determinant of intelligence, the test scores of the children would not regress toward the mean for the entire population. Instead, the children of professional parents would move to higher levels of intelligence, while children in the lower socioeconomic groupings would either remain constant or decline further. The reason for this expectation is that, as parents are upwardly mobile socially, they are able to give their children many opportunities which they themselves lacked, and to provide their children with kinds of intellectual stimulation which they themselves were unable to obtain.

The IQs of children of encouraging, well-educated parents could be expected to increase steadily from generation to generation. Children of stultifying parents could then be expected to be even more stultifying, and their own children would fall considerably below the mean IQ for the population. Thus, if environment were the dominant factor in intelligence, instead of regression toward the mean in succeeding generations for each social class, there would be continually greater differences between classes in mean IQ scores.

Intergenerational Constancy of Population Mean. Another argument for the predominance of genetic factors in socioeconomic variations in intelligence is the relative constancy of IQ levels over generations despite improvements in the educational and economic levels of the general population. In her discussion of the heredity-environment controversy, Conway compares the working-class children in the Burt studies in London in 1922–1927 with studies by Floud in two English cities in 1952–1953. The Floud investigations utilize an intelligence test comparable to the one used in the Burt studies. Conway remarks that "we find that the standardization of the two is much the same; if anything, the Moray House tests [used by Floud] appear slightly easier, though the differences are not significant statistically."[25] The overall working-class averages for the Floud and Burt studies are similar. The working-class children in the Burt studies have a mean IQ of 98.3, while those in the Floud data have a mean of 98.2. Conway comments:

> There can be no question that the environmental conditions of working class children in Hertfordshire and Middlesex today are far superior to those of working class children in London at the time of the pre-war surveys, which, it should be remembered, include a period of marked economic depression. Yet it seems clear that the improvement in social circumstances has in no way produced a rise in the level of intelligence as assessed by the intelligence tests. Hence, there seems no cogent ground for supposing that the lower averages of children from the lower occupational groups are in any important degree due to economic handicaps.[26]

Twin Studies. Conway presents a strong case for the role of heredity in intelligence by her reference to twin studies. She refers to studies by Burt and Conway, Shields, and the earlier Newman, Freeman, and Holzinger investigation. In the Burt and Conway studies, identical twins reared together had a .92 correlation on an individually administered test (as opposed to a group test), whereas forty-two identical twins reared apart from early infancy had a .85 correlation on this test. They found that nonidentical twins reared together had a correlation similar to those of ordinary siblings reared together — nonidentical twins .53 and ordinary siblings .49. The correlation between IQ and socioeconomic rating of the homes was .26 and, according to Conway, could not account for the high correlation for identical twins.[27]

The findings in the Shields study are comparable to those of the Burt and Conway investigation. Shields studied only identical twins who had been reared apart. He found twenty-five female and thirteen male sets of twins, most of whom were over twenty years of age. They came from all parts of England, and twenty-five of them had been separated during the first year of life, most of them not long after birth. Information was obtained on the home environment, and, according to Shields, often the environment was very different for each of the twins. The correlations between twins were .77 on a non-verbal intelligence test and .74 on a verbal test.[28] These correlations indicate a great similarity in intellectual development despite the lack of common experience.

The Newman, Freeman, and Holzinger study has served as a model for later investigations of twins. This study involved nineteen pairs of identical twins who had been reared apart. Individual tests given to these twins resulted in a correlation of .67, while identical twins reared together were found by Newman and his associates to have a .91 correlation. The average difference between members of pairs reared apart was 8.2 IQ points. IQ differences correlated .51 with judged discrepancy in social environment. For comparison, Newman and his associates found that nonidentical twins reared together also showed a .74 correlation in IQ, which was similar to the findings for identical twins reared apart.[29] While this investigation shows some contribution by the environment to intellectual development, it emphasizes the role of heredity.

Erlenmeyer-Kimling and Jarvik have reviewed fifty-two studies based on intelligence test scores of the general population and have concluded that "the composite data are compatible with the polygenic hypothesis which is generally favored in accounting for inherited differences in mental ability." They found that median correlations between parent and child, between siblings reared together, and between dizygotic (fraternal) twins were all around .50. The median correlation for unrelated persons reared apart was −.01. However, the median correlations between monozygotic (identical) twins reared together was .87 and those brought up apart .75.[30] The findings of the review of IQ studies have been corroborated in a study by Vandenberg. By computing heritability indices based on differences in correlations for identical and fraternal twin pairs, Vandenberg estimated heritability of most factors related to intelligence to be around .6. This estimate is somewhat lower than that proposed by other investigators (around .8).[31] At any rate, the findings imply that heredity plays a significant role in intellectual development and social structure.

THE ENVIRONMENTAL POSITION

Studies of social mobility, social factors in IQ, changes in IQ of individuals over time, and findings on the amount of variance of IQ scores of children "explained" by parental IQ scores favor the environmental position. Evidence from investigations of environmental influence on intelligence and stratification will be presented below.[32]

Social Mobility. Burt's position that social structure results from genetic differences is weakened by his findings on the relationship between intelligence and social mobility. As a part of his longitudinal studies of children in London, Burt and his colleagues obtained data for about 200 children of normal intelligence who "have already reached an age when it is possible to say either that they have already moved out of their original class, in one direction or the other, or else that it is now practically certain that they will never do so."[33] With mobility data on intellectually superior and subnormal children, they found that, first of all, those children whose intelligence was below the minimum estimated for the occupational class to which they were born indicated no upward mobility; instead, about a third of them dropped to a lower social class. In contrast, about 40 percent who had an intelligence above the maximum estimated by Burt for the occupational class into which they were born rose above this class. Intelligence, however, was not the only factor involved in social mobility. Poor motivation contributed more to downward social mobility than poor intelligence did. Nor was motivation itself sufficient to promote upward mobility. Rather, the combination of high intelligence and strong motivation was responsible for almost all of the upward mobility. "A good home background" was a secondary factor in upward mobility. "In the case of the child of the lower classes what chiefly count are the social aspirations, the ambitious aims, and the constant urging that often characterizes the most earnest working-class parents; with children from higher levels it is rather the intellectual and cultural character of the home that helps."[34]

Burt maintains that some degree of social mobility is necessary to readjust the population to appropriate occupations. In the regression toward the mean, the children of highly intelligent parents tend to have a somewhat lower mean intelligence than their parents, and the children of very dull parents have somewhat higher mean intelligence than theirs.[35] According to Burt, some social mobility is then needed in both directions in order to obtain a good fit between occupation and intelligence. In his study, he found that "only 55% of the population could be regarded as correctly placed if intelligence were the sole criterion: nearly 23% are in a class too high, and, with a perfect scheme of vocational selection, ought to be moved down: 22%

are in a class too low, and would have to be moved up."[36] Burt suggests that these figures indicate the amount of mobility that will occur in a society in a "steady state," and he calls this "basic mobility." Each generation then requires a reshuffling if the class system is to persist through an effective division of labor.

A. H. Halsey raises several questions about the Burt and Conway analysis. Halsey argues that intelligence does not operate as a pressure toward social mobility but merely as a selective factor. For example, the Burt and Conway rate of "basic mobility" for maintaining a stable society requires a 20 percent mobility both in and out of the professional class. Yet studies of social mobility indicate both a much lower rate than 20 percent of upward mobility and an infinitesimal downward mobility from the professional class to the manual working class.[37] Halsey's statements suggest that either Miss Conway is wrong in her assumptions or that British society is much more rigid in its class structure than "basic mobility" requires. Halsey also questions the importance of intelligence even as a selective factor in upward social mobility. He presents the variances in IQ for the different socioeconomic levels in England (based on the Hertfordshire and Middlesex data). The variance of the IQ scores for children in high socioeconomic levels is about 67 percent of the total, while the variance for children of unskilled manual workers is 88 percent of the total. With this great overlap in scores throughout the entire socioeconomic structure, Halsey suggests that intelligence plays only a small role in determining social and occupational status. Instead, educational and economic opportunity appear to Halsey to be the major factors in the distribution of persons in the social structure.[38]

Social Factors in Intelligence.   The hereditarians pay more attention to central tendencies in correlations between intelligence and genetic situations, while the environmentalists focus on deviant cases. The environmentalists are concerned much more with nonlinear factors in intelligence than the hereditarians are. It makes little difference to the environmentalist that individuals with identical hereditary traits tend to produce similar IQ scores on tests or to react to illness in similar ways. The fact is that only a small minority of the population consists of identical twins, and these twins differ widely from other individuals in the population, as well. Therefore, for practical purposes in the discussion of social structure and social mobility, heredity accounts for only about one-fourth of the variance in comparisons between parents and children, between siblings, and between husband and wife. It accounts for even less explained variance in dealing with differences between social classes and racial and ethnic groups.

Another argument used by environmentalists is the effect of age on intelligence test scores. In his review of literature on Negro intelligence, Pettigrew points out that when thorough socioeconomic controls are applied, there is little difference in intelligence test scores between Caucasian and Negro children through kindergarten. But, as the children progress in school, the difference between Caucasian and Negro children increases.[39] Anastasi has noted a comparable tendency for IQ scores to diminish with increasing age among groups who have been considered as environmentally deprived, such as mountain and other rural isolated children in the United States, and canal-boat and gypsy children in England. Not only environmental deprivation but also the large number of children raised in families with reduced parental contact may influence performance on intelligence tests.[40] Pettigrew also indicates that Negro children score below Caucasian children, especially in verbal performance and in spatial perception.[41] Studies in which Negro and Caucasian children were given special training on spatial perception have indicated that the Negro children benefit more from practice.[42] Perhaps this deficiency can be attributed to social factors.

The relevance of family relationships for intellectual development is indicated persuasively by Honzik's investigation of persons who were examined at the age of twenty-one months and (with intervening testings) again at thirty years of age. Her data show the following family factors (reported at twenty-one months) to be predictive of high scores at thirty years of age: (a) a friendly relationship between mother and father (predictive for males); (b) parental concern for the child's educational achievement; (c) close father-child relationship (predictive for males); (d) parental concern with the child's health (predictive for females). Significantly, marital compatibility between the parents declines in predictive effectiveness of IQ between the ages of eighteen and thirty years. After the individual leaves his parents' home, the emotional problems in his family of orientation decline in their effect on his intellectual performance.[43]

A major difference between the environmentalists and the hereditarians is their belief as to the extent to which the maximum of individual potentiality in intelligence is actually attained. The hereditarians assume that people tend to approach their maximum intellectual development, while the environmentalists regard individuals generally as capable of attaining much more than their apparent levels of intellectual functioning.[44] For example, Elizabeth Fraser, in her study of the relationship between the home environment and the school, found that the correlation between parental encouragement and the child's IQ was .60. The correlation between parental education and the child's IQ was in the same direction but of smaller magnitude (.42).[45]

Although social aspects of mental retardation ought not be ignored, it would be a mistake to attribute retardation only to social relations as such. For example, Pasamanick and Knobloch found a greater dispersion of infant intelligence among Negro babies than among Caucasians. This finding is consistent with the tendencies of Negro mothers to vary more widely in age, to have dietary deficiencies, and to have less prenatal care than Caucasian mothers.[46] While these differences are related to position in the social structure, the effects are far more indirect than those relating to social interaction.

Instability of IQ Scores.   Most evidence concerning the instability of IQ scores is found in investigations of special class training and of migration. Goldstein, Moss, and Jordan studied children who had been diagnosed as mentally retarded at age six and placed in special programs. When the children were retested the following year, many of them had made significant gains in IQ scores. After the program had been in effect another year, a few of the children were performing well enough to be taken out of the special classes. Since some of the children in control groups made somewhat comparable increases in IQ, the change could not be attributed to the program itself, but to the general school experience.[47]

Skeels and Dye moved thirteen mentally retarded children, aged seven to thirty months, from an orphanage to an institution for the mentally retarded. Older educable retarded girls were given the responsibility for caring for one baby each. These girls gave much attention to their charges. After two years, the Kuhlmann test was applied, and the children were found to have increased a median of about 27 IQ points over the pretest. The range of the increase was 7 to 58 IQ points. In contrast, a group of twelve children with somewhat higher intelligence test scores remained in the orphanage from which the babies were taken. This orphanage could not provide the children with much attention. When the control children were retested, it was found after two years that their IQ scores had decreased a median of 26 points.[48] Twenty-one years later, Skeels followed up the thirteen children who had been placed in the institution for the mentally retarded and the twelve children remaining in the orphanage. He found that all the experimental children were now self-supporting and had completed a median of twelve years of school. The twelve children who had remained in the orphanage had completed a median of only three years of school, and four of the eleven individuals still living were in institutions.[49]

Kirk undertook the early education of mildly mentally retarded children both in institutions and in the home. The children were in the program from one to three years. In the institutions, fifteen four-year-old children were given intensive preschool experience each day. Twelve other children of similar age and mental ability were tested but remained on the wards, performing ordinary routines. Kirk found that the experimental group gained an average of over ten points in IQ while the children remaining in the wards lost six points. Eventually, six of the experimental children were paroled from the institution, but none of the children remaining in the wards was paroled. In his study of children remaining in the home, Kirk used siblings as controls. He found that, like the children in the institution preschools, those children placed in the program showed marked increases in IQ after being entered in the preschool at the age of four. Their siblings showed some increase also when they entered school at the age of six but were unable to catch up to their brothers and sisters who had had preschool training. Kirk found that the greatest increases were made by those children with no organic defects who had been placed in foster homes, away from their parents, during the course of the program.[50] It is noteworthy that one of the children in the preschool program, after having been classified as an educable mentally retarded child early in life, has been a successful college student.[51]

Another source of evidence relating to the instability of the IQ or of intellectual functioning is the performance of children who migrate. In the 1930s Otto Klineberg evaluated over 3,000 ten-to-twelve-year-old Harlem Negroes on an array of intelligence tests. He found that the longer southern-born children lived in New York City, the higher their intelligence test scores were. Those children who had lived in New York for a number of years approached the

levels attained by New York-born Negroes.[52] In 1951, Lee replicated
the Klineberg study in Philadelphia. He analyzed the scores of the
children as they progressed through the schools. Although the southern Negro migrants did not quite reach the scores attained by the
Philadelphia-born Negroes, with each grade they completed in
Philadelphia they gained regularly in IQ. Moreover, the younger
the children were when they entered the Philadelphia schools, the
greater was their general increase in IQ.[53] The migration studies of
Klineberg and Lee provide additional evidence of the depressing
effects of environment on the intelligence of large segments of the
organizationally surplus population.

IQ Scores of Parents and Children.   One difficulty in the genetic
explanation of the relationship between parents' and children's IQ
scores is the low amount of variance in children's IQ scores explained
by the size of the correlation. According to L. Erlenmeyer and Lissy
F. Jarvik, "The average genetic correlation between parent and child
. . . is .50." As indicated previously in this chapter, in their collation
of twelve studies of similarity between parents and children on IQ,
they found a median correlation coefficient of .50 — as expected on
the assumption of polygenic inheritance.[54]

With this finding, the extent to which the IQ of *both* parents
generally accounts for the intelligence of their children can be estimated. First, assume that the correlation between IQ scores of husbands and wives is zero and that the correlation between IQs for
children and each of their parents is .50. On the basis of these
intercorrelations, the multiple correlation for children with their
mothers and fathers would be .66, and about 44 percent of the variance
in children's IQ scores would be explained.

Because of assortive mating, whereby persons tend to choose marital
partners with fairly similar levels of intelligence, the amount of
variance explained by the parents' IQ scores would be lower than .44,
since the actual correlation in IQ between husbands and wives is not
zero. In her review of studies of mental resemblance in married
couples, Helen Richardson reported a range of correlations from .42
to .59 and a median of .49. The samples in these studies represented
a wide range of socioeconomic characteristics. (These correlations are
shown in Table 9.)

Also shown in the table is the result of the study of relatives in the
genealogies of mental retardates in Minnesota reported by Reed and

TABLE 9

Correlations of Intelligence Between Husband and Wife

Investigator[1]	Tests Used	Correlation Coefficients	Number of Couples	Sample Characteristics
Willoughby	Verbal Nonverbal	.44 .44	90	"A representative group" from Palo Alto, California
Jones	Army Alpha	.59	105	Representative of general Vermont population in socioeconomic status
Burks	Stanford Stanford	.42 .55	174 100	"Groups chiefly from skilled labor, business, and professional classes"
Freeman	Otis (S-A)	.49	150	(Same characteristics as Burks samples)
Schooley	Otis (S-A)	.56	80	"Range of school attendance for the men was 5 to 22 years"
Reed and Reed	Various tests administered prior to marriage	.46	1,866	Relatives of probands in family study of retardation, many distantly related to probands; diverse socioeconomic backgrounds in Minnesota
Mean for 7 samples	——	.49	——	——

[1] Bibliographical references for Willoughby, Jones, Burks, Freeman, and Schooley investigations appear in Helen Richardson, "Studies of Mental Resemblance Between Husbands and Wives and Between Friends," *Psychological Bulletin*, 36 (1939), pp. 104–120. For Reed and Reed study, see Elizabeth W. Reed and Sheldon C. Reed, *Mental Retardation: A Family Study* (Philadelphia: Saunders, 1965).

Reed. The 1866 couples in the Minnesota Study were examined on a variety of intelligence tests, and the correlation between husbands and wives was .46. As the IQ tests for these persons were administered in school prior to their marriages, the couples' interaction could not have contaminated the results of the Reed and Reed investigation.[55]

If we assume that all the correlations between husbands and wives and between parents and children are .5, then the multiple correlation between the IQs of children and those of their mothers and fathers is .58, with 33 percent of the variance explained. Therefore, even if we accept assumptions of polygenic determination of intelligence, at most 44 percent of the variance in children's IQs (or more likely, about 33 percent) would be explained in terms of heredity.[56]

Yet, as indicated earlier, some psychologists (such as Burt and Conway) suggest that about 80 percent of intelligence in children can be explained by their parents' level of intelligence. However, in order for even 65 percent of the variance in children's IQ to be explained in terms of heredity, the correlation between the IQs of the parents and children would have to be .7. Few investigations of parent-child IQs have found a correlation coefficient approaching .7. We must therefore assume that social and cultural factors predominate in determining the degree of children's intelligence.[57]

HEREDITY, ENVIRONMENT, AND SOCIAL STRUCTURE

The heredity-versus-environment controversy presents the problem of deciding whether social structure is to be considered the "cause" or "effect" of intelligence. Significantly, adherents to both positions can find supportive evidence in research. The hereditarians find support in (a) the regression of children's IQ scores toward the population mean; (b) the fact that increases in the adequacy of schooling, communications media, and economic condition do not elevate mean IQ scores from one generation to the next; and (c) high coefficients of hereditability in twin studies. The environmentalists point to (a) the great amount of variance within social classes and the importance of nonintellectual factors in social mobility; (b) the influence of family and other social variables on IQ; (c) changes in IQ through educational procedures and migration; and (d) the low amount of variance in children's IQ scores explained statistically by the scores for both parents.

The norms and values in the social structure determine what is considered "intelligent" or "stupid," and social status is based on these standards. However, birth and behavior do have genetic components, and individuals who are gifted genotypically have a greater probability of success, all other things being equal. Of course, all other things are not equal, and the relationship between heredity, general cultural environment, and social stratification is highly complex.

Differential Fertility and the Prevalence of Mental Retardation

The fertility of the mentally retarded is low. Among the severely mentally retarded, the gross physiological and metabolic problems, of which the retardation represents only one aspect, make fecundity unlikely. The fertility of the educable mentally retarded may be impeded by their inability to compete successfully in the courtship and marriage market.

Reed and Reed examined the reproduction rates of 1450 retardates, of whom only 115 had been institutionalized. They found that 43 percent of the retardates had never had children, although about 750 had been married. Those retardates who married produced 2165 children, or 2.09 children per family. However, 214 children died before the age of two. The 1450 retardates as a group therefore produced an average of only 1.35 children surviving to the age of two. Since about 15 percent of the children were themselves retarded and death rates for low socioeconomic levels of the population tend to be high, there is little likelihood that those who survived to adulthood were sufficient in number to replace their parents in the population.

Because of differences in general socioeconomic characteristics between retarded couples and married couples of normal intelligence, Reed and Reed matched thirteen families by age and social class. All of the children in these families were over forty years of age so that all of the grandchildren had been born at the time of the study. The thirteen families in which both husband and wife were retarded produced 66 children and 155 grandchildren, while the thirteen families in which the parents had normal intelligence gave birth to 62 children and 161 grandchildren. Although the sample is small, it suggests that the fertility rates for retarded couples and those with normal intelligence are comparable when socioeconomic characteristics are taken into account.[58]

In Kalamazoo, Michigan, Bajema also found a lower fertility rate among the mentally retarded. While the average number of offspring for the sample studied was 2.24, those persons with an IQ of 69 to 79 had an average of 1.50 children. Whereas 20 percent of the entire sample had no offspring, 30 percent of those in the 69 to 79 IQ range were without children. The marriage rates showed a similar tendency. Ten percent of the persons of IQ 69 to 79 never married, as compared with 5.6 percent for the entire group. The allover relationship between IQ and subsequent fertility was low; the correlation was .05. High reproductive rates were found among persons with high IQs (120 or over) and those in the low-normal range (80 to 94).[59]

The connection between family size, socioeconomic class, and IQ led Gibson and Young in England to examine the relationship between fertility, IQ, and occupation. They found that there was a low negative correlation between parents' IQ and family size when only those families with children were examined. When the unmarried and childless were included, however, there was a zero correlation between IQ and family size. Although the couples in which the husband was in a manual occupation had a mean of 2.8 children, the inclusion of nonreproductive siblings reduced the mean to 2.08. The reproduction rate of the white-collar classes was much less affected by the inclusion of nonreproductive siblings.[60]

The findings in the investigations cited contradict the traditional assertions that the general level of intelligence is declining. These assertions are based on the following assumptions: (a) Families at low socioeconomic levels tend to have more children than do families at high socioeconomic levels. (b) The larger the number of children in a family, the lower their mean IQ tends to be. (c) Persons at low socioeconomic levels tend to have lower IQ scores than persons at high socioeconomic levels. These assumptions do not take into account the fact that persons at low socioeconomic levels and persons with low IQ scores have lower marriage and fertility rates. Hence the initial assumption is irrelevant, and the conclusion that the general intelligence is declining is false. Possibly, with the increased use of oral contraceptives and intrauterine devices, the differential in fertility between higher and lower socioeconomic groups will disappear. As time goes on, such factors as income, occupation, and education become less important in determining fertility.[61]

Differential Death Rates and Prevalence of the Mentally Retarded

The probability is high that mentally retarded individuals will die at an earlier age than people of normal intelligence. One difficulty in estimating mortality rates of the mentally retarded is that degree of intelligence, for obvious reasons, is not recorded on death records. The studies described below, however, suggest that because of differential mortality rates, the prevalence of mental retardation in a population tends to decline with increasing age. Because of the very high death rate among persons with IQs below 50, a low prevalence of the severely retarded can be expected in adulthood. While many of the educable retarded "pass" in the general population, the hypothesis is suggested that the educable mentally retarded also tend to die sooner.

Bajema computed life-table expectations by IQ in the course of a fertility study. The proportion in his sample (selected at school age) who were alive at the age of forty-five declined at low IQ levels. Although 96 percent of those in the IQ range of 120 or over were still alive at forty-five, there was a successive decrease in chance for survival as IQ became smaller (with one minor exception). For those in the 69 to 79 IQ group, only 87 percent survived to the age of forty-five.[62]

In his panel study of elementary school students, Baller found that seven times as many retarded as normal control subjects matched by age, sex, and nationality had died by young adulthood in 1936 (7 percent versus 1 percent).[63] By 1950, 15 percent of the retarded individuals (now with a mean age of forty-three) had died.[64]

The retarded child's chances of dying are related to residence and to his intellectual ability. Tarjan and his associates reported on the deaths of residents in the Pacific State Hospital in 1948–1952. They found that children up to four years of age had a high death rate, with 20 percent dying during the first year of hospitalization; by the end of the fourth year, 30 percent had died. Generally, children who are institutionalized before the age of five tend to have low intellectual ability; otherwise, their retardation would not be so apparent at an early age. Among patients of all ages with IQs under 20, 19 percent of all first admissions died by the end of four years. (In contrast, those with an IQ of 50 or over had a relatively low mortality rate — about 3 percent.) The high death rate of those with low intelligence is associated with their more general disability. Frequently these individuals have metabolic or other developmental anomalies. Within four years after institutionalization, Mongoloids and other patients with developmental cranial anomalies had an accumulative mortality rate of about 28 percent, with most of the deaths taking place in the first year of institutionalization. Persons classified as familial or undifferentiated, however, had accumulative death rates for the four-year period of 4 percent and 2 percent, respectively.[65]

Inasmuch as Down's Syndrome (mongolism) is easily diagnosed, it can be used as an index of mortality rates for severely retarded, metabolically impaired individuals. In their investigation of a Swedish population, Forssman and Akesson found that Mongoloids had a considerably higher mortality rate than the normal population did. In the age range from one to five years, the Mongoloids had a death rate 11 percent over the normal rate; in the ages from six to thirty-nine, the excess was 6 percent; but for persons 40 years of age or over, the mortality rate of the Mongoloids was 19 percent over the expected rate. With increasing age in adulthood, the mortality rate rose.[66] Similarly, in their construction of life tables for Mongoloids in Australia, Collmann and Stoller reported a low life expectancy for Mongoloids at birth — 16.2 years. In contrast, the normal life expectancy at birth for Australians is about seventy years. If the Mongoloids survive to the age of forty, they can expect to live only another 6.8 years on the average, as compared with over thirty years for the general population.[67]

However, death rates among even severely mentally retarded persons are not fixed. According to Dybwad:

> The longevity of the severely retarded in the institutions has increased considerably in recent years. This increase has been the product of improved medical care, new drugs including antibiotics, and general advances in patient care and diet. At the Woodbine Colony in New Jersey, which holds only severely retarded residents, the median age at death was 27.5 in 1951 and over 38 years of age in 1959. In New York, data from the various institutions in the state show that the median age at death for imbeciles increased from 28.2 in 1951 to 40.1 in 1959 and the age at death of idiots changed from 15.4 years of age in 1951 to 21.5 in 1959.[68]

The ratio of mildly to severely retarded persons is affected by differential death rates in the two major categories of retardation. The severely retarded tend to die at a younger age than the mildly retarded. The exact ratio cannot be determined because of the large proportion of severely retarded persons who die in infancy and early childhood.

Reed and Reed examined the proportions of retardates' relatives dying by classification of etiology. The first group consisted of retardates who had well-defined genetic anomalies, one or more siblings with IQs below 50, or were the offspring of consanguineous matings. In this group, 20.5 percent of the siblings of the retarded did not survive to two years of age.

The second category in the Reed study consisted of those retardates in which the etiology was probably genetic. This group included those families with three generations of retardates in the direct line of descent. In this group, 26 percent of the siblings died before the age of two.

The third group of retardates consisted of those in the primarily environmental category, persons whose retardation seemed to be mainly the result of such events as birth injury, serious disease in infanthood, or congenital syphilis. In the primary environmental category, 20.8 percent of the siblings of the retardates died before the age of two.

The fourth category in the Reed and Reed study was that of unknown causes. This group was a residual category and included the "familial" retardates. Here 23 percent of the siblings of the mentally retarded persons died before they were two years old. The high death rate of the siblings of the mentally retarded suggests that some of the brothers and sisters may also have been retarded but had not yet been diagnosed as such.

TABLE 10

Percentage of Children Dying Before the Age of Two, by Mental Status of Parents (Reed and Reed Study)[1]

Mental Status of Parents	Number of Families	Percent of Children Born Who Died Before Age of Two
Retardate married to retardate	54	15.4
Retardate married to partner of unknown intellectual level	300	9.8
Retardate married to normal	182	8.3

[1] Elizabeth W. Reed and Sheldon C. Reed, *Mental Retardation: A Family Study* (Philadelphia: Saunders, 1965), p. 39.

Since many of the families in the Reed and Reed study had a clear genetic base for their retardation, the effect of the marriage of two retarded persons upon the death rate of their children seems important. The data are shown in Table 10. The probability that a child will die in infancy or early childhood when both parents are retarded seems especially high. When both parents were retarded, about 15 percent of their children died before the age of two, while less than

10 percent of the infants or young children died where only one parent was known to be retarded.[69] Probably some of the children in the families in which both parents were mentally retarded were themselves severely retarded.

TABLE 11

Percentages of Educable and Severely Retarded Persons in Five Surveys of Mental Retardation, United States, 1936–1958

Year of Field Work	Location[1]	Retardates in Educable Range		Retardates in Severely Retarded Range		Age Range
		Criterion	Percent	Criterion	Percent	
1936	Baltimore	50–79 IQ	89	Below 50 IQ	11	7–16
1953	Delaware	Below 10 percent on four criteria[2]	83.3	Below 3 percent on four criteria	16.7	All ages including adults
1953	Onondaga County, New York	50–74 IQ	80	0–49 IQ	20	5–17
1957	Maine	IQ 50 or over	73.8	IQ 49 or under	26.2	5–20
1958	Illinois	Classified "Educable"	79.9	Classified "Trainable or below"	20.1	Under 20

[1] Bibliographical references in Tables 2 and 3.
[2] Those in lowest 9 percent on all four criteria minus those in lowest 2 percent on the four criteria.

Although it cannot be said with certainty that in the Reed and Reed study the retardates' siblings and children who had died in childhood were severely retarded, the probability that some of them were raises some doubt as to the relative prevalence of severely and mildly retarded individuals given in most estimates.

The proportions of mentally retarded in the educable range (roughly 50 to 75 or 80 IQ) and in the severely retarded range (IQ below 50) in various studies are shown in Table 11. Although the data are inconclusive, they do indicate an upward trend over time in the proportion of the severely retarded as compared with persons in the educable range. This increase in the proportion of retardates who were trainable or custodial reflects medical advances since World War II, and it may account for the increased pressure for institutionalizing the severely retarded. Indirectly, it may also be a factor in the rapid growth of the parent-group movement in the 1950s.

In summary, although the death rates for the mentally retarded are higher than those for the general population, and rates for the severely retarded are considerably greater than those for the mildly retarded, differential death rates for the retarded population seem to be declining. Improvements in medical technology, educational programs, and social services can be expected to minimize differences in mortality rates between the general and retarded populations in the future.

SUMMARY

Age and sex variation in the prevalence of mental retardation appear to reflect the interaction between cultural and biological factors. As the child matures, there is increasing pressure upon him to develop the ability to think in abstract terms and to utilize formal logical processes. This expectation is generally greater for boys than for girls. At the same time, genetic as well as cultural factors may inhibit this ability to think abstractly and use formal logical procedures. Both sex-linked chromosomes and participation in deviant cultures may have a similar effect on intellectual development.

Similarly, community characteristics may be associated with differences in the prevalence of retardation. The mentally retarded are evidently less prone to migrate to areas where their economic opportunities would be better, and they may be more readily labeled but given fewer remedial services in small communities. Migration studies have indicated that children who have migrated may increase in their level of intellectual functioning. Thus the retardates who remain in their community, especially in rural areas, may stagnate.

The relationships between socioeconomic variations and intelligence, and between hereditary and environmental influences, are difficult to assess. Reed and Reed indicate that "the crucial question for the cultural-familial type cases is whether social conditions were bad because of the genetic retardation of the parents or were the parents retarded because of cultural deprivation in the families into which the parents were born." They come to the conclusion that "it is entirely clear that socioeconomic conditions will not be satisfactory when one or both parents is retarded."[70] On the other hand, Halsey and others show that social-class variations in IQ are too great for socioeconomic placement to be attributed to genetic factors in intelligence. Moreover, given the phenomenon of assortive mating, the correlation between the IQs of parents and children is too low for a genetic interpretation of intellectual development and social stratification.

The low fertility of mentally retarded persons and others in "high-risk" populations has been demonstrated. At the same time, death rates for all low socioeconomic level families tend to be high, and data in studies of retardates both in institutions and in the community suggest that retardates die disproportionately early. The low net reproduction rates and the high death rates of the mentally retarded tend to depress the prevalence of the mentally retarded population in society. However, with recent improvements in medical technology, the severely retarded are surviving to a greater extent, and the proportion of severely retarded is increasing. This increase may be responsible for widespread attention to mental retardation as a medical and social problem. In addition, the increase may be related to greater pressure to institutionalize severely retarded individuals.

 GENERAL DISCUSSION

In many ways, variations in prevalence of the mentally retarded suggest patterns of distribution for the surplus population in general. First, major areas of poverty tend to be in rural areas and in the slums of the city, which tend to be places with a large out-migration and a general loss in population. Like the chronically ill and the aged, the mentally retarded are not highly mobile. Second, like other segments of the surplus population, the mentally retarded have a low fertility rate, especially when the unmarried and childless persons are taken into account. The death rates also show an affinity between the mentally retarded and other segments of the surplus population in a tendency to die at an early age.

Perhaps the major differences between the mentally retarded and other segments of the surplus population are in age and sex distribution. Unlike the aged surplus population, the mentally retarded show a preponderance of males. Unlike the chronically ill, the mentally retarded tend to be younger. Although these differences present some problems with regard to services or treatment, they do not preclude regarding the surplus population as a social class in society.

NOTES

[1] James J. Gallagher, *The Tutoring of Brain-Injured Mentally Retarded Children* (Springfield, Ill.: Charles C Thomas, 1960), p. 156.

[2] From *The Growth of Logical Thinking from Childhood to Adolescence,* by Bärbel Inhelder and Jean Piaget, translated by Anne Parsons and Stanley Milgram (New York: Basic Books, 1958), pp. 282–283.

[3] *Ibid.,* pp. 292–293.

[4] *Ibid.,* p. 338.

[5] See Elizabeth J. Levinson, *Retarded Children in Maine: A Survey and Analysis* (Orono, Maine: University of Maine Press, 1962), p. 14.

[6] *Ibid.,* p. 96.

[7] Samuel A. Kirk and Bluma Weiner, "The Onondaga Census—Fact or Artifact," *Exceptional Children,* 25 (January, 1959), p. 230.

[8] Levinson, *op. cit.*

[9] Richard L. Masland, Seymour B. Sarason, and Thomas Gladwin, *Mental Subnormality* (New York: Basic Books, 1958), pp. 260–274; P. V. Lemkau, C. Tietze, and M. Cooper, "Mental Health Problems in an Urban District," *Mental Hygiene,* 26 (1942), pp. 275–288.

[10] Joseph F. Jastak, Halsey M. MacPhee, and Martin Whiteman, *Mental Retardation, Its Nature and Incidence* (Newark, Delaware: University of Delaware Press, 1963).

[11] Levinson, *op. cit.,* p. 205.

[12] Bernard Farber, *Prevalence of Exceptional Children in Illinois in 1958* (Springfield: Illinois Superintendent of Public Instruction, 1959), Circular—Census IA.

[13] Hans Olof Akesson, *Epidemiology and Genetics of Mental Deficiency in a Southern Swedish Population* (Uppsala: The Institute for Medical Genetics of the University of Uppsala, 1961). Note, however, that it is not necessary to assume that selective migration operates at all levels of intelligence. The concern here is with selective migration of the retarded versus persons of normal intelligence. (See references to studies by Klineberg and Lee later in this chapter.)

[14] U.S. Bureau of the Census, *County and City Data Book, 1962,* (A Statistical Abstract Supplement) (Washington, D.C.: Government Printing Office, 1962), Table 2.

[15] Lee G. Burchinal and Hilda Siff, "Rural Poverty," *Journal of Marriage and the Family,* 26 (November, 1964), pp. 399–405.

[16] R. Fairbank, "The Subnormal Child Seventeen Years After," *Mental Hygiene,* 17 (1933), pp. 177–208.

[17] W. R. Baller, "A Study of the Present Social Status of a Group of Adults, Who, When They Were in Elementary Schools, Were Classified as

Mentally Deficient," *Genetic Psychology Monographs,* 18 (1936), pp. 165–244.

18 Frances A. Mullen and Mary M. Nee, "Distribution of Mental Retardation in an Urban School Population," *American Journal of Mental Deficiency,* 56 (1952), pp. 777–790.

19 Bernard Farber, "Effects of a Severely Mentally Retarded Child on Family Integration," *Monographs of the Society for Research on Child Development,* 24 (1959), No. 2, Serial No. 71, pp. 95–96. See also Gerhart Saenger, *Factors Influencing the Institutionalization of Mentally Retarded Individuals in New York* (New York: State Interdepartmental Health Resources Board, January, 1960), pp. 45–50.

20 Karre Svalastoga, *Prestige, Class, and Mobility* (Toronto: William Heinemann, 1959), p. 402.

21 Cyril Burt, "Intelligence and Social Mobility," *British Journal of Statistical Psychology,* 14 (1961), pp. 2–24.

22 Marjorie P. Honzik, "Environmental Correlates of Mental Growth: Prediction from the Family Setting at 21 Months," *Child Development,* 38 (June, 1967), p. 342.

23 Vera P. John, "The Intellectual Development of Slum Children: Some Preliminary Findings," *American Journal of Orthopsychiatry,* 33 (October, 1963), pp. 813–822.

24 Burt, *op. cit.,* p. 15.

25 J. Conway, "The Inheritance of Intelligence and its Social Implications," *British Journal of Statistical Psychology,* 11 (November, 1958), pp. 178–179.

26 *Ibid.,* p. 179.

27 *Ibid.,* pp. 171–189.

28 J. Shields, "Twins Brought up Apart," *Eugenics Review,* 50 (1958), pp. 113–123.

29 Horatio H. Newman, Frank N. Freeman, and Karl J. Holzinger, *Twins: A Study of Heredity and Environment* (Chicago: University of Chicago Press, 1937).

30 L. Erlenmeyer-Kimling and Lissy F. Jarvik, "Genetics and Intelligence: A Review," *Science,* 142 (December 13, 1963).

31 Steven G. Vandenberg, "The Heredity Abilities Study: Hereditary Components in a Psychological Test Battery," *American Journal of Human Genetics,* 14 (1962), pp. 220–237; B. S. Burks, "The Nature and Limit of Improvement Due to Training," in the *28th Yearbook of the National Society for the Study of Education, Part I* (Chicago: University of Chicago Press, 1928); J. Conway, "Class Differences in General Intelligence: II," *British Journal of Statistical Psychology,* 12 (1959), pp. 4–15; Robert C. Nichols, "The National Merit Twin Study," in Steven G. Vandenberg, ed., *Methods and Goals in Human Behavior Genetics* (New York: Academic Press, 1965).

32 Supportive findings from animal studies can be found in Harry F. Harlow and Gary Griffin, "Induced Mental and Social Deficits in Rhesus Monkeys," Sonia F. Osler and Robert E. Cooke, eds., *The Biosocial Basis of Mental Retardation* (Baltimore: Johns Hopkins Press, 1965), pp. 87–106.

33 Burt, *op. cit.,* p. 19.

34 *Ibid.,* p. 21.

35 See also Elizabeth W. Reed and Sheldon C. Reed, *Mental Retardation: A Family Study* (Philadelphia: W. B. Saunders, 1965).

36 Burt, *op. cit.,* p. 12.

37 In D. V. Glass, ed., *Social Mobility in Britain* (London: Routledge and Kegan Paul, 1954). See also C. Arnold Anderson, James C. Brown, and

Mary Jean Bowman, "Intelligence and Occupational Mobility," *Journal of Political Economy,* 60 (June, 1952), pp. 218–239.

[38] See A. H. Halsey, "Genetics, Social Structure and Intelligence," *British Journal of Sociology,* 9 (March, 1958), pp. 15–28; and A. H. Halsey, "Class Differences in General Intelligence," *British Journal of Statistical Psychology,* 12 (May, 1959), pp. 1–14.

[39] Thomas F. Pettigrew, "Race, Mental Illness, and Intelligence: A Social Psychological View," *Eugenics Quarterly,* 11 (December, 1964), pp. 189–215.

[40] Anne Anastasi, *Differential Psychology* (New York: Macmillan, 1958).

[41] Pettigrew, *op. cit.*

[42] J. H. Boger, "An Experimental Study of the Effects of Perceptual Training on Group IQ Test Scores of Elementary Pupils in Rural Ungraded Schools," *Journal of Educational Research,* 46 (1952), pp. 43–52; O. W. Eagleson, "Comparative Studies of White and Negro Subjects in Learning to Discriminate Visual Magnitude," *Journal of Psychology,* 4 (1937), pp. 167–197.

[43] Honzik, *op. cit.,* pp. 337–364.

[44] See Reed and Reed, *op. cit.,* "To be sure, cultural deprivation may be able to lower the intellectual performance . . . ," p. 75.

[45] Elizabeth Fraser, *Home Environment and the School* (London: University of London Press, 1959).

[46] Jerry Hirsch, "Discussion: The Role of Assumptions in the Analysis and Interpretation of Data," *American Journal of Orthopsychiatry,* 31 (July, 1961), p. 478.

[47] Herbert Goldstein, James W. Moss, and Laura J. Jordan, *The Efficacy of Special Class Training on the Development of Mentally Retarded Children* (Urbana: Institute for Research on Exceptional Children, University of Illinois, 1965), (USOE Cooperative Research Project No. 619).

[48] H. M. Skeels and H. B. Dye, "A Study of the Effects of Differential Stimulation on Mentally Retarded Children," *Proceedings of the American Association of Mental Deficiency,* 44 (1939), pp. 114–136.

[49] Harold M. Skeels, "Effects of Adoption on Children from Institutions," in Joe J. Frost and Glenn R. Hawkes, eds., *The Disadvantaged Child* (Boston: Houghton Mifflin, 1966), pp. 116–119.

[50] Samuel A. Kirk, *Early Education of the Mentally Retarded* (Urbana: University of Illinois Press, 1958).

[51] Personal communication.

[52] Otto Klineberg, *Negro Intelligence and Selective Migration* (New York: Columbia University Press, 1935).

[53] Everett S. Lee, "Negro Intelligence and Selective Migration: A Philadelphia Test of the Klineberg Hypothesis," *American Sociological Review,* 16 (1951), pp. 227–233.

[54] Erlenmeyer-Kimling and Jarvik, *op. cit.*

[55] Helen Richardson, "Studies of Mental Resemblance Between Husbands and Wives and Between Friends," *Psychological Bulletin,* 36 (1939), pp. 104–120. See also Reed and Reed, *op. cit.*

[56] Cf. Lionel S. Penrose, *The Biology of Mental Defect* (London: Sidgwick and Jackson, 1949), p. 118.

[57] Formula for multiple correlation coefficient in Helen M. Walker and Joseph Lev, *Statistical Inference* (New York: Holt, Rinehart, and Winston 1953), p. 344.

[58] Reed and Reed, *op. cit.*

[59] Carl Jay Bajema, "Estimation of the Direction and Intensity of Natural

Selection in Relation to Human Intelligence by Means of Intrinsic Rate of Natural Increase," *Eugenics Quarterly*, 10 (December, 1963), pp. 175–187.

60 John Gibson and Michael Young, "Social Mobility and Fertility," in J. E. Meade and A. S. Parkes, eds., *Biological Aspects of Social Problems* (New York: Plenum Press, 1965), pp. 69–80.

61 See Richard F. Tomasson, "Why Has American Fertility Been So High?" in Bernard Farber, ed., *Kinship and Family Organization* (New York: Wiley, 1966), pp. 327–338.

62 Bajema, *op. cit.*

63 W. R. Baller, "A Study of the Present Social Status of a Group of Adults Who, When They Were in Elementary Schools, Were Classified as Mentally Deficient," *Genetic Psychological Monographs*, 18 (1936), pp. 168–244.

64 Don C. Charles, "Ability and Accomplishment of Persons Earlier Judged Mentally Deficient," *Genetic Psychological Monographs*, 47 (1953), pp. 3–71.

65 George Tarjan *et al.*, "The Natural History of Mental Deficiency in a State Hospital," *AMA Journal of Diseases of Children*, 96 (July, 1958), pp. 64–70.

66 H. Forssman and H. O. Akesson, "Mortality Patterns with Down's Syndrome," *Journal of Mental Deficiency Research*, 9 (June, 1965), pp. 146–149.

67 R. D. Colmann and S. Stoller, "Data on Mongolism in Victoria, Australia: Prevalence and Life Expectation," *Journal of Mental Deficiency Research*, 7 (June, 1963), pp. 60–68.

68 Gunnar Dybwad, *Challenges in Mental Retardation* (New York: Columbia University Press, 1964), p. 174.

69 Reed and Reed, *op. cit.*

70 *Ibid.*, pp. 73–74.

5.

Cultural Variations and Mental Retardation

Various investigators have indicated general community and family characteristics that are correlated with intellectual functioning. They have cited low socioeconomic status, disorganized family life, isolation, a crowded home, and lack of stimulation as factors in inadequate functioning.[1] When these investigators have found mental retardation among persons living in conditions such as those listed, they have labeled these people as having suffered from cultural deprivation, social or cultural disadvantage, exogenous mental retardation, or environmental-psychological deprivation. This chapter describes a conceptual scheme indicating the relationship between cultural characteristics and mental retardation. Because of the importance generally assigned to intelligence tests in the assessment of mental retardation, cultural variations in intellectual functioning will be described in terms of aptitudes ordinarily tested.

Psychologists and educators have often criticized intelligence tests for their lack of conceptual adequacy.[2] Yet most intelligence tests were not developed to investigate theoretical problems. They were created to enable school officials to distinguish between potentially successful and unsuccessful students. Since they were invented to solve an institutional problem, their continued use must be explained in terms of their functioning as a mechanism designed to affect the selection of personnel and to sustain social norms. Thus their ability to identify potential deviants in the educational system and the cultural system on which it is based constitutes their major utility.

Because intelligence tests have been devised to identify potential deviants from norms, insofar as they are efficient they will do so regardless of the basis for deviance. Children who deviate from norms associated with the school as an institution will generally have lower intelligence test scores than children who conform. The relationship between intelligence and conformity to school rules has been found in numerous investigations.[3]

Moreover, the association between intelligence test scores and deviance appears not only in studies related to school but in research pertaining to other institutions as well. For example, juvenile delinquents and adult criminals generally have a lower IQ than the general population does. Still other studies have indicated that school deviance and poor performance on intelligence tests are related to family problems, deviant neighborhood interaction, and economic problems. The intelligent judgment that is supposed to be measured by the IQ tests thus refers not simply to conduct in school but also to "successful" participation in other institutions.[4]

Wofle has criticized the use of standardized intelligence tests as selection devices because of their conformity to a single standard. Although "it is advantageous for a society to seek the greatest achievable diversity of talent," he suggests that "many of the methods that have been developed for dealing with people in groups have the effect of reducing the variability among group members."[5] However, Dunn and Kirk point out that in the USSR, where tests of perception, concept formation, language disorder, or neurological disability are used in place of IQ tests to select children for special classes consisting of "debiles," the socioeconomic characteristics of the parents of these children resemble those of American parents with educable mentally retarded children.[6] The precise mode of testing, therefore, does not seem to be the crucial factor in determining the characteristics of children identified as retarded.

This chapter will regard intelligence tests as indicators of both the physiological intellectual capacity of individuals and adherence to norms of conduct in contemporary society considered "intelligent." Since the kind of judgment considered intelligent depends on the standards by which it is evaluated, this approach sees intelligence tests as a product of folk wisdom consistent with the norms and values associated with a particular social structure. The identification of these norms and values would suggest the kinds of family and community interaction patterns and social relationships which stimulate and reinforce "intelligent" judgment.

The chapter is organized into two sections:

1. *Public Culture and Private Cultures.* Intelligent judgment and action in any society are evaluated and rewarded in terms of the dominant norms and values in that society. In American society, rewards are distributed in accordance with participation in economic and political institutions. Because of the nature of their integration and bureaucratization, these institutions require particular cultural attributes, which constitute the public culture. Coexisting with the public culture are segmented groupings with recognizable ethnic, religious, familial, and socioeconomic characteristics. These segmented groupings, related tangentially to the highly interdependent core of political and economic institutions, are characterized by private cultures.

2. *Private Self and Public Self.* A distinction is made between private self and public self as reflecting either one's private, segmentary culture or the public culture that integrates the major institutions of the society. The intelligence tests are regarded as consistent with the attributes of public culture.

Public Culture and Private Cultures

In a highly industrialized society, large-scale social networks develop to integrate the major institutions of that society. Industrial and political bureaucracies require particular kinds of behavior for their operation. The educational system is necessarily connected with the industrial and political systems as well as with the religious organization of the society.[7] With the diffusion of literacy, forms of worship and belief systems change, the relationship between government and the individual is modified, and more complex economic organization becomes possible.[8] And the emergence of integrative networks of institutions evokes the need for a public culture to facilitate this integration.

The public culture required to sustain the interdependence of large-scale organization consists of norms and skills associated with efficiency of communication, rational organization of personnel and machines, planning of future operations, and maintenance of the individual's position in the system. (Position maintenance is necessary because the bureaucracy cannot operate effectively without stability of personnel in recognizable statuses.) This culture is supported by the system of rewards in the society. In American society, the distribution of rewards is justified in terms of the ability of persons to perform successfully in the complex of integrated institutions.[9] Intelligent judgment and action in a society are generally evaluated in terms of the system of distributive justice. Thus, in modern American society, intelligent action is interpreted in terms of the incorporation of the individual into this public culture, and intelligence testing is considered valuable insofar as test scores describe or predict the individual's ability to do so.

Coexisting with the integrated network of social relationships and its cultural paraphernalia are small, fragmented, somewhat autonomous groupings that have bases for existence outside the public culture. The family, for example, exists in almost all societies; but, in modern society, families do not have the particular political or economic production activities that would integrate them directly into the public culture. Instead, families are incorporated this way only tangentially, through the fortuitous participation of individual members. There is, therefore, a great deal of variation in the extent to which families are integrated into the general public culture.

Those families and individuals whose way of life is incompatible with the public culture are superfluous population; if anything, their private worlds generally inhibit the smooth operation of the economic, educational, and political institutions. The extent of integration into the public culture depends in part upon various other groupings with which the family is involved. For example, the father provides the major economic support in fostering family solidarity. His absence may produce disastrous effects on the children; the intelligence of lower-class children from fatherless homes continually declines throughout grade school.[10] In addition, some religious groupings have norms and patterns of conduct that are consistent with the public culture, while others are in conflict with it. To the extent that these religious groupings are consonant with the public culture, their members tend to act intelligently with respect to the dominant industrial and political systems. Similarly, ethnic groupings vary in the degree of their incorporation into the public culture. Some ethnic groups are characterized by norms and values that facilitate their members' successful participation in modern educational, political, and economic institutions. Others have norms and values that run counter to the norms of distributive justice of the public culture.[11]

Ethnic groups seem to differ markedly in the kinds of mental aptitudes they encourage in their children. An example given by Gladwin which is appropriate to cultural variations is that of the Trukese islanders, who were able to navigate over thousands of miles of ocean to find a small island but were unable to understand the operation of a gasoline motor.[12]

In another context, Lesser, Fifer, and Clark compared Chinese, Jewish, Negro, and Puerto Rican children on selected mental aptitudes. This included tests for verbal ability, reasoning, number ability, and space-organizing ability. For all four groups, middle-class children made considerably higher scores on all tests than lower-class groups. Jewish children were above the median for all tests. Chinese children were below the median for verbal tests but above it for reasoning, number, and space tests. The Negro children were at the median for the verbal tests, below the median for the remaining ones. The Puerto Rican children were below the median on all tests. In addition, each group presented a different profile. The Jewish children made their highest scores on verbal tests, second highest on number tests, third on reasoning, and lowest on space factors. The Chinese children were low on the verbal tests but generally made about the same scores for reasoning, number, and space. The Negro children made their highest scores on the verbal tests, second highest on reasoning, third highest on space, and lowest on number. The Puerto Rican children made their lowest scores on verbal tests, the next higher score on reasoning, then number; their highest score was on the space test.[13]

The relative scores for verbal abilities for ethnic groups probably reflect their language assimilation, although tests were given in the children's most proficient language. The Jewish and Negro children have the least contact with foreign languages, the Chinese probably retain some contact with their mother tongue, and the Puerto Ricans, as the newest immigrant group, probably do most of their communicating in Spanish.

Caution must be observed in interpreting the findings in terms of social class differences. The same general patterns occurred for both the middle- and lower-class children within each ethnic group. Unfortunately, since each of these ethnic groups tends to be isolated from the others with respect to gene pools, possibly the differences reflect genetic patterns as well as cultural differences. Conceivably, the cultural differences emerge in part to accommodate variations in genetic structure. The results of the Lesser, Fifer, and Clark study cannot be interpreted with confidence at this time without reference to data on specific cultural differences and on extensive genealogies. There is, however, as little reason to believe that all Puerto Ricans come from a common genetic pool as there is to believe that all Chinese, Jews, or Negroes do. Within each group there is considerable selective mating by social class.

If it were assumed that public culture is more efficient in meeting the needs of people than deviant private cultures are, the explanation for the persistence of private cultures would probably be that its proponents simply do not know better; they do not know what is best for them. The ameliorative response would then be to acquaint the children with the public culture and to stimulate acculturation by showing them how public culture is "good." This view assumes that the deviant private culture sprouts under its own power and sustains itself independently.

Alternately, it may be assumed that the public culture itself nurtures and sustains private cultures. Public culture is generally considered as having emerged to accommodate the technological, communications, and organizational developments in society. A question can be raised with respect to private cultures: How does society sustain the existence of deviant private cultures?

In those segments of the society which do not receive the major rewards of the institutions related to the public culture, other justifications must be sought for living. Mysticism, chance, and fate, which emphasize the anti-intellectual norms and values to be found in the society, must furnish explanations for events. This anti-intellectualism thus coexists with an intellectual tradition related to the dominant public culture. Since the intellectual explanations do not provide a satisfactory reason for existence for the population segment that does not receive the major rewards, this segment is stimulated to rely on anti-intellectual justification for action.

With the continued automation of industry, education, and government of society, the gulf between those who are involved in the dominant public culture and those who are isolated from it may increase. The isolation itself enhances the use of private linguistic patterns to set the adherents of the private cultures apart as a reaction to their exclusion from the public culture. There is a glorification of private vocabulary and private semantic and grammatical structures. The language of the "hepcat" as opposed to the "square" and the popularity of the anti-intellectual art forms thrive in the counter-cultures that develop in opposition to the public culture.[14] Moreover, as automation continues to expand, there is a concurrent trend toward the exclusion of the large bulk of the population from the public culture, and this portion of the population feels less and less able to control its destiny. Here again, the elements of chance, disorder, and mysticism enter as factors in the outcast population's interpretation of the causation of events. The private cultures are not subject to the same kinds of proof or the same kind of evaluation to justify their existence. The public culture is required to be coherent and rational; the private culture can incorporate contradictory elements in its structure. Hence the social and cognitive processes that are basic to the continuity or persistence of the public culture need not be present in the private culture. In short, individuals immersed in deviant private culture do not need to develop the capacity for intelligent judgment and action with respect to public culture.

The transformation of deviance into incompetence can occur under various conditions. The plight of the Negro families in Harlem provides one example. In his study of Harlem youth, Michael Lewis indicates that the failure of Negro family members to carry out acceptable academic, familial, and economic roles derives from the patterns of family organization in the rural South. In the southern rural culture, Negro life exists as a deviant pattern. The public white culture of the South demands the presence of a Negro private culture to sustain the social and economic structure. The Negro rural culture is one that denies social mobility to the Negro. As the Negro family moves into a community such as Harlem, the structural supports (such as white paternalism) which sustained the southern Negro culture and made it at least livable are removed. The institutionalized incapacity to develop modes of life appropriate to upward social mobility is transformed from a deviant pattern to one that is ill-equipped to meet the demands of an urban, open-class system. Family breakup, the inability to delay gratifications, and the unstable role of the male (which had been part of a deviant culture in the rural South) become a basis for personal incompetence in Harlem.[15]

In brief, in defining intelligence in terms of the public culture, society regards as unintelligent all those who deviate. By its structure, modern society encourages certain segments of the population to deviate from the public culture. This encouragement of deviance promotes the development of fragmentary private cultures which conflict with the public culture. The conflicting private cultures involve, by definition, unintelligent action; and, since the private cultures are reflected in individuals, these cultures impede the development of intelligence. The characteristics of personal development in relation to private and public culture are described in the following section.

Private Self and Public Self

Most conceptions of personality are based upon dualism. Freud discussed the interaction between the id and the ego (and its extension, the superego); Mead distinguished between the "I" and the "me"; Piaget separated egocentric from decentered thinking; and, in common-sense terms, individuals separate understanding a thing intellectually from understanding it emotionally.[16] In most of these conceptions, there is the assumption that a part of the personality is unsocialized (the id, the "I," egocentric thinking, and emotional understanding). Yet, with the possible exception of portions of the id, the individual is aware of even the "unsocialized" aspects of his personality; he has particular ideas and norms regarding his wants and desires. This awareness suggests that these unsocialized wants and desires, like the socialized aspects of personality, emerge in social relationships. Secret desires, inclinations toward deviance, personal perceptions are as social as public motivations, consensual understandings, and group rationalization.

George Herbert Mead regarded the self as "an individual reflection of the general systematic pattern of social or group behavior in which it and the [other selves] are all involved—a pattern which enters as a whole into the individual's experience in terms of these organized group attitudes which . . . he takes toward himself."[17] Moreover, according to Mead, the self is composed of more elementary selves, each one dependent upon the set of social relationships involved.[18] The distinction between private and public selves represents norms, vocabulary, and values in different kinds of social relationships. The *private* self refers to the organization of perceptions, norms, vocabulary, and values with respect to a fragmented, somewhat autonomous grouping in the society, and contains those elements often regarded as "unsocialized." The *public* self refers to the individual's organization with respect to the central, highly interdependent grouping in the society. Briefly, then, the distinction between private and public selves results from a differentiation between private and public cultures in society.

The distinction between public and private self as representing different kinds of cultures suggests that the child's socialization is different with respect to the public culture than it is in relation to private cultures. The following sections discuss socialization pertaining to private and public cultures in terms of norms of conduct, communication and language, and rationality and expressiveness.

NORMS OF CONDUCT

One aspect of socialization influenced by public culture is internalization of "intelligent" norms of judgment and action. The public culture is based upon highly integrated elements in the society, with interlacing bureaucracies. Private cultures, on the other hand, are based on segmented, autonomous groupings. Socialization consistent with public culture should then reflect the highly integrated, interdependent nature of the public culture. First, there should be much emphasis upon enabling the child to become an active individual in groups capable of great cooperation. Accordingly, parents should stress internalization of (rather than obedience to) norms and values relating to cooperative action for the child who will participate in public culture. But private culture, by definition, stands apart from the highly interdependent aspects of society; private culture coexists with public culture. To maintain this separate existence, the private culture must contain norms that sustain its independent identity. There are appropriate socialization practices for this purpose. For example, socialization consistent with private culture would focus upon this coexistence in expecting the child to be obedient and yet to maintain a separate identity through occasional deviance from parental expectations, which could be regarded as an expression of "spirit" or "mischief."[19] Hence, the continued existence of private cultures requires socialization practices that prevent children from internalizing norms appropriate to the public culture.

Kohn found that the emphasis upon obedience and internalization varies by social class. Low socioeconomic status parents insist upon obedience but not upon internalization. Middle-class parents, however, are more interested in internalization, and their childrearing practices are based upon the intentions of the child and whether he has internalized norms rather than upon obedience as such.[20]

COMMUNICATION AND LANGUAGE

A second aspect of socialization consists of the development of means of communication. For the interlacing economic, political, and educational institutions to operate efficiently, the public culture communication must be maximized. Moreover, patterns of communication must be standardized in order to permit the mutual dependence of all elements in the system. Consistent with these communication needs is the development of public, formal, linguistic patterns in the socialization of children. There is much emphasis upon that grammatical form which would permit a high degree of integration. In contrast to the requirements of the public culture, the segmented private cultures are more concerned with expressive, individualized meanings and language patterns.

Private cultures may even emphasize distinct patterns that set them off from the public culture and stress their own unique identity. Hence, in socialization, language patterns accentuate personal and private symbolism.[21] However, Deutsch suggests that since lower-class children are aware of their grammatical deficiencies, they are reticent to communicate across class lines.[22] Apparently, they then regard themselves as different and, presumably, inferior.

RATIONALITY AND EXPRESSIVENESS

The third element in the public culture is its rational basis. Bureaucratic structures can continue to exist only insofar as they maintain a semblance of efficiency and rationality.[23] Hence, the kind of socialization appropriate to the public culture is one that focuses upon intellectual endeavor in terms of rational causation, rational explanations, and operating according to time schedules.[24] Private cultures, however, are sustained through mysticism and intuitive explanations of events. Private cultures are in a way antirational. They may be heavily endowed with modes of behavior that often evoke fear, anxiety, and discouragement in children.[25] Socialization, then, in private cultures would tend to be anti-intellectual and based mainly on expressive-emotional motivations and modes of conduct.

For the institutional structures upon which public cultures are based to continue to exist, the individuals must develop norms that maintain their position in the system.[26] Thus a part of the socialization with respect to public culture would be the incorporation of norms and values related to status maintenance. On the other hand, the persistence of private cultures depends upon the fluidity and flexibility of movement by individuals in the large social system. This mobility inhibits incorporation into the public culture; the *luftmensch,* the hobo, and the gypsy are examples of social types who refuse to be drawn into the major public culture. Socialization practices consistent with this fluidity in the system (rather than status maintenance) would involve norms that denote restlessness and emphasize excitement and residential mobility, lack of interest in institutions related to the public culture, and a contrasting interest in "fun."

NORMS, COMMUNICATION, AND RATIONALITY

The kinds of norms of conduct, means of communication, and emphasis on rationality that distinguish public from private cultures are expressed as folk wisdom in intelligence tests. Intellectual aptitude tests accompanied the development of public education and large-scale industrial and political organizations. Intelligence tests came into vogue after large-scale social networks encompassing various institutions of society had been developed.

Implicitly, the view of intelligence tests as artifacts reflecting folk wisdom assumes the distinction between public and private self. For example, Wechsler, in discussing the utility of the general comprehension test, indicates that this test is useful not only in determining intelligence but in providing clinical information, which is, by definition, insight into the private life of the respondent. Wechsler indicates that the comprehension test "is frequently of value in diagnosing psychopathic personalities, sometimes suggests the presence of schizophrenic trends (as revealed by perverse and bizzare responses) and almost always tells us something about the subject's social and cultural background."[27]

Similarly, Piaget and Inhelder suggest that the process of decentering tends to occur in adolescence because the adolescent "begins to think of the future—*i.e.,* of his present or future work in society . . . his life program, and his plan for changing the society he sees."[28] This process of decentering or "continual refocusing of perspective"[29] occurs especially among students and in the intellectual classes. Among workers, apprentices, and peasants, there would be "fewer family and still fewer religious crises, and especially a lower degree of abstraction."[30]

Piaget and Inhelder thus regard the decentering process as not just a biological unfolding but as a response to a particular set of institutions. Insofar as individuals are involved in these institutions, they will be absorbed into a public culture that demands intellectual objectivity and abstraction.

SUMMARY

This chapter has discussed cultural variations in intellectual functioning. It has suggested the existence of a public culture that is organized around the major economic, political, and educational institutions of the society. Norms of behavior and judgment consistent with the public culture are regarded as "intelligent"; other forms are "stupid," "foolish," and irrational. However, these so-called stupid, foolish, and irrational norms are part of the numerous private cultures, which are not required to be internally consistent or "success-oriented." In one sense, there is a retardation of intelligent behavior in all private cultures, some more extreme than others.

These private cultures emerge and/or persist to make life tolerable for surplus populations, which themselves grow out of the inability to find acceptable slots in the tables of organization in economic, political, and educational institutions. There is a circularity—people do not find acceptable slots in tables of organization because they have not internalized the norms of the public culture; because parents do not have acceptable slots in the major economic, political, and educational institutions, their children are unable to internalize public culture norms effectively; and so on.

The mechanism relating public culture participation to the individual is to be found in selves corresponding to the public and private cultures. Those who are not deeply immersed in the public culture are not required (a) to develop norms related to highly cooperative behavior (with accompanying inhibition of show of hostility); (b) to incorporate the vocabulary and grammar of the language of the public culture into their everyday lives; (c) to emphasize rationality rather than fun or luck; and (d) to be highly motivated toward social mobility.

GENERAL DISCUSSION

Cultural Deprivation. Private cultures are significant for the study of mental retardation because they seem to inhibit rather than promote the development of those intellectual processes commonly regarded as "intelligent." They do not provide individuals with the kinds of norms that are required in the major public culture institutions. While private cultures may not reduce the intellectual performance of an extremely bright individual to that of a dullard, they may prevent children of normal intelligence from doing the kinds of conceptual tasks expected of them. If a child consistently produces intelligence test results ten to twenty IQ points below his physiological capacity, this performance may place him in the category of the educable mentally retarded. Possibly, in some situations the deleterious effects may be more extreme.

The perspective described in this chapter suggests that the controversy over whether "cultural deprivation" is primarily a familial or a school and community problem focuses upon the wrong issue. If it is primarily a family problem, the solution is to strengthen family relationships (especially the role of the father) in populations that are organizationally surplus. If it is mainly a school and community problem, the quality of schooling and after-school activities must be improved. The public-private culture viewpoint places the emphasis on the cultural content rather than on the institutions engaged in socialization; it suggests investigating the circumstances under which the family, the community, and the school affect the incorporation of the individual into the public culture. Perhaps by isolating the child from slum community and school influences, a family strongly immersed in the public culture can avoid deviant socialization; early childhood education may compensate for a family life dominated by private-culture norms and values (if this compensatory education continues into adolescence); and strengthening the role of the father in many instances may assist the schools in socializing the child into the public culture. Eventual remediation of so-called cultural deprivation depends in the final analysis on determining the particular cultural content associated with kinds of family, school, and community organization.[31]

Folk Culture of Child Development. One aspect of socialization in modern society about which little is known is the folk culture of child development. Social scientists have not investigated how much the games people play with infants, the songs they sing, the cuddling, or other interactions are practiced and valued by parents or the extent to which parents believe that these activities are necessary for the child's intellectual development. Similarly, little systematic observation has been made of folk beliefs and practices related to intellectual growth after early childhood. These too might increase understanding of the significance of private cultures for intellectual development.

Problem of Values.   The assumption that institutions in the public culture nurture and sustain private cultures suggests further that amelioration requires a revision in the distribution of rewards in the society. Institutions in the public culture could then be expanded to include activities now regarded as recreational or as mere time-wasters. In many primitive societies that are generally noncompetitive in their value systems there is no sharp distinction between work and leisure. In much the same way ability can be divorced from productivity (and therefore the specific amount of earning power) for large segments of the population now considered as surplus. As long as institutional efficiency, rather than personal, intellectual, and emotional growth, remains as the criterion for participation in economic, political, and educational institutions, organizationally surplus populations, with their deviant private cultures, will persist. This persistence will continue to be reflected in the production of mentally retarded individuals.

NOTES

[1] See Richard Masland, Seymour Sarason, and Thomas Gladwin, *Mental Subnormality* (New York: Basic Books, 1958); Alfred L. Baldwin, J. Kalhorn, F. H. Breese, "Patterns of Parent Behavior," *Psychological Monographs,* 58 (1945), No. 268; Esther Milner, "A Study of the Relationship of Parent-Child Interaction," *Child Development,* 22 (June, 1951), pp. 95–112; Elizabeth Fraser, *Home Environment and the School* (London: University of London Press, 1959); Martin Deutsch, "Minority Group and the Class Status as Related to Social and Personality Factors in Scholastic Achievement," *The Society for Applied Anthropology,* Monograph #2, 1960; J. McV. Hunt, *Intelligence and Experience* (New York: Ronald Press, 1961); Samuel A. Kirk, *Early Education of the Mentally Retarded* (Urbana: University of Illinois Press, 1958).

[2] Masland, Sarason, and Gladwin, *op. cit.;* Hunt, *op. cit.;* Frank Riessman, *The Culturally Deprived Child* (New York: Harper, 1962).

[3] See Sanford Unger, "Relation Between Intelligence and Socially-Approved Behavior: Methodological Cautionary Note," *Child Development,* 35 (1964), pp. 299–301.

[4] See studies cited in Chapter 3. See also M. Pollack, "Brain Damage, Mental Retardation, and Childhood Schizophrenia," *American Journal of Psychiatry,* 415 (1958), pp. 422–428; and Simon H. Tulchin, *Intelligence and Crime: A Study of Penitentiary and Reformatory Offenders* (Chicago: University of Chicago Press, 1939).

[5] Dael L. Wofle, "Diversity of Talent," *American Psychologist,* 15 (August, 1960), p. 539.

[6] Lloyd M. Dunn and Samuel A. Kirk, "Impressions of Soviet Psycho-

Educational Service and Research in Mental Retardation," *Exceptional Children,* 29 (March, 1963), pp. 299–311.

[7] For example, Henry David Aiken, "The Revolt Against Ideology," *Commentary,* 37 (April, 1964), p. 29. "Indeed, our universities and governments, along with our great industrial complexes, look increasingly like the interlocking arms of a great, if also headless, political establishment."

[8] Talcott Parsons, *Societies* (Englewood Cliffs, N.J.: Prentice-Hall, 1966), pp. 26–27.

[9] For example, see Talcott Parsons, "An Analytical Approach to the Theory of Social Stratification," *American Journal of Sociology,* 45 (1940), pp. 841–862.

[10] M. Deutsch and B. Brown, "Social Influences in Negro-White Intelligence Differences," *Journal of Social Issues,* 20 (1964), pp. 24–35.

[11] Although individuals who are inept in matters pertaining to the public culture may achieve positions of prominence in economic and political organizations, they cannot function without knowledgeable assistants (e.g., Harry Brock in the play *Born Yesterday*). In small companies, this assistance is performed by accountants, tax and business consultants, attorneys, and agencies with whom the small enterprises are involved. Chambers of commerce, professional organizations, cooperative arrangements, short courses, merchandising meetings and conventions, and training programs serve to acquaint marginal entrepreneurs, union leaders, and public officials with elements of the public culture.

[12] Masland, Sarason, and Gladwin, *op. cit.*

[13] Gerald S. Lesser, Gordon Fifer, and Donald H. Clark, *Mental Abilities of Children in Different Social and Cultural Groups,* report to Cooperative Research Program of the U.S. Office of Education, Cooperative Research Number 1635, 1964.

[14] See Harold Finestone, "Cats, Kicks, and Color," *Social Problems,* 5 (1957), pp. 3–13. In contrast, for some intellectual "squares," the occupation itself becomes the focus of the life organization, taking on religious overtones. In a study of religious commitments of University of Illinois professors, Henry Cohen found a sizable number whose major belief system was embedded in their academic commitment. This commitment was based upon a philosophy of naturalism involving scientific method, humanistic efficient causation, and the hope of eventual controllability of human events through knowledge. The academic commitment thus appears to place high value upon the characteristics of public culture, and the committed academic may be regarded as the antithesis of the "cat," who focuses upon "kicks." (The Cohen study is described briefly in Marshall Sklare, "Intermarriage and the Jewish Future," (*Commentary,* 37 [April, 1964], pp. 49–50.)

[15] Michael Lewis, "Competence and the American Racial Dichotomy: A Study in the Dynamics of Victimization," unpublished doctoral dissertation, Princeton University, 1967. See also R. J. Goldman and Francine M. Taylor, "Coloured Immigrant Children: A Survey of Research, Studies and Literature on their Educational Problems and Potential — in Britain," *Educational Review,* 8 (June, 1966), pp. 163–183.

[16] Sigmund Freud, *The Ego and the Id* (London: Hogarth Press, 1947); George Herbert Mead, *Mind, Self, and Society* (Chicago: University of Chicago Press, 1934); and Bärbel Inhelder and Jean Piaget, *The Growth of Logical Thinking from Childhood to Adolescence* (New York: Basic Books, 1958).

[17] Mead, *op. cit.,* p. 158.

118   *Mental Retardation as a Social Product*

¹⁸ *Ibid.*, p. 143; see also George A. Kelly, *The Psychology of Personal Constructs* (New York: Norton, 1955), pp. 8–12.

¹⁹ Cf. T. Adorno, *et al.*, *The Authoritarian Personality* (New York: Harper, 1950). Research on the authoritarian personality indicates a co-existence of tendencies toward both obedience and aggressiveness.

²⁰ Melvin Kohn, "Social Class and Parent-Child Relationships: An Interpretation," *American Journal of Sociology*, 68 (1963), pp. 471–480.

²¹ Basil Bernstein, "Social Structure, Language and Learning," *Educational Research*, 3 (June, 1961), pp. 163–176. Formal language as described by Bernstein includes "accurate grammatical order and syntax as well as logical modifications mediated through a grammatically complex sentence construction." Formal language facilitates participation in the various interdependent institutions which are the core of the public culture. In contrast to formal language is the language used in informal and segmented groupings. Bernstein regards *informal* language as characterized by "short, grammatically simple, often unfinished sentences with a poor syntactical form stressing the active voice." See also Goldman and Taylor, *op. cit.*, pp. 173–174.

²² Martin Deutsch, "The Role of Social Class in Language Development and Cognition," *American Journal of Orthopsychiatry*, 35 (January, 1965), pp. 78–88.

²³ See discussion in Alvin Gouldner, "Organizational Analysis," in Robert K. Merton *et al.*, eds., *Sociology Today* (New York: Basic Books, 1959), pp. 400–407.

²⁴ For example, Klineberg reported that white children exceeded Indian and Negro children in the speed but not the accuracy of performance. Indian and lower-class Negro cultures pay little attention to time scheduling. See Otto Klineberg, "An Experimental Study of Speed and Other Factors in 'Racial' Differences," *Archives of Psychology*, 15 (1928), No. 93.

²⁵ For example, see Jeannette S. Vosk, "Study of Negro Children with Learning Difficulties at the Outset of their School Careers," *American Journal of Orthopsychiatry*, 36 (January, 1966), pp. 32–40.

²⁶ For example, Louis Schneider and Sverre Lysgaard, "The Deferred Gratification Pattern: A Preliminary Study," *American Sociological Review*, 18 (1953), pp. 142–149; Ralph H. Turner, *The Social Context of Ambition* (San Francisco: Chandler, 1964); and D. F. Swift, "Social Class and Achievement Motivation," *Educational Research*, 8 (February, 1966), pp. 83–95.

²⁷ David Wechsler, *The Measurement and Appraisal of Adult Intelligence* (Baltimore: Williams and Wilkins, 1958), pp. 6–7.

²⁸ Inhelder and Piaget, *op. cit.*, p. 339 and p. 342.

²⁹ *Ibid.*, p. 345.

³⁰ This decentering is reflected in intelligence tests by the kinds of tasks required of adolescents as indicated in *Ibid.*, pp. 292–293.

³¹ Daniel P. Moynihan, "Employment, Income, and the Negro Family," *Daedalus*, 94 (Fall, 1965), pp. 745–770; Frank Riessman, *The Culturally Deprived Child* (New York: Harper, 1962); Joe L. Frost and Glenn R. Hawkes, eds., *The Disadvantaged Child* (Boston: Houghton Mifflin, 1966), *passim*; Louis Kriesberg, "Rearing Children for Educational Achievement in Fatherless Families," *Journal of Marriage and the Family*, 29 (May, 1967), pp. 288–301.

PART TWO

Treatment of the Retarded in Contemporary Society

6. 🌿

Mental Retardation: A Problem in Social Reform

This chapter is divided into two sections. The first deals with the nineteenth-century social movements related to mental retardation and serves as background to the discussion of the current movement in the United States. The second section is concerned with the current social movement pertaining to mental retardation. It focuses on the National Association for Retarded Children, the organization of local parents' groups, and characteristics of members and volunteer workers. Although the emphasis is on the organizations themselves, the intention of the discussion is to indicate how patterns of organization develop to integrate the special concerns of the movement into the existing social context.

The Nineteenth Century

Social movements related to mental retardation have changed considerably in the past one hundred years. During the nineteenth century, these movements were connected with a variety of "causes"; the emergence of Darwinism provided a focal point for them. Because of the differences in the role of mental retardation in British and in American movements in the nineteenth century, we shall deal with them separately.

SOCIAL MOVEMENTS RELEVANT TO
MENTAL RETARDATION IN ENGLAND

The significance of social movements concerned with mental retardation in England in the latter part of the nineteenth century can best be understood by reviewing some of the status concerns at that time. Banks has suggested that perceptions of status and threats to status are more powerful in determining opinion than the objective situation is. Banks studied influences of the period following the 1873 economic depression in England on family limitation.[1] He took the position that both the rationale (provided by the publication of the Malthus essay on population) and the means for family limitation (i.e., contraceptives) had been widely known in England since the beginning of the nineteenth century. Yet it was only after the depression of 1873 that family limitation was practiced among large segments of the middle class. Banks remarked that "although the success of the neo-Malthusian movement after ... 1877 demonstrated the extent to which the desire for a smaller family already prevailed, it is not immediately obvious why a rapid expansion in the level of living, followed by a sense of restriction, should *necessarily* have led to the acceptance of the idea of adopting birth control by a generation which had rejected it earlier."[2] Prior to the depression of 1873, family limitation was not an ethic of the middle-class style of life. Although the depression did not seriously threaten their level of living, their sense of security was shaken, and child limitation became one way of contracting expenditure, thus enabling the maintenance of the style of life to which the middle class aspired. Banks thus linked the insecurity of the middle class after the 1873 depression with the acceptance of limitation of childbirth.

The threat to the middle-class way of life in England, however, did not emerge suddenly at this time. The growth of the working class and its agitation for improved working and living conditions were prominent throughout the latter half of the nineteenth century. The strength of the working-class movement in politics during the sixties was found in alliance with the lower middle class on the basis of their common exclusion from the franchise. In 1868 the franchise was expanded so that many members of the working class were able to vote. Greater representation in Parliament was given to the large urban areas. This change, as well as others affecting the working class and the trade union movement, influenced subsequent legislation in ways that increased the insecurity of the middle class. In 1870, the Elementary Education Act established the principle of universal education regardless of one's family's financial status. Within the next decade school attendance was made compulsory. Enfranchisement and educational acts operated to minimize a distinction between the middle and working classes and consequently operated to emphasize any status insecurities present in the middle class. The depression of 1873 dramatized this threat to the middle-class style of life.

This status insecurity in England was heightened by commercial difficulties in the 1880s and the presence of a large body of unemployed. Greenwood suggests that the increased industrial capacity of Germany and France shrank the English market. Moreover, technological unemployment, coupled with migration from the English countryside and Eastern Europe, swelled the ranks of the unemployed. "There were unemployable men, too weak, in body or mind, to stick to any job for too long. The very improvements made in the methods for providing for the poor caused an increase in the number of people who preferred to live on others whether as paupers or as 'tramps.' "[3] The combined presence of a working class encroaching upon the style of life of the middle class and a visible body of unemployed provided a constant threat to the middle class in the latter part of the nineteenth century.

The popularity of Darwinism did not reach its height until after 1872. Significantly, Julian Huxley indicates that "the emergence of Darwinism, I would say, covered the 14-year period from 1858 to 1872; and it was in full flower until the 1890s."[4]

The connection between Darwinian thought and English political life is exemplified by the sides taken during the American Civil War. Most English Whig and Conservative statesmen were inclined to favor the South. According to Trevelyan, "While the war was raging (1861–65), opinion in Britain had been largely divided on the issue according as men wished for democracy or aristocracy, a wide or a narrow franchise, in their own country."[5] The victory of the North served to give strength to the democratic, anti-Darwinian proponents in England. This strength, in turn, increased the threat to the middle-class style of life as distinct from that of the lower classes (in schooling, the voting franchise, living standard). Darwinian doctrine justified the previously existing status structure and provided a moral basis for the belief that the lower socioeconomic levels and foreigners represented distinct races that were inferior to the English middle and upper classes. Subjugation of the groups was then justified. The implication here is that the sense of threat and insecurity dramatized by the 1873 depression facilitated the revision of views of the middle-class population regarding the nature of the structure of society—and incidentally mental retardation. In England, Darwinism (and Malthusian doctrine) thus emerged as an explicit issue around which other cultural problems were organized.

SOCIAL MOVEMENTS RELEVANT TO
MENTAL RETARDATION IN THE UNITED STATES

In the United States mental deficiency did not have enough dramatic impact to become a focal issue in social movements in the nineteenth and early twentieth centuries. Instead, it was subordinated to other issues. According to Richard Hofstadter:

> In our political life there have always been certain types of cultural issues, questions of fate and morals, tone and style, freedom and coercion, which become fighting issues. To choose but one example, prohibition was an issue of this kind during the 20's and early 30's. In the struggle over prohibition, economic interests played only the most marginal role; the issue mobilized religious and moral conviction, ethnic habits and hostilities, attitudes toward health and sexuality, and other personal preoccupations.[6]

In the United States, the strength of fundamentalist Protestantism prevented the Darwinist issue from becoming a rallying point. Instead, the focus had to be one that was attractive to both the fundamentalist and the Darwinist. Opposition to the consumption of alcohol provided a common element. At least until the 1930s in the United States, prohibition of alcoholic beverages was identified as a symbol of the "general system of ascetic behavior with which the Protestant middle classes had been identified."[7]

Prohibitionism, however, was not an isolated phenomenon. It was identified with nativism and racial superiority. One prohibitionist journal stated that "the Anglo-Saxon stock is the best improved, hardiest, and fittest. . . . If we are to preserve this nation and the Anglo-Saxon type we must abolish saloons."[8] The relationship between prohibitionism and eugenics was considered especially close by persons holding the Tredgold position that excessive use of alcohol degenerates germ plasm. Here again, the threat was defined by various kinds of decline — social position, standard of living, and genetic quality.

The upsurge of the Americanism movements with fascist leanings in the 1930s was a reaction to the status threat during the Depression. The contraction of standard of living, like those of earlier economic depressions, facilitated emphasis upon exclusion of surplus segments of the population. With the lower-class surplus (as well as other undesirables) excluded from participation in the major institutions of the society, middle-class status would not be endangered.

Before 1930 there were numerous elite groups interested in problems of the mentally retarded. Some of them were connected with eugenics and sterilization. In the early 1900s several states passed laws permitting the sterilization of mental defectives. These laws were enacted in the belief, following Tredgold, that "90 per cent of feeblemindedness was familial in origin." Yet not all organizations concerned with the retarded were repressive. For example, in 1902, at the Vineland Training School, a group of philanthropists and public-spirited men formed the "Feeble-Minded Club" to provide financial assistance for studies of characteristics, causes, and treatment of mental deficiency. In addition, the National Committee for Mental Hygiene organized a Division of Mental Retardation and the Committee on Provision for the Feebleminded was formed in 1914 to promote the establishment of residential institutions. The fact remains, however, that the problem of mental retardation did not stimulate the development of a popular social movement. There was no central organization that nurtured membership and publicized the "cause."[9]

The subordination of concerns about the mildly mentally retarded to other "causes" such as temperance or nativism renders attempts to ameliorate intellectual incompetence ineffective. At some point, efforts to deal with mental retardation as a form of deviance conflict with those pertaining to the dominant "cause." The solution to this conflict is generally to ignore the problems of retardation as such, with the justification that the treatment of the dominant cause will simultaneously ameliorate retardation.

Inasmuch as the etiology and consequences of mental retardation are varied and complex, attention to the dominant "cause" precludes an effective solution to the problem of retardation. Currently, the attempt to explain much mental retardation as a consequence of segregation of and discrimination against Negroes illustrates the point. Initially, in Supreme Court arguments the integration of schools was proposed as a means for reducing intellectual and educational retardation among lower-class Negroes. However, with the passage of time, school integration itself, aside from its consequences for the educational and intellectual development of lower-class Negroes, has become a dominant issue. Since school integration may sometimes interfere with the amelioration of mental retardation, efforts to reduce incompetence are impeded.[10]

The Current Social Movement

The character of the social movements associated with the problem of mental retardation changed following World War II. Prior to the war, social movements concerned with retardation were dominated by those proposing the control and possible elimination of the mentally retarded population. For these persons, the mentally retarded constituted a threat to the well-being of society. Many of the adherents of these movements were nativists who were concerned with the possible debilitating genetic effects of foreigners and Negroes. Others identified the mentally retarded with poverty and immorality. Still others, with humanitarian motives, sought improvements in institutions and segregated colonies to reduce the misery of the mentally retarded. There was also a group of professionals consisting of educators, psychologists, social workers, and personnel in residential institutions seeking ways to improve services to the retarded. The professional personnel interested in the retarded were banded together in the American Association for Mental Deficiency.

After World War II, however, the era of prosperity reduced competition in the labor market, and mildly mentally retarded persons were no longer seen as a threat to the middle class. The focus was shifted to parents and relatives of the severely mentally retarded. The increase in birth rate following World War II produced a larger number of severely mentally retarded children among highly educated and articulate population segments. Improvements in medical technology heightened the chances for survival of the severely retarded. The prosperity of the period stimulated optimism among these parents, both in terms of their own life chances and those of both their normal and retarded children. If the burden of the retarded children were to be to some extent lightened, possibilities of either maintenance of high socioeconomic status or further upward social mobility would be enhanced. Moreover, since middle- and upper-class individuals were affected, the attention was shifted from the previous emphasis upon the transmission of stupidity as a family trait to debilitating diseases (such as rubella among pregnant mothers or encephalitis) and genetic anomalies occurring either through recessive genes or mutation. In addition, the problems of caring for the severely retarded became pressing. Social groups interested in the mentally retarded shifted their concern from problems in social welfare to problems in medicine. Hobbs suggests that "the concepts of public health have finally penetrated the field of mental health." He believes that there is "growing recognition that mental illness [including mental retardation] is not the private organic misery of an individual but a social, ethical and moral problem, a responsibility of the total community."[11] This revision has been accompanied by a change in both personnel involved in the social movement and the kinds of alliances developed. Since World War II, the relationship between those in the mental retardation movement and persons in other health organizations has been strengthened.

This section deals with the National Association for Retarded Children as the formal organization that emerged after World War II to promote the welfare of the mentally retarded. It will indicate how the character of this organization is influenced by the emphasis on the severely retarded and the need to integrate the mental retardation movement with other movements. Attention will also be given to the local parents' groups and their predicaments in developing programs for the mentally retarded while maintaining corporate stability. Finally, the section will describe the participants in agencies and associations for promoting the welfare of the mentally retarded. It will point out some selective factors in membership and volunteer work, and will attempt to indicate ways in which members and volunteers integrate their work with the mentally retarded into a larger pattern of interests.

FORMAL ORGANIZATION OF NARC

The major voluntary association for promoting the welfare of the mentally retarded is the National Association for Retarded Children (NARC). According to its constitution, NARC is nonpolitical and takes no position in matters of governmental policies other than those concerning mental retardation. Its principal objectives as stated in its constitution are as follows:

1. To promote the general welfare of the mentally retarded of all ages everywhere: at home; in the community; in institutions; and in public, private, and religious schools.

2. To further the advancement of all ameliorative and preventive study, research, and therapy in the field of mental retardation.
3. To develop a better understanding of the problems of mental retardation by the public and to cooperate with all public, private, and religious agencies, international, federal, state, and local, and departments of education, health, and institutions.
4. To further the training and education of personnel for work in the field of mental retardation.
5. To encourage the formation of parents' groups, to advise and to aid parents in the solution of their problems, and to coordinate the efforts and activities of these groups.

.   .   .

7. To serve as a clearinghouse for gathering and disseminating information regarding the mentally retarded, and to foster the development of integrated programs in their behalf.

Individual membership in NARC is obtained automatically by persons who are members in good standing of local or state member units. A state organization composed of at least three local member units within the state may request membership in NARC. Only one state member unit may be recognized in each state. Local units may become member units of NARC only when they belong to the state organization. In states where there is no member unit, local units of ten or more members may join NARC. Local and state member units are required to remit NARC membership dues, support payments, and annual reports to NARC.

A sharp distinction is made in the NARC constitution between officers of the association and paid employees. No paid employee is eligible to hold any elective office in NARC. The officers of NARC consist of a president, a senior vice-president, six regional vice-presidents, a secretary, a treasurer, and twenty-four directors elected by the members of NARC. However, major control is vested in an executive committee, which consists of the elected officers of NARC, the immediate past president, and one member of the board of directors. Although the board of directors appoints the executive director, who is a professional administrator with a social work background, the executive committee is responsible for his supervision. The professional staff of NARC serve in sections on community services with field representatives in the six regions (a) community services, (b) governmental affairs, (c) education, (d) public health and nursing, (e) residential care, (f) vocational rehabilitation and adult services,

(g) fund-raising, (h) public information, and (i) membership in international affairs. Coordinate with these staff sections are committees composed of NARC members.[12]

CENTRALIZATION OF POWER

The consequences of the centralization of power for the development and execution of programs has provided a major focus for past studies pertaining to volunteer health or health agencies and bureaucratic organization. The specific concepts used to distinguish between highly centralized and decentralized agencies vary with the organizations studied. Sills used the terms "corporate organization" and "federation" to distinguish between volunteer help agencies on the basis of centralization of power. Truman compared federated with unitary forms of structure in his study of interest groups in the governmental process.[13] Raphael studied the spatial distribution of members of local labor unions in relation to the democratic versus the oligarchical organization of the union movement.[14] Tom Burns and G. M. Stalker compared organizations with organic structures (many different social positions that interact, low centralization, and low formalization of rules) with organizations characterized by mechanical structures (few interacting social positions, high centralization, and high formalization of rules).[15]

Although these investigations have distinguished between centralized and decentralized *types,* as Sills states, no organization is purely corporate or purely federated. Instead, tendencies toward both centralization and decentralization of power (or whatever pairs of concepts are used) exist in all organizations; empirical classifications represent only the predominant tendency. Within each organization, there is a continual interplay of tendencies toward centralization and decentralization of power. A central problem in the study of the associations for the mentally retarded is the extent to which this condition affects the activities of the associations.

The generalizations that have emerged from the investigations of centralization and decentralization of power may provide some insights into the operation of the parent group movement in mental retardation. Some of these generalizations are discussed below.

1. *Decentralized or federated agencies have greater problems in cohesion than centralized or corporate structures.*[16] Federated structures have more difficulty in presenting a united front to the outside

world and to the various segments within the organization. The National Foundation for Infantile Paralysis, which is described by Sills as having a corporate structure, changed its organizational goals when the development of polio vaccine made its initial mission or purpose obsolete. This transition could be accomplished easily because of the unity of purpose afforded by the corporate structure. However, the National Association for Retarded Children, which is a national body supported by local parent groups (each with its own school programs), is a federation. As such, it is susceptible to splintering and overt conflict. One of the board members of the NARC expressed the ambivalence imposed upon the officers and board members by the dual loyalties of the national unit as opposed to the local associations:

> We, in positions of responsibility and trust in NARC, must not use the prestige and influence of our positions to pursue our own objectives if these are at variance with the policies of NARC established by the board and by the convention delegates. We must recognize that in our respective regions we may exert more personal influence than does NARC. They [the parents] may have little knowledge of NARC, but they know and respect us personally.[17]

2. *Organizations that are primarily corporate in structure generally have more limited relationships with other organizations than do those with a federated structure.*[18]   The National Foundation for Infantile Paralysis described by Sills has shown little inclination to merge with other associations. Instead, it changed its organization goals when infantile paralysis ceased to be a major crippling disease in the United States. On the other hand, federated organizations such as the National Society for Crippled Children and Adults, and the United Cerebral Palsy Association have shown many instances of cooperative endeavors with other organizations, including NARC. In contrast to the policy of the National Foundation, NARC has included organizational cooperation as a major aim of the association. Regular liaison arrangements have been made with other welfare agencies to facilitate cooperation on matters of mutual concern. These agencies include the American Association on Mental Deficiency (a professional organization), the Council for Exceptional Children of the National Education Association, and the National Association for Mental Health.[19]   In addition, working relationships are main-

tained with such organizations as the AFL-CIO community services department, Civitan, United Commercial Travellers, State Junior Chamber of Commerce Committees, and United Cerebral Palsy Associations. A representative of NARC sits on the council of the International League of Societies for the Mentally Handicapped. Aside from these cooperative endeavors, NARC has entered into a contract with the United States Department of Labor to provide employment training for mentally retarded persons in national retail stores. This program, initiated through a contract signed late in 1963, has required the cooperative effort of numerous agencies and civic groups. For example, "Early in 1965, Louis C. Lustenberger, President of the Grant Company [W. T. Grant], sent a formal policy statement on employment of the mentally retarded along with a guide to job placement, to each of the company's 1092 stores across the country, urging full cooperation," with the NARC program.[20] Thus the federated structure of NARC has enabled and perhaps stimulated it to develop programs requiring the cooperation of other agencies. Since the mentally retarded represent a diversity of clinical symptoms and social backgrounds, it seems unlikely that a corporate structure could have worked efficiently in handling the numerous problems in both ideology and social relations associated with mental retardation.

3. *When local units gather to combine into a national organization, a federation type of structure usually develops; when an already existing national group creates branches, a corporate structure emerges.*[21] The American Heart Association was initially a professional society composed of physicians. In 1948, after about twenty-five years of existence, the Heart Association established affiliates in other states and has since then maintained a corporate structure. Similarly, the National Foundation for Infantile Paralysis was created in 1937 by President Franklin D. Roosevelt, and affiliates were established only subsequent to the creation of the national organization. The National Foundation has been described by Sills as having a corporate structure. The formation of the National Association for Retarded Children reveals that historically it is a federation of prior-existing local organizations. The earliest parent groups were founded in the 1930s, about the same time as the National Foundation for Infantile Paralysis. The oldest known member group of NARC is the Council for Retarded Children in Cuyahoga County (Ohio), founded in 1933 for families with children who had been excluded from the public schools

in the county. About ten other parents' groups were established in the 1930s and early 1940s. Two of them were associated with residential centers for the mentally retarded. These were the Children's Benevolent League in the State of Washington founded in 1936 (since 1952 called Washington Association for Retarded Children) and the Welfare League for Retarded Children created in 1939 by parents with children at Letchworth Village in New York State. Many of the groups were unaware of the existence of other parent associations. After World War II, the number of parent groups increased. By 1950, there were about ninety local groups with approximately 20,000 members in nineteen states. Some of the groups, such as the Children's Benevolent League, had more than one local unit.

Prior to the organization of a national society, the parents' groups were able to communicate through members' participation in the American Association on Mental Deficiency (AAMD). From 1947 through 1949, parents worked with professional workers in mental retardation in this association. In 1949, the AAMD devoted part of its program to the activities of parents' groups, and again in 1950 sessions were planned with parent participation at the annual AAMD meeting. These meetings provided an opportunity for the parents of the mentally retarded to crystallize their ideas regarding a national organization.

At the AAMD convention in 1950, the parents of retarded children were asked to underwrite a research foundation to be administered by AAMD. The parents met separately for three days to consider the proposal and then decided to reject the AAMD proposal and to organize themselves into a national association. Their immediate goal was that of parent education, and they hoped to develop their own research foundation later.

A steering committee was established, and the Minnesota Association was the host for a meeting to establish a national association. Ninety persons registered at the 1950 organizing convention in Minneapolis. Of these, forty-two were delegates from twenty-three parent-group associations in California, Connecticut, Illinois, Massachusetts, Michigan, Minnesota, Missouri, New Jersey, New York, Ohio, Texas, Vermont, Washington, and Wisconsin. By February 1951, the constitution of NARC (called initially National Association of Parents and Friends of Mentally Retarded Children) was completed. The first annual convention was held in September 1951; by that time fifty-seven charter member units had been accepted. The number of state and local member units of NARC rose from 40 in 1950 to about 350 in 1955, 750 in 1960, and to some 1,000 units in 1965. The number of individual members increased correspondingly. In 1950 there were 5,000 members, and in 1965 there were over 100,000. The local units comprising NARC represent all fifty states, with twenty-three state units organized. In addition, there are six regional divisions, each contributing a vice-president to the national organization.[22]

Not all local associations are affiliated with the National Association for Retarded Children. For example, of the thirty-four parents' groups in Illinois in 1954, only twenty-six were members of the Illinois Council for Retarded Children, and fifteen were members of NARC.[23]

4. *The federated structure of agencies shows greater flexibility in taking on new activities and in developing new positions and roles than the corporate type of structure does.*   Aiken found that in Milwaukee agencies which (a) were decentralized in control, (b) had highly diversified professional specialties, and (c) had a minimum of formal rules of statuses were able to modify their programs and to accept new functions pertaining to the mentally retarded and other clients to a greater extent than agencies with a tight corporate structure.[24] Associated with this finding is the fact that "those national voluntary health associations which have corporate-type formal structures generally devote a much larger percentage of their budgets to research than do those with federation-type structures."[25] Federated structures, with their more decentralized power base, are more susceptible to pressures from a variety of sources in allocation of funds. And, because of their greater sensitivity to public response and the demands of local units, there is more pressure to provide services that would give immediate benefit to the handicapped and their families. Thus the National Association for Retarded Children tends to encounter more opposition in soliciting funds for research than for service. In 1964, the chairman for fund-raising for NARC research wrote:

> To continue the barest minimum of a program of research, our Research Advisory Board has recommended the annual expenditure of $225,000. Yet in 1963, the Research Fund was limited by contributions totaling only slightly in excess of $110,000. Of this amount, $30,000 was contributed by non-member sources—only

$80,000 came from units and individual members. This represents an average giving of $1.00 by each of the 80,000 members of NARC. Why this poor showing? Why did six states contribute not one cent to the Research Fund?[26]

5. *Regardless of age of organization, heterogeneity of composition, or number of members, those organizations with spatially concentrated members are more likely to have "democratic" than "oligarchic" arrangements (or federated rather than corporate structures).*[27] This generalization may account for a tendency for the national office of a federated organization with a widely dispersed membership to attain autonomy and to seek its own corporate identity. The concentration of powerful individuals in the national office permits the development of a group that is prone to set policy informally and, through day-to-day decisions, to create or modify agency policies. This oligarchy need not be on the board of directors or on the professional staff, but they may be in control of sources of funds and publicity media or may lend dignity to the association by their social position. For example, the Scientific Research Advisory Board gives the association respectability among professionals, and it is a source of autonomous action by the national unit. In a sense, the national unit, acting as the corpoarate image of the federated agency, can publish official statements of the organization's position and act as a pressure group in the national government.

By forming close alliances with health agencies, philanthropic foundations, and governmental bodies, the national unit (NARC) can reduce its dependence upon state and local associations for funds and stability. In doing so, it tends to avoid the constraints placed upon it by the federated type of organization. However, the demands of the health agencies, foundations, and government units with which the NARC staff does business offset to some extent the autonomy gained through the decreased reliance upon local and state associations for funds. These national alliances create pressures upon NARC to develop programs different from those of the local associations. While the local associations are interested in schools for the severely retarded and in diagnostic clinics, the national association tends to focus its energy on research support and cooperative programs with other agencies which enhance its reputation and position among health agencies. The tendency toward autonomy of the national unit creates tension between it and the member associations over the allocation of staff and financial resources. The consequences of this tension should be investigated.[28]

Local Parents' Groups

The organization of the NARC as a federation provides the local parents' groups with much autonomy in shaping the destiny of the mental retardation movement. This section deals with topics affecting the organization of the local groups, such as stated goals, power and authority, patterns of leadership, and members of parents groups.

STATED GOALS

The characteristics and purposes of local parent associations depend to a large degree upon the kind of communities in which they exist. About 1960, Goldstein undertook a study of parents' groups in Illinois. He found that associations in large metropolitan areas generally had more members per unit than those in smaller cities. While most members in both metropolitan areas and smaller communities had retarded children age six to fourteen years, the concentration of children in this age range was greater in smaller communities than in the metropolitan areas. There were relatively more parents with preschool children in the metropolitan association than in the associations in smaller communities. This difference can be accounted for by the greater prevalence of public-school provisions for the severely mentally retarded in metropolitan areas than in smaller communities.

Most parents' groups have as their primary task the establishment and operation of special schools for their own severely mentally retarded children. Because of the focus on special schools, parents of retarded children who are either too young or too old for school placement, or who present behavior problems that would disqualify them from these schools, tend not to maintain membership in the parents' associations. Similarly, parents who require services different from those provided by the parents' associations, or whose children are in public school classes for the trainable mentally handicapped, or in institutions, appear to be underrepresented in these groups. Because parents' associations in large metropolitan areas often provide sheltered workshops for the older retarded and nurseries for the preschoolers, there is a greater dispersion in the age of children whose parents belong to associations in these areas than in smaller communities. As the parents' groups expand programs and services, membership will probably increase and become more diverse in age range and in socio-economic characteristics.[29]

POWER AND AUTHORITY

The direct confrontation of parents and professionals occurs more often at the local parents' groups than in the national organization. In his study of the formation of parents' associations, Katz found that initially many parents tended to be active in the association but, as time went on, parental involvement in the association declined and the role of professionals increased. Schools were turned over to professionals, and direct treatment was administered by specialists rather than by parents. With this decline in active participation, the parents became apathetic in the work of the association. Although participation in the parents' groups may provide an outlet for feelings of frustration and assist in solving family problems, only a minority of parents who joined the association remained active in its operation.[30]

The description by Katz is consistent with the view generally attributed to Max Weber and Roberto Michels regarding the development of organizations.[31] Briefly, as presented by Zald and Ash, the Weber-Michels position applied to organizations associated with social movements is:

> An MO [movement organization] attains an economic and social base in the society, as the original charismatic leadership is replaced, a bureaucratic structure emerges, and a general accommodation to the society occurs. The participants in this structure have a stake in preserving the organization, regardless of its ability to attain goals. Analytically there are three types of change involved in this process; empirically they are often fused. The three types of change are goal transformation, a shift to organizational maintenance, and oligarchization.[32]

The transformation of goals refers to accommodating the goals of the organization to those considered "practical" in the society. The shift to organizational maintenance means an increasing emphasis on the requirements for sustaining the organization—funds, retaining members, bureaucratization of activities. Oligarchization is the concentration of power in a minority of the organization's members.[33]

Unlike the national unit, in local groups power in the formation of policies and major decisions is generally not delegated to the professional bureaucracy. The members are close at hand, and the major power remains with the nonprofessional oligarchy. The fact that the power in local associations tends to be concentrated in a small group generally operates to give them a centralized, corporate organization. This concentration of power may create problems for professionals, such as psychologists or teachers, who work with the local associations. In a study of social agencies in Wisconsin, Aiken and Hage found that, in highly centralized and highly formalized structures, staff members felt alienated from the organization and there was little informal interaction. The absence of opportunities for staff to participate in decisions concerning policies and the lack of freedom in determining rules governing jobs created much dissatisfaction. In such a situation, much turnover and a sense of inadequacy among the professional staff can be expected.[34]

PATTERNS OF LEADERSHIP

Centralization of control in local organizations seems to be related to leadership patterns in the division of labor that develops in parents' groups. Some of the participants show greater interest in problems related to programs or purposes, while others become more involved in the means of organization—that is, in ways of making the institution "work." Those participants involved in purposes devote a considerable amount of time and energy to promoting new programs, to proselytizing others, and, in short, to making "the cause" a primary occupation in their lives. The organizing leaders both mobilize the potential membership and try to convince other agencies and the larger community of the legitimacy of their cause. They may become known as Mr. Mental Retardation or Mr. Cerebral Palsy to outsiders and as either charismatic leaders or "fanatics" to others within the movement. In contrast to the organizers are the businesslike leaders, who are more concerned with sustaining the organization than in guiding its purposes. They are interested in developing a corporate structure for the local organization, whereas the organizing leaders are more interested in proliferation and improvement of treatment or educational programs. In most organizations, it is relatively easy to distinguish the organizing leaders from the business-like leaders. Some descriptions of organizing leaders are:[35]

> What we need is a leader. Now Mrs. Carleton over at Southeast Town has done everything. She got the school started, she goes out and raises money, she goes door to door. The Kiwanis support her. Only she has to do everything herself.

Mrs. A. got a list of all those who had had children in public schoolrooms for the educable and had had to take the children out because of lack of mental capacity. She called the people on the telephone to inform them of a meeting and at this meeting it was decided that they should go ahead and organize the parents' group. There were thirty-two names on the list and Mrs. A. wrote personal letters in longhand to all of them about an organizing meeting. Over twenty-eight persons were at the first meeting. According to Mrs. A., "They were just so glad that something was being done, that they said that they would do whatever I said—just go ahead and they'd work." We had to drag the superintendent of special services to a conference. Well, he got all enthused and on the way back he went by several possible locations for a school. Then he called and said we could have one of them. I am personally very active on the state level and nationally. I have gone to every national convention. We have always been in a position to send a delegate and I went as a participant this last time. I am on a committee that's trying to list all of the private residential schools. It is a lot of work. I am chairman of the committee on local programs for the state council. I handle requests for films and records and such things from all over the state. It's quite a job. I am in the speaker's bureau. We have a plan for all handicapped children. It would include schools, sheltered workshop, a plant to work in, and social life facilities. It is the kind of thing to take care of them from the cradle to the grave. I went down to Houston and saw the wonderful programs they have down there. They also have a wonderful program in Toledo and New Jersey—also in California. I read everything I can about retarded children. I study every issue of *Children Limited*. Interest in the parents' group is down right now. We only had six at the last meeting, but it was a real bad night. Usually more come in April and May when we're planning for the next year.

I got together some parents. I had wanted a school all along but that wasn't the thing that they were interested in right then. They already had a school. They were interested in starting a summer program. So we went to the park commission and they let us use Leroy Park. It's a lovely little park. We had ten children the first year and last year we had forty. Of that ten about half were educable and the others were trainable. Well, I wanted to start a school and so I started a room right in the basement of this house. I just took the children I knew about. And then I started the organization to try to work for a permanent room. It is all right to have a private school, but I couldn't be professional. I was just a parent to them. So they started organizing in October and we had the first meeting here.

We had a notice in the paper and then I went and talked to people. We had twenty-five people at that first meeting and then we moved to Albert School and we started meeting there. They had a group come from the outside to tell us how to organize and all that. Someone from the state organization in Chicago told us about by-laws and that kind of thing. I had had my school for two years and I was anxious to get rid of that. Some of them on the board asked me to go ahead and be a teacher but I couldn't. I wanted to be friendly but I wasn't really a teacher. Then the state took over the class as part of the pilot project. A lot of the children were dropped out of the school either because they were too old or too young or because they were too slow mentally. They just kept putting the standards up and up. I was in on the planning meeting down in Midtown and we never said anything about tests or that sort of thing. But as soon as they got it started, boom! We had to have psychological tests and this and that. These children can't do that. So we started the Lake School and we have a Sunday School too. I went personally to talk with everybody before I took the child into the school. Oh, I am still active, but not as active as I used to be. You know you kind of want others to take over for a while. About thirty of the families are really active, they come regularly and are willing to work. About twenty others come depending on what the meaning is. We usually have thirty to fifty parents at a meeting.

The activities of the businesslike leaders are not as dramatic as those of the organizing leaders. Their concern is with the corporate development of the parents' association. In activities, the businesslike or corporate leaders are more involved in providing a stable financial base and physical plant for maintaining a staff of workers to carry out existing programs of the agencies. Zald and Ash suggest that "a pragmatic leadership replaces unattainable goals with diffuse goals so that the organization can pursue a broader range of targets."

Because practical matters and finance are generally less interesting than program development, emphasis on them discourages many members from participating in the business affairs of the association. The businesslike leaders are thereby left as an oligarchy in the group. These leaders appear to emphasize the need for professionalization, which serves to stabilize the program of the organization and to maintain a corporate structure. In connection with this, it should be noted that the National Association for Retarded Children was organized in opposition to professionals and that the professionalization in the national office has served to counterbalance the diffusion of power in the federated structure of NARC.

The discussion below suggests the kinds of conflict which may emerge as corporate leaders in an association transform its primary goals from expansion of services to providing a stable organization.[36]

> Mr. H. has a number of objections to the way the group is being run. He noted that the treasurer's books are simply a listing of all incoming and outgoing funds and are not arranged so that they could "stand audit." He expressed the feeling that the treasurer, a person with only 8th grade education, was not capable of keeping financial records of an organization which had come to handle relatively large sums of money. In his capacity as chairman of the ways and means committee, Mr. H. has been working with the treasurer trying to put the books in order. Mr. H. reports that when he suggested to the group that they use checks counter-signed by both the president and treasurer, group members said he was accusing the treasurer of dishonesty.[37]

In the classical descriptions of the routinization of charisma, the charismatic organizing leader maintains control until his death or retirement from the organization.[38] However, my observations of the organizing leaders of parents' associations suggest a different sequence of events. Perhaps even at the inception of the association there are dissident members who remain for instrumental reasons although they dislike some personal attributes or plans of the organizing leader. The total involvement of the organizing leader prevents any attempt to displace him, but almost immediately some of the dissidents begin to undermine his influence. In the groups I observed, this undermining generally included a transformation of goals to those which were considered practical, a pressure toward bureaucratization and routinization, and a movement to make the organizing leader a figurehead. In the course of those efforts, members of the organization took sides for or against the organizing leaders, and factions developed. The groups seemed to split into factions focusing on (a) the handling of the business of the organization as opposed to (b) mobilizing the membership to improve the programs of the organization. Squabbles over finances, for example, are expressions of the conflict between the organizing-mobilizing factions and the bureaucratizing-routinizing factions.

These observations suggest the hypothesis that, in spite of pressures toward oligarchy and bureaucratization, the organizing of parents' associations is generally characterized by an ongoing struggle between the factions mentioned above. This hypothesis is presented as an alternative to one formulated by Zald and Ash,[39] namely, "Routinization of charisma is likely to conservatize the dominant core of the movement organization while simultaneously producing increasingly radical splinter groups." Zald and Ash, following the classical Weber-Michels theory, regard routinization as a way of maintaining the program of the charismatic leader; the splinter groups emerge over disagreements in program. My observations, however, suggest that the movement toward routininzation in the parents' associations is created in *response* to the emphasis upon expansion of functions and mobilization of personnel by the organizing leaders.

Perhaps the difference between the classical Weber-Michels statement of leadership and organization and the one presented here stems from the kinds of problems which necessitated the organization. The classical statement is based on political social movements, in which there can be as many organizations as there are solutions to political problems. The associations for the mentally retarded emerge mainly to promote a single solution—to develop school, welfare, and health services for the severely retarded. Hence, developing competing organizations would be unfeasible and parents must join the existing movement to accomplish their ends. Almost immediately, such a situation will force persons who do not regard the organizing leader as charismatic to join the association and possibly to create an opposing faction. The focusing of organization on specific health problems and generally accepted prescribed treatments may differentiate health social movements from political movements in terms of patterns of leadership and organizational dynamics—a difference that should be investigated.

The factions created by rallying around either the organizing or the businesslike leaders suggests the existence of a mutual contempt and suspicion within the subgroups of an organization. Research could be done on the consequences of this split for the power structure of the organization: Since the organizing-leader faction finds its legitimacy in the recruitment and stirring up of members, this faction would tend to favor democratization of power. The businesslike faction, on the other hand, which operates most efficiently as an oligarchy, would rely more upon committee structure and the appropriation of offices for its maintenance. The accrual of specialized knowledge, the appropriation of resources, and skill in the management of others seem to favor the faction supporting businesslike leaders.[40] Tendencies toward oligarchization and bureaucratization would thus appear.[41] These tendencies, however, would not eliminate the organizing leaders' factions, but would stabilize the factional aspects of organization.

The messianic role of the organizing leader is found in many social contexts. Daniel Bell describes the socialist Eugene V. Debs as a man who *"realized* the messianic role of the prophet, [but] he lacked the hard-headedness of the politician, the ability to take the moral absolutes and break them down to the particulars with the fewest necessary compromises."[42] In the study of trade union organization, a distinction has been made between the committed leader, whose dedication to the labor movement is sufficiently strong to be considered a "calling," and bureaucratic leaders, who are careerists.[43] "Men with a 'calling' are likely to be viewed as irresponsible by heads of bureaucracies who prefer to select persons who will work within the framework of the organization's goals as defined by the leaders."[44]

The various descriptions of types of leadership suggest that the organizing and businesslike leaders differ both in personal style and in social and personal characteristics. Inasmuch as the organizing leader must stir up interest in the "cause" both within and outside the interest group, he probably resorts to expressive and dramatic language and activities. His emphasis upon program expansion is itself an expression of his "other-worldliness." In contrast, the businesslike leader bases his position in the group upon his rationality and practicality and therefore must impress others with his matter-of-fact style, his ability to routinize activities, and his competence in obtaining the cooperation of his colleagues in carrying out plans.[45]

The putative difference between expressive and rational styles of leadership in parents' associations implies consistent patterns of personal and social attributes. Organizing leaders, with their motivation elevated to a "calling," probably have more personality problems, more marital and family difficulties, and fewer competing interests than businesslike leaders. In addition, the organizing leader is less likely to be of high socioeconomic and educational status, more likely to be in a minority ethnic or religious group, and unlikely to be an active participant in the decision-making of the dominant economic and educational institutions in the community.

The different styles and abilities required by these two types of leaders are suggested by a study by Willie on the composition of boards of directors of health and welfare voluntary associations over a twenty-seven-year period. In comparing the board members of a fund-raising organization (Community Chest) with those of a health and welfare planning organization (Council of Social Agencies), Willie found out that the fund-raising group consisted more of males, businessmen affiliated with manufacturing industries, and high-ranking officers in business establishments (such as corporation presidents, vice-presidents, secretaries, and treasurers). The planning group had more women, professionals (especially social workers), and managers and administrators. Willie concluded that the dominant leadership made the decisions regarding funding (and thereby selected the services that would be funded), while the subdominant leadership decided on specific plans and policies.[46] The lower socioeconomic status and the greater prevalence of women members suggest a greater emphasis upon mobilization of personnel and program expansion by the board of the service-planning agency than by the fund-raising agency. This difference also indicates the strategy whereby a business-like faction may attempt to control an organizing faction in an association — by attempting to control the financial base and thus restrict the kinds of programs which the organization may undertake.

MEMBERS OF PARENTS' GROUPS

Two types of volunteers can be found in health agencies. First, there are those who are motivated because they themselves are deeply involved with the particular health problem with which the agency deals. A casual observation of membership lists of associations for promoting the welfare of the mentally retarded reveals a predominance of parents of retarded children. However, agencies which list mental retardation among an array of interests do not rely primarily upon parents as volunteers. This section will describe the characteristics both of participants in parents' associations and of volunteers in other types of agencies.

Participating Parents.   There has been little examination of social characteristics of the members of parents' associations. In a study of parents with severely mentally retarded children, Farber obtained mailing lists from parents' groups in the Chicago area which included about 490 families. Farber coded the residences of these families by socioeconomic rank of the census tracts in which they lived. A comparison of socioeconomic rank of census tracts of families listed by parents' associations and all adults living in Chicago in 1950 is shown in Table 12. The table indicates a tendency for parents at the upper and especially middle socioeconomic ranks to contact

TABLE 12

Socioeconomic Rank of Census Tracts of Residence of 489 Families Listed by Parents' Associations in 1956 and All Adults, Aged 21 and over, Living in Chicago, 1950[1]

Socioeconomic Rank of Census Tracts	Families Listed by Associations		Percent of Actual Chicago Adult Population
	No. of Families	Percent	
High (Ranks 7–10)	179	36.7	33.1
Medium (Ranks 3–6)	194	39.6	36.2
Low (Ranks 0–2)	116	23.7	30.8
Total	489	100.0	100.1

[1] Bernard Farber, "Effects of a Severely Mentally Retarded Child on Family Integration," *Monographs of the Society for Research in Child Development*, 24 (1959), No. 2 (Serial No. 71), p. 95.

parents' associations to a greater extent than might be expected on the basis of the actual adult population distribution. Farber's analysis also showed an underrepresentation from tracts where a majority of the inhabitants are Negroes.[47] Since low socioeconomic areas tend to produce a high rate of both trainable and educable children, we can conclude that membership in parents' associations tends to be a middle-class phenomenon and is not representative socioeconomically of the population of parents of either educable or trainable mentally retarded children. Unlike the National Foundation for Infantile Paralysis, the associations consist of individuals with personal experience with the handicap rather than those who tend to participate generally in community organizations for humanitarian or "good citizenship" reasons. Like the volunteers for the National Foundation, the members of the parents' associations tend to be white-collar rather than blue-collar families and to have children under twenty-one.

Parents who participate in associations for the mentally retarded are probably better informed and more involved in a communication network relevant to mental retardation than other parents. Menzel undertook a study of parents with cerebral-palsied children to determine how information pertaining to handicapping conditions is disseminated. He found that parents who have obtained information in publications also see more professionals, talk with more parents of cerebral-palsied children, attend more organizational activities, and in general are exposed to many sources of information. Parents with a high degree of exposure to information about cerebral palsy tend to be people of higher socioeconomic positions and to have more than one child. "The parents of an only child who is handicapped are less likely to talk with other parents (79 per cent to 51 per cent), are less likely to think that professionals have been helpful (46 per cent to 13 per cent), and are even less likely to know the elementary facts about cerebral palsy."[48] Menzel found that the older the handicapped children are, the less do their parents appreciate contact with other parents of cerebral-palsied children. These parents find that facilities for treating their children have become less adequate for their needs. In general, the parents who are most likely to have contact with other parents of cerebral-palsied children (a) are members of parents' associations or generally of high socioeconomic status, (b) make abundant utilization of cerebral-palsied services, and (c) report high participation in community activities related to cerebral palsy.

Volunteers.   Most studies of volunteer agencies focus upon the work of those nonprofessionals who carry on the organizational activities of the group. However, volunteers also perform such direct service as assisting in hospitals or in classrooms. Ethel Miller Adams studied direct-service volunteers in five community agencies. The Adams study showed:

> Women are volunteers more often than men. They usually live in the city or less often in a suburb. Generally they are housewives, although a large number work in a professional or technical occupation. A smaller number work in clerical positions. A few are retired. More of the volunteers have had a high school education than college training although the difference is not great. The reasons they gave for entering volunteer work showed that there were many other considerations aside from the desire to give service. Most of them expected some satisfaction or benefit from giving their services. More volunteers had worked in their agency up to three years than any other length of time, although the range of service

was up to 50 years. More than half of the volunteers have done work in more than one agency.[49]

The characteristics of volunteers in direct service necessarily vary with the kind of service performed and the social climate in which this service occurs. The Welfare Council of Metropolitan Chicago undertook an investigation of the characteristics of Head Start volunteers recruited by the Volunteer Service Corps in 1965. Like the volunteers in the Adams study, the Head Start volunteers tended to be housewives (54 percent), but about one-fifth (21 percent) were students. About two-thirds of the volunteers were married, and 97 percent were women. The single persons were generally students under twenty-six years of age. About one-third of the volunteers were twenty-five or younger (30 percent), and about 60 percent were aged twenty-six to fifty-five. Although the Volunteer Service Corps tried to recruit older retired adults, only 1 percent of the Volunteers were over sixty-five. Religion was also a factor in volunteering. One-third of the volunteers (33 percent) were Jewish, although only 5 percent of all Cook County residents are classified as Jewish. The tendency for students to volunteer for Head Start programs meant that a large proportion of the volunteers had college training. Two-thirds of the volunteers had at least one year of college, and many were still attending. (In contrast, in the Adams study, only one-third of the volunteers had had some college training.) About one-third of the volunteers lived in the suburbs of Chicago, with the preponderance coming from the northern suburbs which have a large Jewish population. Very few of the volunteers worked in their own community area. Three-fourths of the volunteers felt that their work was interesting and challenging and that their talents and skills were being used effectively.[50]

The direct-service volunteers differ from the administrative volunteers in that the service itself is an integral part of the program of the agency, whereas the administrative volunteer is involved with the maintenance of the agency. The direct-service volunteer, therefore, probably identifies more with the professional staff of the agency and its mission than with the fiscal matters or organizational problems. The fact that the direct-service volunteers tend to be women who are also housewives and students who want to contribute something significant to society may involve them in the programmatic aspects of agency work rather than in the fiscal and organizational matters.

Since volunteers frequently work in more than one agency, their apparent concern is not so much with the specific problems with which any single agency is identified as with the idea of contributing to the welfare of society. In general, the characteristics of the direct-service volunteers resemble those of organizing rather than corporate leaders.

SUMMARY

Whereas the social movements pertaining to mental retardation during the nineteenth and early twentieth centuries were dominated by groups who were unsympathetic to the mentally retarded, after World War II the character of the social movements changed. The nativists and moralists, who were threatened by the presence of the mentally retarded and especially by populations that were considered to be highly productive of the mentally retarded, faded into the background.

Historically, in the late nineteenth and early twentieth centuries, when mental retardation was defined primarily in terms of deviance, the social movement was in the hands of outsiders. The ferment created by these outsiders was directed toward the treatment of the large bulk of the retarded — the educable group. After 1950, with the domination of the movement by parents of the severely retarded, the concerns shifted to the medical and care problems of these severely retarded children. At the same time, retardation was generally redefined as incompetence. In the course of this redefinition, the mental retardation movement seems to have achieved respectability.

After World War II, with prosperity and the increased life span of the severely retarded, the focus of efforts in dealing with mental retardation shifted from the mildly retarded to the severely mentally retarded and from problems of deviant behavior (such as delinquency) to medical problems. Consequently the mental retardation movement became identified with agencies dealing with health concerns.

By the 1950s middle-class parents deeply involved in providing schools and services for their severely retarded children dominated the movement. It seems inevitable that the national organization, the National Association for Retarded Children, should have had a federated structure rather than a unified corporate structure. Federated organization gives considerable power to the member groups and emphasizes the diversity of needs of the retarded. This diversity has required an ever-expanding liaison with other agencies in the community and a constant pressure upon government. The effectiveness of the association in government was enhanced considerably in 1960 by the election of President John F. Kennedy, who facilitated the association's striving for prestige as a health agency and its attempts to reconceptualize mental retardation as a health problem.

Like other federated organizations, the National Association for Retarded Children and its member groups are continually faced with the problem of maintaining corporate stability in the face of the need for diversity of services and activities required to accommodate the needs of the retarded. Two kinds of leadership have emerged. The first is the organizational leader, an intensely devoted person who seeks to promote the welfare of the retarded in a variety of ways. To some these leaders seem to be charismatic; by others in the movement they are regarded as fanatics. These organizing leaders try to stir interest in their fellowman and operate to prevent the formalization of programs in the associations. The second type of leader is the corporate leader who tries to promote a firm financial base, the stability of programs, and a well-organized corporate structure. The corporate leader emphasizes the need for professional persons to carry out the existing programs; the apathy of a large portion of the membership facilitates the work of an oligarchy of corporate leaders. Parents' associations often contain factions that rally around organizing as opposed to corporate leaders.

The agencies that rely on nonparents as volunteers differ in clientele from those associated with parents' groups. The clients of the agencies operated by parents' groups (generally special schools and sheltered workshops) are the severely retarded children of the members. Ordinarily, if the parents want their child to attend the special school or to receive its services, they are required to join the association. Most of the sustained services for the retarded and their families probably take place within this context. However, governmental and private agencies that do not rely upon parents for policy-making, financing, or volunteer work generally serve a clientele more diverse in terms of both degree of retardation and socioeconomic characteristics. The services of these agencies are ordinarily of a sporadic nature (such as emergency or temporary hospitalization, diagnosis, or medical treatment). As a result of the differences in clientele between parent-sponsored agencies (including special schools) and government or private agencies dealing with the retarded, the major effort in medical, welfare, and educational services and research is applied to a minority of the retarded — the children of members of the parents' associations.

GENERAL DISCUSSION

The tendency for corporate leaders to dominate social movements (as indicated by Katz's findings) suggests that the social movement connected with mental retardation will continue to serve a middle-class clientele and focus its efforts on the severely mentally retarded. Since, ironically, the severely mentally retarded represent a minority of retardates, the effectiveness of the National Association for Retarded Children and of associated groups will likely be more symbolic than practical in promoting the welfare of the majority of retardates. By focusing upon the severely mentally retarded, the NARC and other health agencies have appropriated the power and leadership, while the parents of the educable mentally retarded have little voice in either the associations or in health and government agencies. Perhaps even more significant, the major resources are allocated to the severely retarded, and the majority of the retarded — the educable group — receive little special treatment or attention. Inadvertently, the social movements pertinent to the retarded have stabilized the position of the educable retarded in society. Only paternalistic action on the part of the associations is of benefit to the educable retardates, and paternalism stabilizes the perception of the subordinate as a dependent "child."

NOTES

[1] J. A. Banks, *Prosperity and Parenthood* (London: Routledge and Kegan Paul, 1954).

[2] *Ibid.*, p. 201.

[3] Alice Drayton Greenwood, *History of the People of England* (London: Sheldon, 1929), Vol. 4, p. 129.

[4] Julian Huxley, "The Emergence of Darwinism," in Sol Tax, ed., *Evolution after Darwin* (Chicago: University of Chicago Press, 1960), Vol. I, p. 10; article on pages 1–21.

[5] G. M. Trevelyan, *History of England* (Garden City, New York: Doubleday, 1953), Vol. 3, p. 204.

[6] Richard Hofstadter, "Pseudo-Conservatism Reprinted: A Postscript, 1962," in Daniel Bell, ed., *The Radical Right* (New York: Anchor, 1963), pp. 81–86.

[7] Joseph R. Gusfield, *Symbolic Crusade* (Urbana: University of Illinois Press, 1963), p. 123.

[8] *The American Issue*, 20 (April, 1912), p. 1, quoted in Gusfield, *op. cit.*, p. 100.

[9] See Eugene E. Doll, "A Historical Survey of Research and Management

of Mental Retardation in the United States," in E. Philip Trapp and Philip Himelstein, eds., *Readings on the Exceptional Child* (New York: Appleton-Century-Crofts, 1962), pp. 31–40; and especially Stanley P. Davies, *The Mentally Retarded in Society* (New York: Columbia University Press, 1959), pp. 65–70.

10 The solution implied in this discussion is not, of course, to continue school segregation, but to separate the issue of civil rights from that of retardation. The civil rights of Negroes demand prompt integration of the schools. Elimination of effects of past segregation and discrimination, however, requries *superior* educational services and facilities in many instances.

11 Nicholas Hobbs, "Mental Health's Third Revolution," *American Journal of Orthopsychiatry*, 34 (1964), p. 824.

12 See constitution and bylaws of National Association for Retarded Children, Inc., November, 1965, and annual reports of NARC for 1964 and 1965.

13 David L. Sills, *The Volunteers: Means and Ends in a National Organization* (Glencoe, Illinois: Free Press, 1957). David B. Truman, *The Governmental Process* (New York: Alfred A. Knopf, 1951).

14 Edna E. Raphael, "Power Structure and Membership Dispersion in Unions," *American Journal of Sociology*, 71 (November, 1965), pp. 274–283.

15 Tom Burns and G. M. Stalker, *The Management of Innovation* (London: Tavistock Publications, 1961).

16 Based on statement relating sources of power to consensus in Seymour M. Lipset, "The Political Process in Trade Unions: A Theoretical Statement," in Morroe Berger, Theodore Abel, and Charles H. Page, eds., *Freedom and Control in Modern Society* (New York: Van Nostrand, 1954), p. 106.

17 James K. Gould, "Board Members' Rights Versus Responsibilities," *Children Limited*, 13 (April, 1964), p. 14.

18 Ray E. Johns, *The Cooperative Process Among National Social Agencies* (New York: Association Press, 1946).

19 *Children Limited*, 15 (February–March, 1966), p. 10.

20 National Association for Retarded Children, *1965, Action with Vision*, Annual Report of NARC. See also *1964, A Threshold Year*.

21 Sills, *op. cit.*, p. 6.

22 Letha L. Patterson, "How the National Association for Retarded Children, Incorporated, Came into Being," issued by National Association for Retarded Children, 1954; *Children Limited*, 15 (February–March, 1966), p. 10; *Voices in Chorus* (New York: National Association for Retarded Children, ND), pp. 2–3.

23 William R. Arnold, "Social Movements of Parents in Five Communities for Better Care of Mentally Retarded Children," Master of Arts thesis, University of Illinois, 1956.

24 Jerald Hage and Michael T. Aiken, "Program Change and Organizational Properties: A Comparative Analysis," *American Journal of Sociology*, 72 (March, 1967), pp. 503–519.

25 Sills, *op. cit.*, p. 73.

26 G. Franklyn Ward, "Greatest Hope of All Parents Is in Research," *Children Limited*, 13 (June, 1954), p. 6.

27 Raphael, *op. cit.*, p. 282.

28 The alliance of the national unit with other agencies, foundations, and government bodies represents a mutual co-optation whereby "new elements are absorbed into the leadership or policy-determining structure of [the national organizations] as a means of averting threats to [their] stability

or existence." Philip Selznick, *TVA and the Grass Roots* (New York: Harper Torchbooks, 1966), p. 13.

[29] Herbert Goldstein, "A Study of the Status of Parents' Groups in Illinois: Unmet Needs," unpublished paper, Institute for Research on Exceptional Children, University of Illinois.

[30] Alfred H. Katz, *Parents of the Handicapped* (Springfield, Illinois: Thomas, 1961).

[31] See H. J. Gerth and C. Wright Mills, *From Max Weber: Essays in Sociology* (New York: Oxford University Press, 1946), pp. 297–301; and Roberto Michels, *Political Parties* (New York: Free Press, 1949).

[32] Mayer N. Zald and Roberta Ash, "Social Movement Organizations: Growth, Decay and Change," *Social Forces*, 44 (March, 1966), p. 327.

[33] *Ibid.*, pp. 327–328.

[34] Michael Aiken and Jerald Hage, "Organizational Alienation: A Comparative Analysis," *American Sociological Review*, 31 (August, 1966), pp. 497–507.

[35] Excerpts from interviews from Arnold, *op. cit.*

[36] Zald and Ash, *op. cit.*, pp. 327–341.

[37] Arnold, *op. cit.*

[38] Zald and Ash, *op. cit.*

[39] *Ibid.*, p. 338.

[40] Seymour Martin Lipset, Introduction to Michels, *op. cit.*, p. 16.

[41] Katz, *op. cit.*

[42] Daniel Bell, *The End of Ideology* (New York: Collier Books, 1961), p. 286.

[43] See Seymour Martin Lipset, *Political Man* (New York: Doubleday Anchor Books, 1963), pp. 417–424.

[44] *Ibid.*, p. 421.

[45] See Talcott Parsons and Robert F. Bales, *Family, Socialization and Interaction* (New York: Free Press, 1955); and Robert F. Bales, "Task Roles and Social Roles in Problem-Solving Groups," in Eleanor E. Maccoby, T. M. Newcomb, and E. L. Hartley, eds., *Readings in Social Psychology* (New York: Holt, 1958), pp. 437–447.

[46] Charles V. Willie, "Community Leadership in the Voluntary Health and Welfare System," in Alvin W. Gouldner and S. M. Miller, eds., *Applied Sociology* (New York: Free Press, 1965), pp. 207–214.

[47] Bernard Farber, "Effects of a Severely Mentally Retarded Child on Family Integration," *Monographs of the Society for Research in Child Development*, 1959, No. 71, pp. 95–97.

[48] Herbert Menzel, *The Dissemination of Information among Parents of Handicapped Children* (New York: Association for the Aid to Crippled Children, April, 1961), p. 76.

[49] Ethel Miller Adams, "A Study of Volunteers in Five Community Areas," unpublished Ph.D. dissertation, University of Pennsylvania, 1964, pp. 83–84.

[50] Francis E. Burke, "A Study of Head Start Volunteers Recruited by the Volunteer Service Corps — Their Characteristics and Reactions to the Program, Chicago Summer, 1965," Welfare Council of Metropolitan Chicago, Publication #1017, July, 1966.

7.

The Family

This chapter will discuss the immediate social matrix in which most mentally retarded persons live — the family. However, the significance of family life for the severely mentally retarded is considerably different from that for the educable, mildly retarded. Unless the severely retarded person is institutionalized, he will undoubtedly spend all of his life with his parents and siblings. The mildly retarded individual, on the other hand, may eventually marry and have children. Moreover, the characteristics of families of the severely retarded differ from those of families of mildly retarded individuals. For these reasons, this chapter will deal separately with the family lives of severely and mildly retarded persons.[1]

Families of the Severely Mentally Retarded

Families with severely mentally retarded children exist in all segments of society. Since social factors do not appear to play an important role in the prevalence of the severely retarded, these families constitute an unselected cross-section of kinds of family life prior to the birth and diagnosis of the retarded child. The major concern for investigation is determining the retarded child's impact on family relationships.

This chapter discusses the consequences of labeling the child as retarded for families in different social contexts. Two kinds of consequences will be considered. First, the chapter will focus upon the revisions in age and sex roles in family relationships; then it will deal with the modifications in the interaction between family and community.

Labeling the Child as Mentally Retarded

The impact of the retarded child on family relations begins at the point of the parents' definition or labeling of the child as retarded. The definition of the child as mentally retarded will be discussed under three topics: the extent to which the parents redefine the child's role, the various types of redefinition, and factors that influence redefinition.

EXTENT OF REDEFINITION OF THE CHILD

The extent of parental redefinition of a child as retarded has received some systematic investigation. Parents tend to rate their retarded child less favorably than their normal children on personality traits.[2] However, Zuk found that parents tend to overestimate the social quotient of the retarded child but that this distortion is most pronounced when children are relatively normal in motor functioning.[3] Jensen and Kogan suggest that this tendency declines over time. They report that parents overrate the intellectual potential of younger cerebral-palsied children to a greater extent than they do that of older children.[4] On the other hand, Schulman and Stern and Rosen indicate that parents are fairly realistic in judging the IQ of their children.[5] For the Schulman and Stern study, the correlation coefficient between tested and parent-estimated Stanford-Binet IQ was .67 at the time that the families first sought help. Yet Barclay and Vaught[6] found neither age nor physical disability related to maternal estimation of the intellectual potential of cerebral-palsied children. This discrepancy in findings may have resulted from differences between the samples with respect to age, severity of retardation, physical deformities, or social status.

KINDS OF LABELS

There is little question that the actual labeling of an individual as mentally retarded by a physician or psychologist generally produces tremendous emotional turmoil in the parents. In modern society, an individual's destiny depends on many labels, such as race, religion, occupation, and age and sex attributes, as well as on personal attributes. Groups differ with respect to the importance they attach to these labels. The label of mental retardation may be more important in some groups than others in determining participation. In our society the combinations and permutations of socioeconomic and other labels are probably more significant in determining life chances for the mentally retarded than the label of mental retardation itself. Viewing the label of mental retardation as only one in a series suggests that this label will have different consequences for family relationships to the extent that it represents a contrast to other labels. These remarks call forth the following hypotheses.

The first hypothesis is: The higher the socioeconomic status of the family, the greater the impact on family relationships of labeling a child as mentally retarded. This effect emerges through the discrepancy between the mental retardation label and other labels ascribed to family members by society. In low socioeconomic status families, the label of mental retardation is not greatly divergent from other labels associated with low status. There is a multiplicity of stigma. Therefore the label of mental retardation would have less impact on family relationships in these families. This hypothesis is consistent with a finding in research that parents of high socioeconomic levels tend to have a greater initial emotional reaction to the diagnosis of retardation, whereas low socioeconomic level mothers are often not as severely shaken by the diagnosis.[7]

The second hypothesis is: The potency of child-care problems associated with mental retardation is related to socioeconomic status in affecting family relationships. As long as high socioeconomic status parents are uncertain about the potential intellectual development of the retarded child, their family relationships may not be profoundly affected. However, as soon as the child is diagnosed as *severely retarded,* the discrepancy between his other familial, social, and economic labels and his intellectual label is sufficiently great to produce great emotional impact. If the child is considered as an *educable* retarded individual, the discrepancy is not so severe, and family relationships may not be as profoundly affected. For low socioeconomic level families, however, since the label itself is presumably not the primary crisis-evoking factor, child-care problems themselves provide the basis for family tension. Regardless of the degree of retardation, if the physical disabilities of the child do not require a great deal of effort and attention, the consequences for family relationships would not be severe at lower socioeconomic levels.

The latter hypothesis concerning the redefinition of the child is related to the kind of problem the child presents. A study by Korkes showed that many parents of mentally ill children blamed themselves for the child's handicap. The parents did not regard these children as basically different from themselves. Other parents, however, viewed the child as "unhuman." By regarding the child as unhuman, incomprehensible, or uncontrollable, the parent could then institutionalize the child without guilt.[8] In her investigation of families who had institutionalized their retarded children, Mercer made a somewhat similar differentiation between the burden of care and interpersonal stress as precipitators of family crisis.[9]

Earlier, Farber made a comparable distinction between tragic crisis and role-organization crisis. Tragic crisis deals more with the social context of family life, role-organization crisis with care problems. For middle-class mothers, the major problems concern the frustration of aims and aspirations for themselves and their families. They see the retarded child as interfering with the attainment of certain ends in family life; they define the situation as tragic. In contrast to this, low socioeconomic status mothers are confronted with a different kind of crisis. They are concerned with their inability to organize their domestic roles in ways that permit them to have an acceptable family life. As the mother becomes more involved in caring for the retarded child, she becomes more alienated from other family members. The lower-class mother is often faced with a role-organization crisis. Thus, whether the crisis is defined as tragic or role-organization seems to hinge upon the part played by the label of mental retardation in each socioeconomic group. Parents facing role-organization crisis were found by Farber to be more receptive of institutionalization as a solution than were tragic-crisis parents.[10]

Hence there seems to be a convergence of findings relating to the kind of problem presented by the child and the definition of this child as an intruder in family life. The child who is uncontrollable, incomprehensibly "unhuman," and a care problem may become "dehumanized"; while the child whose retardation is considered a tragedy inducing personal stress may become the "invalid" of the family.

Factors Affecting Redefinition of the Handicapped Child

Which factors are relevant for the particular redefinition of the retarded child's role in the family? The redefinition of the child may depend on age and sex (of both child and parent), etiology as perceived by parents, social and religious background, and the interaction between intrafamily and extrafamily relationships.[11] The studies reported in this section suggest that these factors interact in a complex way in affecting parents' perceptions of their retarded children.

The role of the child in the family may be more important than the professional diagnosis in defining the child as a handicapped individual. Klebanoff indicated that child-rearing attitudes of mothers of retarded and mentally ill children were generally similar, but much different from those of mothers of intellectually normal children.[12] Yet a mental abnormality seems to provide the child with a family role different from that of a physical invalid. Cummings, Bayley, and Rie reported that middle-class mothers of retarded children showed more signs of personal stress than did mothers of chronically ill children.[13] The role of the child, in addition, depends upon the mother's conception of her own role. Nelson found that younger mothers of handicapped children rejected the maternal role more often than did older mothers.[14] Presumably, young mothers have to contend with other small children as well as with the handicapped child. The mothers' perceptions thus seem to vary with the kinds of stress placed upon them in performing their maternal roles.

The complex interaction of factors affecting parental perceptions of retarded children is also revealed in findings on fathers. In the Tallman study of eighty families with severely mentally retarded children in the San Francisco area, fathers tended to be more highly motivated in coping with problems of retarded boys than with those of retarded girls. Similarly, fathers were better able to cope with non-Mongoloid children. Tallman also found that whereas the mother's ability to cope with the child was associated with factors intrinsic to the parent-child relationship (such as the child's IQ and social competence), the father's ability to cope with the child was related to the child's sex and diagnostic classification. These results suggested to Tallman that the fathers' expectations for their retarded children were highly influenced by nonfamily social factors.[15]

Farber, Jenné, and Toigo found that the initial stress on the parent appears to be somewhat sex-linked, with the mother indicating a slightly greater impact if the retarded child is a girl and the father a markedly greater impact (regardless of social status) if the retarded child is a boy. In the low status families, where sex differentiation in family roles is probably greatest, mothers suffered a much greater impact when the retarded child was a girl. With time, however, the nature of the impact on the mother tended to shift; that is, eventually mothers of retarded boys were confronted with more severe problems than mothers of retarded girls. Hence the Farber, Jenné, Toigo findings suggest that the problems of "living through the children" and other emotional factors in identification are associated with the early tragic crisis and feelings of guilt. Later problems are associated with the development of family roles; and at this point a retarded boy may provide more difficult role problems than a retarded girl.[16]

The problem of guilt has been investigated by Zuk, who found that Catholic mothers were more acceptant than non-Catholic mothers with older retarded children but that sex of child, socioeconomic status, and size of family were not related to parental acceptance. Zuk found that Catholic mothers, as compared with Protestant mothers, also were more faithful in church attendance, more loyal to the religious training of their own parents, more prone to attend church when everything was going well (not just in crisis situations), and more consistent in prayer practice.[17] Unfortunately, he was unable to hold religious fervency constant in the comparison between Catholic and Protestant mothers. Therefore it is impossible to determine whether religiosity or Catholicism was responsible for the Catholic-Protestant differences.

There also is a tendency to equate religious duties with a sense of guilt. A study by Ray indicated that Catholic parents were helped in the denial of their responsibility for the child's condition. The majority of the mothers felt that God had given them a handicapped child as a "cross to bear."[18] Zwerling found that about 25 percent of his respondents indicated that religion was an important factor in accepting the retarded child.[19] Jordan identified a "martyrdom" constellation in his study of attitudes of mothers of retarded children.[20] Waterman noted a similar response based on his clinical experiences and labeled this response a "martyr or chosen people syndrome."[21] However, in none of these studies was the nature of the religious belief system investigated. Although some parents have reported that "my greatest mission in life is to care for my slow child,"[22] the religious implications of this statement have not been drawn out. The mission may signify saintliness as well as guilt for the parent. Because past investigations have failed to explore specific belief systems, the influence of religion on parental reaction to retarded children remains unclear.

Revision of Age and Sex Roles

The revision of age and sex roles in coping with a severely retarded child occurs mainly for the siblings. Parental responsibilities are increased because of the high degree of dependence and the special treatment required by the retarded child. The normal siblings, however, are more directly affected. The revision of age and sex roles is discussed under the following headings: (a) how birth-order is revised socially through the process of arrest in the family life-cycle and (b) how this revision affects the normal siblings in the family.

ARREST IN THE FAMILY LIFE CYCLE

The presence of a severely handicapped child in the family is regarded as a factor in the arrest of the family cycle.[23] This assumption is made on the following basis:

1. In interaction with their children, parents tend to assign a status to each child commensurate with the capabilities they impute to him.

   a. The roles embodied in the status are classified on the basis of age grading. By definition, normally, mental age is approximately equal to chronological age.

   b. Age grading in a culture is regarded more as a psychological and social activity than as a chronological variable, e.g., the chronologically middle-aged severely retarded individual is generally regarded as a "boy" or "girl" by those with whom he interacts. According to Eaton and Weil, the Hutterite religious group excludes the mentally retarded from adult responsibility by cancelling baptism requirements, thereby giving them the moral status of children.[24]

2. As the child proceeds in his career, the parents normally tend to revise their self-concepts and roles. With respect to their normal children, ideally, parents continually redefine their roles, obligations, and values to adjust to the changing role of the child. With respect to their retarded children, the parental role is fairly constant. Regardless of his birth order in the family, the severely handicapped child eventually becomes the youngest child socially. A very severely handicapped child at home would not engage in dating and courtship, belong to organizations, seek part-time employment, or take part in other activities characteristic of adolescents. In his progressive movement to the youngest-child status, the severely retarded child would not merely slow down movement in the family cycle but also prevent

the development of the later stages in the cycle.[25] Dexter suggests an evaluation of roles that derive from retardation may provide many insights into family relations.[26]

EFFECT ON SIBLINGS

The relative ages of a retarded child and his siblings seem to affect the extent to which there will be a revision in birth-order roles. Shere investigated thirty pairs of twins. Within each pair, one child was cerebral-palsied. The behavior of the parents toward the twins differed in certain respects: (1) the parents generally expected the non-cerebral-palsied child to assume more responsibilities and to act older than his age or capabilities would warrant; (2) the parents tended to be more responsive to the problems of the cerebral-palsied child and oblivious to those of his twin; (3) the parents overprotected the cerebral-palsied twin, permitting him little discretion in his activities. The non-cerebral-palsied twin was more curious and adventurous, less patient, more excitable, less cheerful, more resistant to authority, and more prone to emotional outbursts than the cerebral-palsied twin.[27]

The Farber study of 240 Chicago area families with severely retarded children investigated characteristics of those normal siblings who were closest in age to the retarded child. Farber found that the retarded child's siblings were affected by his high degree of dependency, which adversely affected the siblings' relationships with their mother. When the children were young, interaction between the normal and the retarded brothers and sisters tended to be on an equalitarian basis. As they grew older, the normal siblings frequently assumed a superordinate position in the relationship. However, siblings who did not interact frequently with their retarded brother or sister generally were affected less than those who interacted frequently.[28]

In contrast to the findings by Shere and Farber, the investigation by Graliker, Fishler, and Koch revealed the retarded child had little influence on siblings who were considerably older (for example, a ten-year difference in age).[29] These findings suggest that when the normal siblings are much older than the retarded child, there is little need to modify the birth-order roles in the family. Without this revision of roles, apparently, the normal siblings are not profoundly affected by the presence of the retarded child.

The family constellation influences the adjustment of the parents in a variety of ways. In a study by Bergheim, mothers exhibited an accepting attitude when cerebral-palsied children were the youngest in the family and a relatively rejecting attitude when the cerebral-palsied children were the oldest or without siblings.[30]

A more profound effect involves the restriction of fertility. A study by Holt of 201 families with retarded children in England indicated that although additional pregnancies were theoretically possible in 160 of the families, 101 of them did not want more children. In ninety of these families, the restriction appeared to stem directly from the presence of the retarded child.[31] Similarly, Tizard and Grad found in a sample of London families that there was a tendency to avoid having additional children. In each study, however, there was a very small percentage of families in which other children were conceived to compensate for the disappointment over the defective child.[32]

Revision of Community Relationships

The effect of the retarded child on the family's community relationships can be dealt with from both short-run and long-range perspectives. The short-run effects concern day-to-day interaction between family members and others in the community. The long-run effects involve the social mobility of parents and siblings.

Day-to-day Interaction in the Community

One of the most consistent research findings is the limitation on participation of parents of severely retarded children in extra-family relationships, such as organizational membership or recreation. For example, in England, Holt found that 40 percent of the parents were unable to go out together and a smaller percentage were unable to take a vacation.[33] Similarly, in the studies of Australian families by Schonell *et al.*, about half of the families reported that their visits to other peoples' homes and their shopping arrangements were affected. Parents also found it impossible to indulge in daily social activities.[34] Tizard and Grad discovered that about half of their families with a retarded individual living at home reported that their social contacts were limited by the presence of the child;[35] other investigators report a similar pattern.[36] In his study of cerebral-palsied children, Hall found that mothers of the more severely handicapped group were more likely to remain in the home than to take outside employment.[37] Meyerowitz and Kaplan indicated that mothers of children with cystic fibrosis often ceased their outside employment, while fathers might take on a second job and limit their activities as husbands and fathers. Their data also showed that parents who went out socially without the child with cystic fibrosis also displayed more somatic symptoms of stress (such as ulcers) than did other parents.[38] This tendency is consistent with Farber's findings on families with severely retarded children, where women faced with role-organization crises often developed physical symptoms and many parents who spent considerable time in voluntary associations or in neighboring had low marital integration scores.[39] Taken together, the findings of the various studies concerned with the extent of community relationships suggest that the families with severely handicapped children tend to disengage themselves from these activities and to focus attention on problems within the family. The data also indicate that failure to do so may lead to conflict and disturbance in family relationships.

One question that can be asked regarding community relations is: How does the family present the handicapped child to the community? An attempt to answer this question has been made by Barsch, who studied explanations offered by parents and siblings of brain-injured children. He found that parents of brain-injured children used the term "brain injury" freely in discussing their child with others. However, when the child was only mildly neurologically involved, the parents were reluctant to say he was brain-injured and hesitated to apply any label to the child. Others used the term "cerebral-palsied" even if no diagnosis had been given, since this term is generally understandable to others. Ordinarily, siblings followed the parents' lead in describing the handicapped child to their playmates. According to Barsch, the nature and severity of the child's handicap did not significantly alter the parental explanation.[40]

The problem of how to present the handicapped child to other people is not the only problem with which parents must deal. At the same time, the parents are actually suggesting a reciprocal role to outsiders. Research is needed on a variety of topics: What kinds of roles do these parents set up for their friends, for strangers, or for neighbors? Do they expect them to behave like kin, grandparents, or therapists, or do the parents wish the outsider to treat the child as a nonperson? Similarly, we do not know how the manner in which the parent presents himself is related to the manner in which he presents his handicapped child to others. There must be numerous ways of presenting one's self in economic situations, hospital situations, neighborhood situations, and in transient relations. Do the parents present themselves as sick and thereby invite sympathy for themselves and perhaps hostility for the child? Or do they present themselves as defining the handicap as irrelevant to their own relationship with the outsider?

Finally, we can ask: How do parents maintain a consistent manner of presenting the child to others in a particular role? The findings on relationships within the family suggest that the more severe the handicap, the more areas of social life are affected. It was noted by Hall that residence was more stable among the families of the severely handicapped cerebral-palsied children than among the lesser handicapped.[41] Apparently, stable presentation of the severely handicapped child to persons outside the family can be maintained in the neighborhood; but the handicap becomes a relevant factor in change of residence when the neighbors refuse to accept the parents' mode of presenting the child.

The topic of presenting the retarded child to the community implies the presence of particular reference groups and significant individuals for the parents. Little investigation, however, has been performed in this area with respect to handicapped children. Farber found that when the parents of a retarded child were in frequent contact with the wife's mother, marital integration tended to be high. However, when they were in frequent contact with the husband's mother, marital integration tended to be low. Ordinarily, the wife's mother showed much sympathy and understanding for her daughter's situation; but the husband's mother generally blamed the wife for the retarded child. Sometimes there was an implication that the mother-in-law regarded the retarded child as punishment for her daughter-in-law's wrongdoing; such a view might then reinforce the mother's definition of the handicapped child.[42] These findings on the reactions of grandmothers suggest that extended family relations be explored as an area of investigation relating to the effects of handicapping conditions on family relations. Perhaps intervention in the kinship process by social workers, psychiatrists, or psychologists can be applied eventually as a therapeutic device.[43]

Although supportive community relations (as with the maternal grandmother) can be contrasted with isolation, they also can be discussed in contrast to nonsupportive community relations.[44] Just as "differential association" has been applied to the conformity of delinquents and criminals to a "criminal" way of life, so can interaction with groups who do not support the conventional norms and values relating to marriage stimulate types of interaction in the family disruptive to its internal organization.[45]

SOCIAL MOBILITY OF PARENTS AND SIBLINGS

Most studies on the effects of a severely mentally retarded child on family relationships have focused upon emotional problems and personal difficulties generated by the child. Another applicable perspective pertains to the subsequent place of the retarded child's family in the social structure. From this viewpoint, research can be framed in terms of the question: How does the presence of a severely mentally retarded child in the family affect the long-run social destinies of the other family members? An effort can then be made to determine the conditions under which various consequences occur.

Max Culver has investigated social mobility patterns of parents of severely mentally retarded children. He has compared the fathers' occupations with those of the child's grandparents. This study utilized data collected in the Chicago metropolitan area in 1958–1959 on approximately 400 families with severely mentally retarded children living either at home or in an institution. The investigation showed that the timing of the birth of the mentally retarded child was related to the upward or downward social mobility of the parents. The earlier in the marriage the child was born, the greater were the chances of his having a depressing effect on social mobility. Thus, when a couple had a retarded child early in their marriage, the husband's chances of moving upward occupationally were impeded. Moreover, among families in which the grandfathers of the retarded child had white-collar occupations, the parents who kept their severely retarded child at home were more often downwardly socially mobile than were those who institutionalized their retarded child.[46]

The Culver study on social mobility utilized gross categories and presented little analysis of the occupational history of the retarded child's parents. Insight into the retarded child's impact on his parents' and siblings' destinies would be enhanced by more detailed study of the occupational and educational histories and aspirations of fathers and mothers, brothers and sisters, and grandparents of retarded children.

The concept of life chances can be applied in yet another way to families of the severely retarded. Children who interact constantly with their retarded siblings seem to develop a more socially conscious outlook on life. A study by Farber and Jenné showed that both boys and girls who interact daily with their retarded siblings emphasized as life goals "devotion to a worthwhile cause" or "making a contribution to mankind," while those who do not interact so frequently with their retarded siblings are more oriented to success in personal relations.[47] Normal siblings who act as parent-surrogates apparently internalize welfare norms and turn their life careers toward the improvement of mankind, or at least toward the achievement of goals they believe will enhance social welfare. It might be valuable to determine the extent to which siblings of retarded children differ from others in their occupational and leisure time patterns. Such a study might reveal how a number of factors, such as frequency of interaction and sex of the child (in addition to relative ages), affect the life chances of the retarded child's siblings. In some social circumstances, parents may be more tolerant of deviance in normal children and of their lack of achievement, and in other instances the parents may apply great pressure toward achievement.

The effect of the retarded child on the life chances of his siblings extends beyond occupation to marriage. Especially where the normal siblings have a close relationship with the retarded child, his presence may influence the choice of a marriage partner. Presumably, the siblings would not marry an individual who could not tolerate his or her retarded sibling. Yet the extent to which a mentally retarded child's presence influences mate selection of his siblings has not been investigated. If the presence of a retarded child is highly disturbing to an upwardly mobile potential husband, the retarded child's sisters may reject marriages that would enhance their life chances.

Knowledge about the organization of families with a retarded child is necessary in order to assess the long-run effects on parents and siblings. An earlier study by Farber described three pure or theoretical types of family organization developed by parents with a retarded child. These types of organization were called "parent-oriented," "child-oriented," and "home-oriented."[48] The parent-oriented families focused upon the father's and mother's occupational and social careers, and assigned to the retarded child a secondary position in determining the life chances of family members; husband and wife considered themselves as colleagues in a family enterprise. The second group of families, classified as child-oriented, subordinated the relationship between the parents somewhat to maximize the life chances of their children. The division of labor was such that the husband would specialize in work activities (sometimes to the exclusion of other activities) while the wife cared for the home and family. Here again, great expenditure of time and effort compensated for the depressing effect of the retarded child on their upward social mobility. In the third kind of family organization, the home-oriented, the parents completely sacrificed their life chances for family cohesion. In home-oriented families the husband disregarded his personal career in order to maintain family unity; consequently, the life chances of all the members might be markedly affected. However, there was a large proportion of families in the investigation who did not present a clear-cut type of orientation. This fourth or residual category was not consistently parent-oriented, child-oriented, or home-oriented. There was considerable disagreement between the parents with regard to orientation, and in many instances the orientation itself was not crystallized. Families in the residual category were probably the most affected in their life chances by the retarded child. Perhaps the numerous problems that had beset them interfered with any concerted effort to promote upward social mobility. Study of the long-run consequences of particular types of family organization on the life chances of family members may provide important knowledge about families with retarded children.

In general, research on health problems indicates a relationship between poor health and downward social mobility.[49] However, little is known about the circumstances under which a child's chronic illness or severe disability interferes with the social mobility of his family. Institutionalization, birth order, family organization, and parents' position in the social structure represent only a few of the factors that might be studied. Investigation of families with severely retarded children would produce knowledge necessary for an adequate understanding of the relationship between a child's disability and his family's life chances.

Families of the Educable Mentally Retarded

Educable mentally retarded individuals exist as a segment of the population which is not required for carrying out the work of the society. Nor have individuals classified themselves voluntarily as educably retarded. This section deals with the family life of these persons. First, their families of orientation will be described, then their families of procreation. In many instances, persons designated as mentally retarded are not downwardly mobile; instead, they perpetuate a marginal existence. Where low socioeconomic status is perpetuated from one generation to the next, there seems to be continual departure from conventional standards and from ways of living prevalent in the society.

FAMILIES OF ORIENTATION

This section will review research dealing with parental families of the mildly mentally retarded. In socializing the children, the parental families provide them with orientations toward society and its institutions. And, insofar as the families reflect private cultures, they may depress the children's level of intellectual functioning.

In the studies of families of orientation of the educable mentally retarded, attempts have been made to introduce controls for socioeconomic status. Kennedy matched 256 "morons" with 129 intellectually normal persons of similar age and socioeconomic background. At the time of the investigation (in 1946–47), none of the retarded individuals had been institutionalized, and all were living in a city in Connecticut. Most of the retarded were second-generation Italian, with less than an eighth-grade education. Their mean age was 24.5. The retarded males had somewhat more schooling than the females — a mean of 9.4 versus 6.2 years. Although over 90 percent of the retarded individuals had repeated at least one grade in school, only two-thirds of them had ever been in a special class. Among the intellectually normal control group, about 66 percent completed high school, and almost 20 percent attended college.

The Kennedy study produced the following results:

1. Parental families of the retarded showed a greater prevalence of instability through divorce and desertion, and a greater frequency of commitments of family members to state institutions for mental difficulties.
2. The families of the retarded had greater contact with social work agencies. This assistance included help from more than one agency, and emergency medical care and work relief.
3. Members of the parental families of the retarded appeared more frequently in court records.

The Kennedy study thus indicated greater marginality of the retarded in terms of family stability and economic sufficiency.[50]

Meyerowitz and Farber reported a comparison of 120 educable mentally retarded children with sixty normal children from families of comparable income and occupational status. The retarded and normal children lived in the same slum areas and attended the same schools. About 70 percent of the fathers in both groups had a semiskilled or unskilled occupation. All the families had a six-year-old child entering school (and all retarded children were six years of age). The findings of this study indicated that families with retarded children showed a lower level of integration into the community, provided less adequate resources in the home, were characterized by family relationships reflecting instability, inattentiveness, and overcrowding, and were less capable of motivating the children intellectually and academically.

The lower level of integration into the community by families with a retarded child was indicated by (a) less participation in voluntary associations, (b) membership in isolated religious sects rather than in major denominations, (c) less church attendance, (d) less contact with friends and neighbors, and (e) greater residential mobility.

The inadequacy of parental resources in the retarded group was revealed by (a) lower level of education of the parents, (b) lower income per family member, (c) slightly greater reliance on welfare agencies, (d) poorer health of the mother, and (e) less exposure to mass communications media such as movies, magazines, and newspapers, as well as (f) the lack of a telephone in the home.

The presence of problems in family relationships in the sample with retarded children was suggested by (a) a greater amount of remarriage, (b) birth of the retarded child prior to the current marriage, (c) larger age discrepancy between husband and wife, (d) a greater tendency for the mother to be a teen-ager when the child in the study was born, and (e) overcrowdedness of the home. The retarded child in the study was more often a middle child with several younger siblings than an oldest or youngest child.

Finally, the parents' inadequate motivation was suggested by (a) a tendency for the mother to regard the retarded child as a problem child and (b) either an expectation of low academic achievement for the child or aspirations which indicated that the parent did not comprehend the nature of the educational process. Although most parents were enthusiastic about the importance of education in the lives of their children, often they did not think their child would succeed educationally or, because of their own limited experience, they had little conception of the nature of high school or college work.[51]

Both the Connecticut study by Kennedy and the central Illinois study by Meyerowitz and Farber suggest that persons born into families producing retarded individuals must compensate for deficiencies in their families of orientation. Most families producing educable mentally retarded children can be characterized as "culturally deprived" with respect to the dominant "public" culture in the society. Yet those children who appear to be helped most by educational programs are more often from families similar to those with intellectually normal children than from other families with retarded children. In follow-up testing four years after the retarded children in the central Illinois study had been in school, the following factors were related to a rise in at least 10 IQ points by the children initially classified as retarded: (a) Caucasian rather than Negro, (b) mother had more than eight years of education, (c) mother interacted to a higher degree with neighbors and with friends, (d) parents tended to have a higher marital integration as indicated by their consensus on family values, and (e) the parents were more often in their first marriage. Although family income had been included in the analysis, it was not found to be related to the tendency for the child to increase significantly in IQ.[52]

Perhaps, without the school these factors in themselves would not have been sufficient for the child's intellectual development. The school environment apparently provided the additional stimulation and consistency in social relationships which enabled the child to function at a higher level intellectually. Although the findings in the central Illinois study suggest that the school can help children from families that are only slightly deficient in intellectual stimulation and stability, they do not indicate which supplementary practices are needed to raise the level of intellectual functioning of children from homes that are grossly stagnating and unstable.

One question on the role of the family of orientation in fostering mental retardation is: If the basis for mild mental retardation is not genetic, why are some children retarded while their siblings are not? Research cited indicates that birth order, sex, and mother's marital problems are involved in producing a mildly retarded child. Some attention has been given to a similar question in research on juvenile delinquency and mental illness. The comparison of siblings in the study of juvenile delinquency has indicated that the delinquent tends to be more alienated than his siblings from the family.[53] In her study of schizophrenics, Lu reports that the mothers, who are generally authoritarian, insist on controlling the preschizophrenic child to a much greater extent than their other children. As a result, the preschizophrenic child relies excessively on the parent, while his brothers and sisters seek escape from authoritarian family relationships.[54] Similar research could be undertaken in comparing lower-class families in which none, some, or all children are retarded. Investigation could disclose the conditions under which children learn to be mentally retarded. This research may reveal different kinds of intellectual deficits accruing from interaction with alienating mothers as contrasted with overcontrolling mothers.

FAMILIES OF PROCREATION

If educable mentally retarded individuals tend to come from homes that reflect instability and insufficiency, then, even without the assumption of mental retardation, their families of procreation can be expected to have characteristics comparable to their parental families. The results of numerous studies can be arrayed to show this persistence in style of family life.

Reed and Reed have reported family characteristics relating to the marriage of retarded persons. In their sample of 1450 retardates, only 115 had been institutionalized. Of the remaining 1335 persons living in the community, only 56 percent had ever married. In contrast, according to U.S. census figures during the period from 1890 to 1950, by the time people reached the age of forty, over 80 percent had been married at least once.[55] Among retarded parents, the probability of producing retarded children was high; the risk was especially great when both parents were retarded. About 40 percent of the children in marriages in which both parents were retarded were themslves incompetent (IQ under 70). For marriages with one retarded partner, the rate varied from 8 percent (retarded husband) to about 20 percent (retarded wife). In all instances the probability of having a retarded child was much higher than might be attributed to chance. Yet a majority of the children of retardates were in the normal range of intelligence.[56]

The findings in the Reed and Reed study are consistent with those of other investigations. In a randomly selected sample of 125 adult male retardates, Peck and Stephens found only sixteen men who were married, divorced, or separated. Of these, just five were fathers. Comparing retardates who had married with those who had remained single, Peck and Stephens found that the unmarried retardates had fewer law violations, less "trouble-begetting behavior," and were more safety-conscious. However, those retardates who were still married, rather then divorced or separated, were regarded by their employers as persons who observed rules of safety closely and who worked under pressure satisfactorily. Of the five retardates who had become fathers, two were now divorced or separated. Peck and Stephens considered four of the five fathers as unsuccessful in their roles as parents. Still, many characteristics displayed by the retardates in the Peck and Stephens sample are similar to those of lower-class populations in general, and the precise role of mental retardation in marital relationships is unclear.[57]

Although the emphasis in this discussion has been on the continuity of a style of family life conducive to mental retardation, findings by Fairbank and by Charles on the intellectual development of the children of mentally retarded parents are of interest. In 1933, Fairbank studied 122 adults who had been ascertained as mentally retarded seventeen years earlier. In general, their family life was like that described in the previous studies. As compared with a group of normal individuals, Fairbank found that the retarded showed more broken marriages, slightly more sex delinquency, greater dependence upon charitable organizations, "poorer" living conditions, more juvenile court records, and less migration to the better parts of the city. However, of children tested, only three were defective (mean IQ 66); twenty-four were dull normal (mean IQ 89); fifty were of normal intelligence (mean IQ about 100); and four were of superior intelligence (mean IQ 118).[58]

In 1936, Baller reported the results of a study in which he compared the postschool adjustment of 206 individuals with an IQ of under 70 who had been in "opportunity rooms" in Lincoln, Nebraska, and who were now age twenty-one or over. As a control group he paired individuals with IQs between 100 and 120 with each of his retarded subjects in age, sex, and nationality. He found numerous differences between the two groups in postschool life. Many more of the retarded had court records and had been imprisoned. They tended to come more often from families at lower occupational levels, with virtually no representation at the professional levels. And the mentally retarded individuals had been added in greater numbers to relief rolls than had those of normal intelligence. There was no difference between the two groups in the proportion married or in age at marriage. There was, however, a greater tendency among retarded women than men to improve their social status through marriage.[59]

In 1950 Charles located 127 of the retarded individuals studied by

Baller. Trends in the Baller study had become more pronounced in the intervening fifteen years. The subjects were now a mean age of forty-three, with an age range of thirty-six to forty-nine. About 78 percent of the retarded males and 77 percent of the females had been married at least once. This proportion of persons who had ever been married was lower than that for the entire city of Lincoln in 1950. Generally, the marriages were unstable. Only 63 percent of the males who married were living with their first wives; 44 percent of the married females were still with their first husbands. The proportion of individuals having children was also lower than that for the entire city. Seventy-five percent of the married males and 85 percent of the married females had children. Most of the children, however, were not mentally retarded and had achieved a grade-school education. Only two children were known to be institutionalized, and another two had been in a special education class.

Charles believed that the original IQ tests had been affected by such things as a foreign language background, behavior problems and delinquency, and social and economic deprivation. He regarded about two-thirds of the subjects as being now in the dull-normal or average range of intelligence. Conceivably, over the years and with increasing experience, the intellectual level of these individuals may have risen. In spite of this increase, however, many of the characteristics that marked the population segment as "marginal" or "surplus" were still present.[60]

The families of procreation of individuals in the Kennedy study in Connecticut show similar traits. Kennedy found that more persons in her retarded than in her comparison sample had marriages terminated by divorce, and more of their families included stepchildren and adopted children. Moreover, fewer retarded than normal subjects in the Connecticut study had any children. Thirty-five percent of the females among the retarded were childless as compared with 24 percent of the normal females. Illegitimacy was slightly more prevalent in the retarded group (2.3 versus 1.7 percent). The age discrepancy between husband and wife was greater for the retarded persons than for normal individuals. In addition, the retarded tended more often to marry into families with court records, more retarded individuals than normals had court records and went to prison, and they also committed a greater number of offenses. The social participation of the retarded individuals resembled that of their parental families. The retarded persons tended to participate less in formal voluntary organizations, to vote less, and their leisure time showed much aimless and random behavior.[61]

Similarly, Peterson and Smith found in Cedar Rapids, Iowa, that graduates of classes for the educable mentally handicapped had more family problems than normal adults who had come from low socio-economic status families. As compared with the normal adults, the retardates were often renters, owned less personal property, migrated less frequently, tended to live in substandard housing, more often remained single, had a higher divorce rate, belonged to fewer voluntary associations, and participated less in family-group activities.[62]

The study by Jastak and his associates of mental retardation in Delaware presents a picture like those of the other investigations. Comparing retarded and nonretarded respondents in a probability sample, the Delaware study showed that (a) a greater proportion of the nonretarded were married (64 as compared with 55 percent); (b) a slightly larger proportion of the retarded were in common-law marriages (6.5 as compared with 2.3 percent), and (c) more retarded were widowed (6.5 as compared with 2.4 percent). Of those in-dividuals who had been married, a larger proportion of the non-retarded were now in their first marriage (83 as compared with 78 percent). On the other hand, the retarded individuals tended to marry at an earlier age, with 32 percent of the retarded but only 21 percent of the nonretarded marrying below age nineteen. The re-tarded individuals also showed a slightly greater inclination to separa-tion, even during the current marriage (15 as compared with 11 percent). The nonretarded tended to show a greater participation in both formal and informal activities outside the family.

The retarded in the Jastak study had little more contact with social and legal agencies. They had dealings with social agencies only slightly more than the nonretarded (8 vs. 4 percent). To a much greater extent, the retarded's contact with social agencies pertained to health rather than to family or welfare problems. With regard to legal problems, the retarded individuals in the Jastak study had only slightly more contact with the courts than did the nonretarded re-spondents (12 vs. 10 percent). However, of those persons having court contact, the retarded were more prone to repeated contacts than were the nonretarded (58 vs. 38 percent).

The findings of the Delaware study are less extreme than those of the other investigations of families of procreation of mentally retarded individuals. They do, however, indicate the same proclivities of family instability and insufficiency in handling social relationships associated with family life.[63]

The findings of problems in families of procreation of retarded individuals are not confined to the United States. Ramer reported a study of 626 special school students and 589 individuals of normal intelligence in Stockholm. The study, undertaken in 1943, was aimed at examining how many of the mentally retarded remained as dependent or delinquent in adulthood. The subjects were between twenty-six and thirty-eight years of age, and the retarded individuals had tested IQs of 70 to 84 as children. Ramer examined official records concerning relief, pensions, court records, and other indications of dependency or delinquency. Inasmuch as Swedish social records are generally reliable, the coverage offered by them was probably thorough. As might be expected, more of the retarded than the control individuals came from broken or unstable homes. The retarded persons had higher rates of mortality, a lower marriage rate, and a higher divorce rate; they were more frequently recipients of relief or pensions and more often inmates in institutions. There were no differences in criminal records or in types of crime. Yet, considering that the retarded individuals tended to be drawn from a lower socioeconomic status on the whole, a question still remains as to the extent to which mental retardation itself was a factor in the greater instability and insufficiency in family life.[64]

Akesson also found that "feebleminded" males have significantly lower marriage rates than their control group. However, they produced a larger number of children per individual as compared with their controls. There was no important difference between the "feebleminded" and the control group in extramatrimonial births.[65]

SUMMARY

Families of the severely retarded are found in all segments of society. Prior to the birth of the severely retarded child, these families are similar to others. All parents with offspring in the severely retarded range of intelligence eventually label their child as mentally retarded. However, the mentally retarded label seems to affect families differently. The hypothesis was suggested that the higher the socioeconomic status of the family, the greater the impact on family relationships of labeling a child as mentally retarded. Consistent with this hypothesis, it was also speculated that the impact of child-care problems connected with mental retardation on family relationships is associated with socioeconomic status. For low socioeconomic level families, since the label itself is presumably not the primary crisis-evoking factor, child-care problems themselves provide the basis for family tensions. Various family characteristics affect the parental reaction to the retarded child: age of the mother, sex of the child and parent, and religion.

Adjustment to the retarded child frequently means a revision of age and sex roles in the family, which can be conceptualized as an arrest in the family life-cycle whereby the retarded child (regardless of his actual birth-order rank) becomes the youngest child socially and never matures. The brothers and sisters are also affected in this revision. Apparently, the closer in age they are to the retarded child, the more they are affected in personality and social destiny.

Interaction between the family and community is also revised by the presence of a severely retarded child. The data indicate that the families tend to disengage themselves from community relationships and to focus their attention on problems within the family. Failure to do so may lead to conflict and disturbance of family relationships. Long-range community relationships of families are also influenced by the presence of the severely retarded child. Findings indicate patterns of downward social mobility by the retarded child's parents. Retarded children born early in the marriage have the most profound influence on parental social mobility, but placing the retarded child in an institution seems to inhibit downward mobility. Siblings appear to be influenced in their choice of life goals by their relationship with the retarded child. Those brothers and sisters who interact frequently with the retarded child seem to be oriented toward the improvement of mankind and the enhancement of social welfare. However, the specific conditions of parental downward mobility and siblings' choice of career require further study.

The family life of the mildly retarded population presents a different picture from that of the severely retarded group. Families of orientation of educable retardates display environments that are unstable and stultifying. These families show much instability through divorce and desertion, a high degree of contact with social welfare agencies, and a large number of police arrests. Moreover, when lower-class families are considered, those with a mildly retarded child reveal a low degree of participation in voluntary associations, a tendency to belong to isolated religious sects rather than to major denominations, infrequent church attendance, relatively little contact with friends and neighbors, and high residential mobility. There tends to be a low level of education of the parents, low income per family member, poor health, and little exposure to mass communication media such as movies, magazines, and newspapers. The home tends to be overcrowded, and (as is characteristic of most remarriages) there is a large age discrepancy between husband and wife.

Although the marriage rate of the mentally retarded is low, the home life of families of procreation of those who do marry tends to duplicate that of their parental families. The retarded adults often have a history of marital instability, criminal violations, and low participation in voluntary organizations. Perhaps most important, they seem to be inadequate as parents. The extent to which intellectual incompetence, apart from socioeconomic factors, is responsible for family problems and intellectual deficits in children is unknown.

GENERAL DISCUSSION

The families of the severely and mildly retarded present contrasting pictures. The families of the severely retarded provide an example of ways in which one member's incompetence generates deviant patterns of conduct among other family members. The kinds of deviance provoked depends upon the social context of the family—its socioeconomic position, and ethnic and religious background. However, the families of the mildly retarded seem to carry traditions of incompetence in social and economic affairs from one generation to the next. From the viewpoint of the observer, these traditions foment deviance from acceptable conduct and stabilize the position of the family in the social structure. Still, since many educable retardates marry persons of normal intelligence, the role played by the normal spouse in these families should be investigated. This research could indicate how marital interaction and parent-child behavior differ in families in which (a) both parents are retarded, (b) both parents are normal in intelligence, and (c) one parent is retarded and the other is normal. With regard to the mildly retarded, there is still a question as to the ways in which intellectual incompetence influences family role under different social conditions.[66]

There has been little research on the retardate's perceptions of his family and kin. If mental retardation implies an inability to develop an adequate "cultural map" of society, the retardate's view of his family, the kinship structure, and nonfamily relationships is probably distorted. Study of family life from the perspective of the severely retarded as well as the mildly retarded may provide many insights into the nuances of family and kinship in modern society.

NOTES

1 Several summaries of research related to the impact of retarded children on the family have appeared in recent years. These include Thomas E. Jordan, *The Mentally Retarded* (Columbus, Ohio: Merrill, 1961); Richard Koch *et al.*, *A Multidisciplinary Approach to the Young Retarded Child and His Family* (Los Angeles: Children's Hospital, 1962); A. O. Ross, *The Exceptional Child in the Family* (New York: Grune and Stratton, 1964); Bernard Farber and David B. Ryckman, "Effects of Severely Mentally Retarded Children on Family Relationships," *Mental Retardation Abstracts*, 2 (January-March, 1965), pp. 1–17; Bernard Farber and Shirley M. Clark, "The Handicapped Child in the Family: A Literature Summary," in B. V. Sheets and B. Farber, eds., *The Handicapped Child in the Family* (New York: United Cerebral Palsy Research and Educational Foundation, N.D.), pp. 1–37.

2 Jean R. Hebeler, "A Factor Analysis of an Attitude Scale Toward Retardation with a Population of Parents of Educable Mentally Retarded Children," *Dissertation Abstracts*, 22 (1961), p. 154; and T. L. Worchel and P. Worchel, "The Parental Concept of the Mentally Retarded Child," *American Journal of Mental Deficiency*, 61 (1961), pp. 782–788.

3 Gerald H. Zuk, "Autistic Distortions in Parents of Retarded Children," *Journal of Consulting Psychology*, 23 (1959), pp. 171–176.

4 G. D. Jensen and K. L. Kogan, "Parental Estimates of the Future Achievement of Children with Cerebral Palsy," *Journal of Mental Deficiency*, 6 (1962), pp. 56–64.

5 J. L. Schulman and S. Stern, "Parents' Estimate of the Intelligence of Retarded Children," *American Journal of Mental Deficiency*, 63 (1959), pp. 696–698; L. Rosen, "Selected Aspects in the Development of the Mother's Understanding of Her Mentally Retarded Child," *American Journal of Mental Deficiency*, 59 (1955), pp. 522–528.

6 A. Barclay and G. Vaught, "Maternal Estimates of Future Achievement in Cerebral Palsied Children," *American Journal of Mental Deficiency*, 69 (1964), pp. 62–65.

7 Bernard Farber, "Perceptions of Crisis and Related Variables in the Impact of a Retarded Child on the Mother," *Journal of Health and Human Behavior*, I (1960), pp. 108–118. Reprinted in Marvin B. Sussman, ed., *Sourcebook on Marriage and the Family* (Boston: Houghton Mifflin, 1963).

8 Lenore Korkes, *A Study of the Impact of Mentally Ill Children Upon Their Families* (Trenton: New Jersey Department of Institutions and Agencies, 1956).

9 Jane R. Mercer, "Patterns of Family Crisis Related to Reacceptance of the Retardate," *American Jouranl of Mental Deficiency*, 71 (July, 1966), pp. 19–32.

10 Farber, "Perceptions of Crisis . . .," *op. cit.*

11 Cf. E. A. Miller, "Cerebral-Palsied Children and their Parents," *Exceptional Children*, 24 (1958), pp. 298–302.

12 Louis Klebanoff, "Parental Attitudes of Mothers of Schizophrenic, Brain-Injured and Retarded, and Normal Children," *American Journal of Orthopsychiatry*, 29 (1959), pp. 445–454.

[13] S. Thomas Cummings, Helen C. Bayley, and Herbert E. Rie, "Effects of the Child's Deficiency on the Mother: A Study of Mothers of Mentally Retarded, Chronically Ill and Neurotic Children," *American Journal of Orthopsychiatry*, 36 (July, 1966), pp. 595–609.

[14] Martha Nelson, "The Parental Attitudes Expressed by Mothers of Exceptional Children," unpublished master's thesis, Purdue University, 1959.

[15] Irving Tallman, in Leo F. Cain and Samuel Levine, "Effects of Community and Institutional School Programs on Trainable Mentally Retarded Children," *Council for Exceptional Children, NEA, Research Monograph Series*, 1963, No. B-1. See also Irving Tallman, "Spousal Role Differentiation and Socialization of Severely Retarded Children," *Journal of Marriage and the Family*, 27 (February, 1965), pp. 37–42.

[16] Bernard Farber, William C. Jenné, and Romolo Toigo, "Family Crisis and the Decision to Institutionalize the Retarded Child," *Council for Exceptional Children, NEA, Research Monograph Series*, 1960, No. A-1.

[17] Gerald H. Zuk, "The Religious Factor and Role of Guilt in Parental Acceptance of the Retarded Child," *American Journal of Mental Deficiency*, 63 (1959), pp. 139–147; and Gerald H. Zuk, "The Cultural Dilemma and Spiritual Crisis of the Family with a Handicapped Child," *Exceptional Children*, 28 (1962), pp. 405–408; Gerald H. Zuk, R. L. Miller, J. B. Bertram, and F. Kling, "Material Acceptance of Retarded Children: A Questionnaire Study of Attitudes and Religious Background," *Child Development*, 32 (1961), pp. 525–540.

[18] I. Ray, "A Study to Develop a Guide of Education for Parents of Cerebral-Palsied Children," unpublished master's thesis, University of Iowa, 1951.

[19] I. Zwerling, "The Initial Counseling of Parents with Mentally Retarded Children," *Journal of Pediatrics*, 44 (1954), pp. 469–479.

[20] Jordan, *op. cit.*

[21] J. H. Waterman, "Psychogenic Factors in Parental Acceptance of Feebleminded Children," *Diseases of the Nervous System*, 9 (1948), pp. 184–187.

[22] Zuk, *op. cit.*

[23] Bernard Farber. "Effects of a Severely Mentally Retarded Child on Family Integration," *Monographs of the Society for Research in Child Development*, 1959, No. 71.

[24] Joseph W. Eaton and R. J. Weil, *Culture and Mental Disorders: A Comparative Study of the Hutterites and Other Populations* (New York: Free Press, 1955).

[25] See Farber. "Effects of a Severely Mentally Retarded Child . . . ," *op. cit.*, pp. 6–11; and Bernard Farber, "Family Organization and Crisis: Maintenance of Integration in Families with a Severely Mentally Retarded Child," *Monographs of the Society for Research in Child Development*, 1960, No. 75, pp. 78–84.

[26] Lewis A. Dexter, "Research on Problems of Mental Subnormality," *American Journal of Mental Deficiency*, 64 (1960), pp. 835–838.

[27] Marie O. Shere, "Socioemotional Factors in Families of One Twin with Cerebral Palsy, *Exceptional Children*, 22 (1955), pp. 197–199, 206, and 208.

[28] Farber, "Effects of a Severely Mentally Retarded Child on Family Integration," *op. cit.*; Bernard Farber, "Family Organization and Crisis: Maintenance of Integration on Families with a Severely Mentally Retarded Child," *op. cit.*

[29] Betty V. Graliker, K. Fishler, and Richard Koch, "Teenage Reaction to a Mentally Retarded Sibling," *American Journal of Mental Deficiency*, 66 (1962), pp. 838–843.

[30] G. M. Bergheim, "A Study of Social and Emotional Factors Related to the Rehabilitation of Cerebral Palsied Children and a Study of Unmet Educational

Needs of Sixty-Seven Cerebral Palsied Children," unpublished master's thesis, Bryn Mawr College, 1950.

[31] K. S. Holt, "The Influence of a Retarded Child on Family Limitation," *Journal of Mental Deficiency*, 2 (1958), pp. 28–36.

[32] J. Tizard and Jacqueline C. Grad, *The Mentally Handicapped and Their Families* (New York: Oxford University Press, 1961).

[33] K. S. Holt, "The Home Care of the Severely Mentally Retarded," *Pediatrics*, 22 (1958), pp. 744–755.

[34] F. J. Schonell, I. G. Middleton, B. H. Watts, and M. W. Rorke, "First and Second Surveys of the Effects of a Subnormal Child on the Family Unit," *University of Queensland Papers*, Brisbane, Australia, 1959; F. J. Schonell and B. H. Watts, "A First Study of the Effects of a Subnormal Child on the Family Unit," *American Journal of Mental Deficiency*, 61 (1956), pp. 210–219; F. J. Schonell and Meg Rorke, "A Second Survey of the Effects of a Subnormal Child on the Family Unit," *American Journal of Mental Deficiency*, 64 (1960), pp. 862–868.

[35] Tizard and Grad, *op. cit.*

[36] J. R. Peck and W. B. Stephens, "A Study of the Relationship Between Attitude and Behavior of Parents and That of Their Mentally Defective Child," *American Journal of Mental Deficiency*, 64 (1960), pp. 839–844; J. T. Weingold and R. P. Hormuth, "Group Counseling of Mentally Retarded Children," *Journal of Clinical Psychology*, 9 (1953), pp. 118–124.

[37] W. T. Hall, "Family Disorganization as Associated with Severity of Handicap (by Cerebral Palsy) of a Minor Child," unpublished doctoral dissertation, University of Minnesota, 1961.

[38] Joseph H. Meyerowitz and Howard B. Kaplan, "Familial Responses to Stress: The Case of Cystic Fibrosis," *Social Science and Medicine*, 1 (1967), pp. 249–266.

[39] Bernard Farber, "Effects of a Severely Mentally Retarded Child on Family Integration," *op. cit.*; and Farber, "Perceptions of Crisis. . . ," *op. cit.*

[40] Ray Barsch, "Explanations Offered by Parents and Siblings of Brain-Injured Children," *Exceptional Children*, 27 (1961), pp. 286–291.

[41] Hall, *op. cit.*

[42] Farber, "Effects of a Severely Mentally Retarded Child . . .," *op. cit.*

[43] Hope J. Leichter and William E. Mitchell, *Kinship and Casework* (New York: Russell Sage Foundation, 1967).

[44] See Farber, "Effects of a Severely Mentally Retarded Child . . .," *op. cit.*, p. 24.

[45] See Daniel Glaser, "The Differential-Association Theory of Crime," in Arnold M. Rose, ed. *Human Behavior and Social Processes* (Boston: Houghton Mifflin, 1962), pp. 425–442.

[46] Max Culver, "Intergenerational Social Mobility Among Families with a Severely Mentally Retarded Child," unpublished Ph.D. dissertation, University of Illinois, 1967.

[47] Bernard Farber and William C. Jenné, "Interaction with Retarded Siblings and Life Goals of Children," *Marriage and Family Living*, 25 (1963), pp. 96–98.

[48] Farber, "Family Organization and Crisis," *op. cit.*

[49] See P. S. Lawrence, "Chronic Illness and Socioeconomic Status," in E. Gartly Jaco, ed., *Patients, Physicians, and Illness* (New York: Free Press 1958), pp. 37–49; and Meyerowitz and Kaplan, *op. cit.*

[50] Ruby Jo Reeves Kennedy, *The Social Adjustment of Morons in a Connecticut City* (Hartford: State Office Building, 1948).

51 Joseph H. Meyerowitz and Bernard Farber, "Family Background of Educable Mentally Retarded Children," in Bernard Farber, ed., *Kinship and Family Organization* (New York: Wiley, 1966), pp. 388–398.

52 Goldstein, Moss, and Jordan, *op. cit.*, pp. 45–48.

53 F. Ivan Nye, *Family Relationships and Delinquent Behavior* (New York: Wiley, 1958).

54 Yi-Chuang Lu, "Mother-Child Role Relationships in Schizophrenia," *Psychiatry*, 24 (1961), pp. 133–142

55 Paul H. Jacobson, *American Marriage and Divorce* (New York: Rinehart, 1959), p. 62.

56 Elizabeth W. Reed and Sheldon C. Reed, *Mental Retardation: A Family Study* (Philadelphia: Saunders, 1965), p. 40 (Table 28).

57 John R. Peck and Will Beth Stephens, "Marriage of Young Adult Male Retardates," *American Journal of Mental Deficiency*, 69 (May, 1965), pp. 818–827. See also Medora Steedman Bass, "Marriage, Parenthood, and Prevention of Pregnancy," *American Journal of Mental Deficiency*, 69 (November, 1963), pp. 318–333. A summary of research literature by Bass suggests that marital success among the retarded is greater for couples with few children and that sterilization is an effective means for limiting fertility.

58 R. E. Fairbank, "The Subnormal Child—Seventeen Years After," *Mental Hygiene*, 17 (1933), pp. 177–208.

59 W. R. Baller, "A Study of the Present Social Status of a Group of Adults Who, When They Were in Elementary Schools, Were Classified as Mentally Deficient," *Genetic Psychology Monographs*, 18 (1936), pp. 165–244.

60 D. C. Charles, "Ability and Accomplishment of Persons Earlier Judged Mentally Deficient," *Genetic Psychology Monographs*, 47 (1953), pp. 3–71.

61 Kennedy, *op. cit.*

62 LeRoy Peterson and Lloyd L. Smith, "A Comparison of the Post-School Adjustment of Educable Mentally Retarded Adults with That of Adults of Normal Intelligence," *Exceptional Children*, 26 (April, 1960), pp. 404–408. Dinger reported that the family characteristics of retardates who had been in special education classes in Altoona, Pennsylvania, were much like those in the Peterson and Smith study. (Jack C. Dinger, "Post-School Adjustment of Former Educable Retarded Pupils," *Exceptional Children*, 27 [March, 1961], pp. 353–360.)

63 Joseph F. Jastak, Halsey M. MacPhee, and Martin Whiteman, *Mental Retardation, Its Nature and Incidence* (Newark: University of Delaware Press, 1963), pp. 113–126.

64 T. Ramer, "The Prognosis of Mentally Retarded Children," *Acta Psychiat. Neurol. Supplement*, 4–1 (1946) pp. 1–42.

65 Hans Olof Akesson, *Epidemiology and Genetics of Mental Deficiency in a Southern Swedish Population* (Uppsala: The Institute for Medical Genetics of the University of Uppsala, 1961), p. 99.

66 A study by Edgerton of mildly retarded adults released from Pacific State Hospital indicates that those who remain in the community generally need a benefactor of normal intelligence (often a spouse) to carry on activities requiring literacy or the manipulation of numbers and symbols (such as telling time, reading instructions, or planning). Robert Edgerton, *The Cloak of Competence* (Berkeley and Los Angeles: University of California Press, 1967).

8.

Residential Institutions

The character of residential institutions for the mentally retarded in the United States has changed in the past century. These changes have occurred, however, not so much through rational planning but because of shifts in the political and social structure of the society. Even the kinds of proposals for radically modifying the life conditions of the mentally retarded echo those voiced over a century ago. For example, Samuel Gridley Howe, who founded the first residential institution in the United States, wrote in 1857:

> Being called upon lately to give advice about the establishment of Institutions for the Blind and the Deaf Mutes in a new state, I have counselled a course different from the one I myself followed many years ago. It is to dispense with any great costly building, having common dormitories, dining rooms, chapel, and the like. To make no preparation for any great common household at all; but to build a simple building, with all the conveniences for structuring classes, and make provision for boarding the pupils in private families. In a word, to reduce the Institutions, as we would any machine, to the simplest form. This is perfectly feasible in many small towns and villages.[1]

Howe's statement can be compared with the proposed program of the President's Panel on Mental Retardation, published in 1962. This program is intended to take into account the most recent and novel

180

suggestions for the improvement of services to the retarded. The report of the President's Panel states:

> The challenge to State institutions is how to accelerate the change from large isolated facilities to smaller units close to the home of the patients and to the health, education, and social resources of the community; and the challenge to both State and private residential facilities is how to replace the old concept of custodial care, wherever it still exists, with modern programs of therapy, education, and research.[2]

Even the emphasis by the President's Panel upon treatment and rehabilitation of the mentally retarded mirrors Howe's view. In his letter to the governor of Massachusetts quoted above, Howe indicated:

> An institution had been incorporated and organized under the title of the Massachusetts School for Idiotic and Feeble-minded Youth; and, at the expiration of the three experimental years, the Legislature doubled the appropriation by making an annual grant of five thousand dollars a year to the new school. It soon became clear to all who examined the subject closely, that this institution was really doing a needful work, which could not be done elsewhere, and that there should be a proper building to do it in. The Legislature, therefore, in 1855, voted the sum of twenty-five thousand dollars for such a building. The edifice was erected in a very short time. The pupils were removed to it during the last year, and more new ones applied for admission than could be supported by means at command.
>
> I claim, then, that the experiment of teaching and training idiots has been carefully and patiently made, and has proved successful, and that this institution has done all that its real friends promised. True, it has not changed the nature of any born idiot and given him common sense, and no honest and wise persons have pretended that this could be done. But this experiment has done much good in various ways. It has shown that idiots form no exception to the law that every form of organized life is capable of being changed for better or worse by surrounding influences. It has rescued some children of merely feeble minds from the imbecility into which they had fallen, either through abuse or neglect or unwise treatment—children who were considered as idiots and who would have sunk into hopeless idiocy but for the help of this school. It has given speech to some who were dumb, and who, if left without special aid, would have remained dumb. It has greatly improved the condition of more

than four-fifths of its pupils, as their friends will testify. They have been put to a higher state of health and vigor. They have been trained to the command and use of muscle limb. They feed themselves, dress themselves, and conduct themselves with decorum. Their gluttonous and unseemly habits have been broken up. They have been trained to temperance, cleanliness, and order, until the habits have become as second nature. Their powers of self-control have been increased, and they strive to make themselves less unsightly and disagreeable to others. Many have been trained to habits of industry, so that they may at least be less burdensome to their friends. Their mental faculties and moral sentiments have been developed by lessons and exercises suitable to their feeble condition, and they have been raised in the scale of humanity.[3]

Recent proposals to increase participation by the mentally retarded in the community do not differ essentially from Howe's position. Dexter's suggestion that a community be planned on the assumption that about one-fourth of its adults would be "feebleminded" and that day care centers and other institutions in the community be geared to a place and level comprehended by the feebleminded is not inconsistent with Howe's views.[4] The proposal by Kirk, Karnes, and Kirk for community centers for the mentally retarded offers a compromise between the Howe position and that of those who favor residential institutions. The Kirk proposal differs from the Howe view only in that it would include a temporary residential unit as a "half-way house" for those who are being released from state institutions, for children who are awaiting admission to residential schools, or for retarded children whose parents require temporary relief from the problems of caring for the child.[5]

To date, however, no proposals have been brought forth which are essentially different from the Howe position. The fact that no really radical proposals have been made suggests that possibly public institutions with all of their inadequacies are actually performing the functions the parents and public really want, since people may not care to have unsightly (as some of the severely retarded are) or uncouth and inept persons free to move about in the society. The residential institutions can at least absorb those retardates who are most threatening to parents and the community. The fact that the institutions are understaffed, stultifying in their effects on intellectual functioning, and impersonal is probably less important to most people than the removal of undesirable persons from society.

This chapter will first present a brief history of residential institutions in the United States. It will then discuss factors of admission to and release from institutions. Finally, it will touch upon the social organization of patients in residential institutions for the mentally retarded. The discussion will emphasize the ways in which the outside world imposes itself upon the residential institution and how the institution attempts to maintain its integrity. As a case in point, because of political influences on welfare programs in the United States, state residential institutions cannot develop factories in which inmates could earn not only privileges in a commissary but also perhaps residential privileges in special areas of the institution. In other words, unlike some European institutions that provide for wages and other community-like norms, because of political pressures in our state government, entrepreneurial activities and wage-earning are not integrated into the organization of American residential institutions.

History of Institutions in the United States

Throughout their history, state residential institutions for the mentally retarded have been at the mercy of political whims and patronage practices. This was true of the first American institution in Massachusetts, founded by Samuel Gridley Howe, and it is true of most institutions at the present time. For example, regarding the governor's veto of a bill to increase the grant made by the state of Massachusetts for the support of his institution for the mentally retarded, Howe wrote, "I know indeed that in some states the sacred interests of public Charitable Institutions are often wickedly sacrificed for political purposes, but I did not suspect that in this case there was anything to endanger them . . .This particular school may be crushed, either by reason of the weakness of its friends, or the strength of its enemies, but the charity will reappear in some other form."[6] A century later, residential institutions are still being built, not where they will produce the greatest benefits for the welfare of the mentally retarded, but where powerful persons in legislatures draw their support. Moreover, state institutions often have two lines of authority. One is the official line shown on the table of organization with the superintendent at the head. The second line of authority, however, is based on patronage positions or political appointments, and it undercuts the capability of the superintendent to perform his duties efficiently. The precise role of political maneuvering in the history of residential institutions in the

United States is difficult to determine because of the secrecy and informal arrangements involved. Still, it would be a mistake to ignore the fact that politics has played a role in determining the character of residential institutions for the mentally retarded.

In 1857, Howe described the circumstances that led to the founding of the first residential institution in the United States:

> About twelve years ago, some persons, encouraged by success in attempts to teach children who were apparently beyond the reach of instruction, conceived a plan of improving the condition of Idiots, and brought the subject before the Legislature. By order of the House of Representatives, January 22, 1846, a committee of five members was named "to consider the expedience of appointing Commissioners to inquire into the condition of Idiots in this Commonwealth, to ascertain their number, and whether anything can be done for their relief, and to report to the next General Court." In March, 1846, the Committee reported "that there is no adequate provision by the law for the relief, care and treatment of idiots in the Commonwealth." They set forth strong reasons for the belief that the condition of those unfortunates could be greatly improved. Among other evidence, they gave that of Dr. Woodward, the eminent physician of the State Lunatic Hospital, who said: "My opinion is that nearly all idiots can be made better; the physical condition and personal habits of the lowest order can be improved, and those possessing more mind can be trained to usefulness, and some can be taught to read, write, and labor advantageously, and be useful and happy." The Committee closed by recommending three Commissioners to make a thorough investigation of the subject, and report the results. The Commissioners were appointed, and reported in part, March 31, 1847, and made a full and final report February 26, 1848. This report embodied the greatest amount of information ever collected upon the subject. It gave a minute and accurate description of five-hundred seventy-four idiots. The Legislature was convinced that something should be done by the State but resolved to do it experimentally. By an Act approved May 8, 1848, there was appropriated "a sum not exceeding two-thousand five-hundred dollars a year for three years, for the purpose of training and teaching ten idiotic children, to be selected by the Governor and Council, provided an arrangement can be made with any suitable institution now patronized by the Commonwealth for charitable purposes. The task was undertaken by the Institute for the Blind and was performed satisfactorily. In the meantime, an institution had been incorporated and organized under the title of Massachusetts School for Idiotic and

Feeble-minded Youth; and, at the expiration of the three experimental years, the Legislature doubled the appropriation, by making an annual grant of five thousand dollars a year to the new school.[7]

The reluctance of the legislature to create an institution for the mentally retarded is suggested first by the succession of committees that examined the topic and then by its approval on an experimental basis. However, shortly after Howe established the institution in Massachusetts, other states, such as Pennsylvania, Rhode Island, Connecticut, and Ohio, followed suit. In 1852, the secretary of the board of education for the state of New York wrote to Howe that:

> Dr. Baccus, recently a State Senator, and an enlightened and philanthropic citizen of Rochester, labored with zeal and fidelity, though unsuccessfully, to establish an institution in this state. Very soon after your visit to Albany, a law was passed for an establishment of an institution for idiots; an appropriation of six thousand dollars a year, for two years, was made, and the institution is now in successful operation in the vicinity of this city . . . it may now be regarded as permanently established, and to your visit, more than anything else, are we indebted for this noble charity, so creditable to the liberality and benevolence of this State.[8]

During the latter part of the nineteenth century, residential institutions were constructed not only for the mentally retarded but for the mentally ill as well. Responsibility for the mentally retarded and mentally ill shifted from local and county institutions to the states. It was argued that state institutions were both more efficient and more humanitarian than the poorhouses and prisons for the mentally incompetent. The state institutions were constructed mainly to care for the poor, and the foreign-born contributed disproportionately to the population of these institutions. At a time when the United States was expanding rapidly, the cost of building and maintaining residential institutions constituted an impediment to this expansion.

In spite of the inadequate treatment and housing of the mentally retarded and mentally ill in the large residential institutions of the nineteenth century, these institutions were overcrowded. Strauss and Sabshin suggest that "lower middle-class families (and even families further down in the social scale) were able to lessen chances of their downward mobility by turning over to the state the financial burden of insane family members." In addition, since "a striving but poor family, no matter how modest its aspirations, had an insane member with whom to contend, a state-supported hospital could be a God-sent agent to remove the extra financial burden." Thus Strauss and Sabshin attribute the growth of the large residential institution in the last century to the nation's need to handle its impecunious mental incompetents with minimum expenditure in a period of rapid growth and at the same time to facilitate upward social mobility of immigrant groups.[9]

As the number of inmates in institutions for the mentally retarded grew in the nineteenth century, three different kinds of populations were distinguished—the feebleminded retardates who were amenable to academic programs, the imbecile retardates, and idiots who were unable to function in any kind of program. The rehabilitative and custodial functions of residential institutions were clarified. In the latter part of the century, an apparent trend developed toward grouping the retarded population according to ability and toward the departmentalization of services related to rehabilitation (such as occupational and recreational therapy, and music).

The adult population in institutions increased over time, and the colony system arose. The colonies were for the most part agricultural and were supposed to be self-sufficient. However, as farming became mechanized and scientific methods were introduced, the retarded were unable to operate the colonies efficiently. Moreover, large-scale merchandising and political pressures increased the reliance on outside producers to supply the institutions with food. Finally, because the population that could work a colony had to be small, the system did not solve the problem of overcrowding in institutions.

The early part of the twentieth century saw the establishment of systematic release systems and parole. By 1920, about twenty state institutions had begun a formal parole system, one of the consequences of which was the introduction of social workers to the staffs of institutions. Eventually many institutions added half-way houses and extramural social service departments to ease the adjustment of the released or paroled retardates to the community.

Recently, several states have established institutions for the mentally retarded as research centers, which have a large proportion of well-trained professional persons and generally a highly selected inmate population. The Edward R. Johnstone Training and Research Center at Bordentown, New Jersey, focuses upon educable adolescents. Central Colony, near the University of Wisconsin, has established a close relationship with the medical school at the university. Pacific State Hospital, at Pomona, California, has worked closely with the University of California at Los Angeles Institute of Psychiatry. The Adler Zone Center at the University of Illinois, Urbana, is selecting inmates on the basis of requirements of research projects. With the development of these research-oriented, university-associated facilities, the functions of residential institutions for the mentally retarded have shifted from the traditional ones of rehabilitation and custody. These institutions seem analogous to research and training hospitals in organization as well as in functions.[10]

Admission to Institutions

Dybwad estimates that the two hundred thousand mentally retarded individuals who are in public and private institutions in the United States represent only about 4 percent of the five and a half million mentally retarded. In some states probably only 1 percent of the mentally retarded are in institutions, while other states probably institutionalize 7 or 8 percent.

Figures submitted to Congress by the National Association for Retarded Children would indicate that expenditures properly assigned to the problem of mental retardation, whether from national, state, or local, public or private sources, exceed one billion dollars a year. Of this sum, an unproportionate amount is spent on the four per cent of the mentally retarded in institutions: three hundred million dollars for their care, treatment, and maintenance and an additional one hundred million dollars for institutional construction. Of the remaining sum, approximately one hundred fifty million dollars are spent on publicly and privately sponsored programs of services in the field of education, rehabilitation, recreation, health care, diagnostic testing, etc.[11]

In spite of the relative infrequency of institutionalization of educable mentally retarded persons, there is much public sentiment for this course of action. About 40 percent of the respondents in a random sample of 1 percent of households in a "city of 80,000 persons near Los Angeles" thought that persons who "will always be like a nine-year-old and will always need someone to look after them" should be institutionalized or sent to a special training school. Non-Caucasians, persons with less than twelve years of education, those in low socioeconomic levels, and persons with orthodox religious beliefs were more inclined than others to favor institutionalizing of the educable retarded as a general solution.[12] Perhaps experience with retardates by persons in low socioeconomic levels predisposes them to solutions that would eliminate the retardates from their field of action.

The large majority of institutionalized mentally retarded persons live in public residential institutions, primarily those designated specifically for the mentally retarded. In 1962, about 174,000 mentally retarded persons were in 124 such institutions, an additional 10,000 were in 200 private institutions, and another 43,000 retardates lived in about 280 public mental hospitals. The number of people in public institutions specifically for the mentally retarded has increased steadily at a rate of 2.5 percent each year—from 113,000 in 1946 to over 160,-000 in 1960. The 1960 population in such institutions was 1.4 times the population in 1946. During the same period of time, the total population of the United States had increased only to 1.3 times the size of the 1946 population. Thus the increase in the institutional population was slightly greater than the total population increase and represents an increased pressure to commit the mentally retarded to institutions designated specifically for them.[13]

One factor in the increase in the number of mentally retarded individuals in public institutions is the trend toward the admission of younger, more severely handicapped individuals. The following sections describe trends in first admissions of the mentally retarded by degree of retardation. Although designating the mentally retarded as morons, imbeciles, and idiots is considered outmoded, the U.S. mental health reports used these terms until 1960. Since then they have classified first admissions in five categories of degree of mental deficiency; however, the terminology of the pre-1960 U.S. reports will be used below.

ADMISSION OF MORONS

Table 13 indicates the percentage of morons admitted to public institutions for the mentally retarded in the period from 1922 to 1963. The term "moron" is used in the table as synonymous with educable or mildly retarded persons. The table shows that, after reaching a peak in 1936 to 1940, the proportion of first admissions classified as morons has declined. The data suggest a sensitivity of rates of admission of morons to economic cycles of prosperity and depression. The highest proportions were admitted during the depression of the 1930s.

TABLE 13

Number and Percentage of Morons, Imbeciles, and Idiots Among First Admissions to Public Residential Institutions for the Mentally Retarded in t he United States, 1922–1963[1]

Years	Morons		Imbeciles		Idiots		Total Number Reported[2]
	Number	Percent	Number	Percent	Number	Percent	
1922–23	5,668	40.4	4,948	35.2	2,007	14.3	14,045
1926–30	18,068	44.1	13,078	32.1	6,397	15.7	40,711
1931–35	20,945	45.7	13,776	30.2	7,093	15.6	45,589
1936–40	19,318	48.1	12,462	31.0	6,380	15.9	40,195
1941–45	18,325	43.3	12,130	29.4	6,301	14.9	42,358
1946–50	16,870	38.1	13,859	31.3	8,533	19.3	44,308
1951–55	14,767	32.1	16,370	35.6	10,302	22.4	45,998
1956–60[3]	14,394	28.9	17,231	34.6	12,919	25.9	49,810
1961–63[3]	6,438	23.5	9,959	35.6	6,895	25.2	27,395

[1] U.S. Public Health Service, *Patients in Mental Institutions: 1963*, Publication 1222, Part I: "Public Institutions for the Mentally Retarded" (Washington, D.C.: U.S. Government Printing Office, 1965). For 1950–1962 data, Part I of *Patients in Mental Institutions* series for 1952–1964. For 1922–1949 data, see Herbert Goldstein, "Social Aspects of Mental Deficiency," unpublished Ed.D. dissertation, University of Illinois, 1957.

[2] The total number of first admissions reported included cases classified as "normal," "unknown," or "not classified." The percentages in the table are computed on the basis of the total number of admissions reported and do not add to 100 percent. In addition, not all public institutions report their first admissions.

[3] Of the first admissions for 1960–1963, patients classified as "borderline" or "mildly retarded" are included in this table as morons; those classified as "moderately" or "severely" retarded are placed in the imbeciles category; patients classified as "profoundly retarded" appear in the idiots column.

About 46 percent of all persons admitted to institutions for the mentally retarded in 1931 to 1935 were morons, and 48 percent of first admissions in 1936 to 1940 were morons. With the emergence of full employment in World War II, the admission rates for morons declined considerably. Since World War II the ratio of admissions classified as morons has fallen below 40 percent. Inasmuch as few institutions were constructed during the depression of the 1930s, the high rate of first admissions among morons appears to reflect the economic plight of their families rather than an increase in facilities.

The large proportion of morons among first admissions to public institutions for the mentally retarded during the depression years also represents an increase in actual number of morons institutionalized during that period. As indicated in Table 13, the actual number of morons admitted reached a peak in the years 1931 to 1935 and remained fairly high through the period 1936 to 1940. Since World War II, the actual number of morons admitted to residential institutions has been declining.[14]

ADMISSION OF IMBECILES

The percentages for first admissions of imbeciles (that is, the trainable mentally retarded with IQ roughly from 25–50) to public institutions in the period from 1922 to 1963 are also shown in Table 13. During the depression years from 1931 to 1935 the imbeciles appeared to be crowded out by the morons in admission priorities. Moreover, the marked increase in admission of idiots following World War II precedes that of imbeciles. The high growth in the proportion of imbeciles in admissions to institutions does not appear until the 1950s. Apparently, more first admissions are now classified as imbeciles (moderately or severely retarded) than as either of the other categories.

Table 13 also presents the number of imbeciles admitted to public institutions for the mentally retarded in the years 1922 to 1963. Before World War II the peak number of imbeciles admitted per year was during the height of the depression, 1931 to 1935. However, this number only slightly exceeds the average annual admissions for the preceding period from 1926 to 1930. Since World War II, the number of imbeciles admitted has risen considerably, and their admissions exhibit the same trends as admissions for idiots depicted below.

ADMISSION OF IDIOTS

The percentages of persons admitted to public institutions as idiots are shown in Table 13. In the years 1922 through 1945 there is little variation in this ratio, with about 15 percent of admissions classified as such. Since 1946, however, the proportion has risen considerably, suggesting that the propensity to admit persons classified as idiots is not greatly affected by economic conditions.

The number of idiots admitted from 1922 to 1963 is also shown in Table 13. There was a slight increase in the number of idiots admitted for the first time in public residential institutions in 1931 to 1935, then admissions reverted to the earlier figure during the following decade. Since World War II, however, the number of idiots admitted to public institutions has risen rapidly. This acceleration reflects the increase both in beds vacated by the educable retarded population and in newly-built institutions. Significantly, the surge in the number of idiots committed following World War II has been much greater than the fluctuations in admissions during the depression.

COMPARISONS OF FIRST ADMISSIONS
FOR MORONS, IMBECILES, AND IDIOTS

The data on first admissions of mentally retarded persons to public residential institutions in the years 1922 to 1963 suggest that the morons' (or mildly retarded) admissions are most affected by variations in the business cycle. The greatest number of mildly retarded were institutionalized in the early part of the depression, from 1931 to 1935. Although somewhat fewer morons were admitted in the following five-year period, from 1936 to 1940, these persons represented almost half of all retardates admitted during that time. Few institutions were constructed during the depression, and the educable retardates, as the least employable persons in the labor force, produced numerous problems in the community. With World War II, however, the demand for workers increased, and the postwar era of full employment (as well as the expansion of special-class programs) has reduced both the number and proportion of morons admitted to public institutions for the mentally retarded.

While the prosperity of the American economy has depressed the rate of admission of educable retardates to public institutions, it appears to have stimulated the commitment of idiots and imbeciles. In other words, the admission rates of idiots and imbeciles to public institutions tend to increase during prosperity. Proportionately more imbeciles and idiots were admitted in the years immediately preceding the depression (1926 to 1930) and in the postwar era than during the depression years.

These tendencies are consistent with the findings of Culver's investigation of social mobility of parents with severely mentally retarded children. He found that among families in which the grandfathers of the retarded child had white-collar occupations, those who keep their severely retarded child in the home are more often downwardly socially mobile (as indicated by the husband's occupation) than are those families who institutionalize their retarded child.[15] Moreover, Culver showed that there is a greater tendency for parents who have attended college to place their retarded child in an institution than there is for parents with a high-school education or less. These findings suggest that when probabilities of upward social mobility are high, families tend to rid themselves of impediments to occupational and social success and, accordingly, institutionalize their severely mentally retarded children. The lower-class families of retardates are less motivated toward effective upward social mobility and hence do not regard their retarded child as an impediment to their socioeconomic aspirations.

The changing proportions of first admissions to residential institutions for the mentally retarded also reflect the increase in the life span of the severely retarded. Children in higher socioeconomic level families are likely to receive a larger amount (and perhaps a better quality) of medical services than children in low socioeconomic level families.[16] The chances of a severely retarded child's survival in a high socioeconomic status family would thus be appreciable. In addition, there is a greater propensity for high socioeconomic level families than for low socioeconomic level families to institutionalize their retarded children voluntarily.[17] These factors converge to produce an increase in admission rates of severely mentally retarded children in residential institutions.

The Family and the Institution: Entrance

Family characteristics of the institutionalized mentally retarded have changed in the past half-century. During the years when the general population feared that immigrant groups with "neuropathic constitutions" would cause the American population to degenerate, there was much interest in the educable mentally retarded or "morons." This interest was stimulated by the belief that high-grade retarded or feebleminded individuals were responsible for much crime, alcoholism, and general degeneracy as a way of life. Official figures showed a large proportion of children of foreign-born parents in institutions. As ideas on heredity changed, the society no longer felt threatened by foreign-born groups; and, as a period of prosperity endured, facilities were constructed for the more severely retarded. This change has resulted in the introduction of new factors leading to institutionalization.[18]

An analysis of the characteristics of families with a retarded member on the waiting list for entry into an institution provides some insight into the selection factors. In 1965, about 1400 persons responsible for a relative on the waiting list for admission to the Lincoln or Dixon State Schools in Illinois were interviewed by public health nurses and volunteer workers. Slightly more than half of the interviews were conducted in the Chicago area. The refusal rate was negligible. The findings included the following:

1. The median age of retardates on the waiting list was eight for males and six for females. Thirty-nine percent of all applicants were under six years of age and 84 percent were under eighteen. Fewer applicants age twelve to seventeen were severely retarded than were the older or younger applicants.

2. Almost half (48 percent) of the applicants on the waiting list were living with their parents. Another 40 percent were living in nursing homes, state hospitals, or private schools. The older the applicant, the greater was the probability of his living at home with his parents. The very young applicants on the waiting list were more often in nursing homes.

3. Forty-four percent of the applicants had one or more physical handicaps; most of them were either partially ambulatory or bedfast. Slightly over half of the applicants with a very low IQ (0–20 range) had a hearing or seeing defect, paralysis, convulsive disorder, or were not completely ambulatory.

4. Only about a third of the school-age applicants had had any formal education experience. Thirty-seven percent of the applicants over eighteen years of age had never been in school, and 90 percent of the applicants between the ages of three and five had never received any preschool education. About 45 percent of those with an IQ of 68 or over had had some formal schooling. Less than 20 percent of those at the trainable level or below had ever attended school.

5. Almost all of the applicants relied on their parents or other

responsible persons for financial assistance and decision-making. (Only four of the 1400 applicants on the waiting list were married.) The families of the applicants tended to be of low socioeconomic level. The median family income was $4,595 as contrasted with about $6,500 median family income in Illinois in 1959. Other characteristics were similar to typical low socioeconomic level families. There was a high rate of divorce for the waiting-list families generally. However, among those families whose retarded child was under six years of age, the proportion of divorce was comparable to that of the United States as a whole. The median age of the persons responsible for applicants under six was only thirty-three as compared with forty-two for all other families in the sample.

6. The retarded individual was generally regarded by his family as troublesome. Over half of the applicants' parents and guardians considered the retarded person's effect on others in the family as an important factor in institutionalization. Four out of ten of the respondents believed that the emotional stress on the family was an important consideration in institutionalizing the retarded person. Over half perceived the retarded person as having at least some harmful emotional effect on other children or adults in the family. Eighty percent of the retardates age six or older were reported by the respondents as displaying behavior serious enough for institutionalization. On the whole, behavior problems were mentioned more frequently among those of high mental levels than among those at low mental levels. Problems prevalent at higher mental levels were stubbornness, temper tantrums, sexual problems, objectionable personal habits, entering other homes, stealing, and setting fires. Those problems mentioned more often at lower mental levels were restlessness or hyperactivity, self-destructiveness, and sleeplessness. Twelve percent of the applicants age six or older had been involved with a law enforcement agency. The most frequent bases for involvement were running away from home, destruction of property, stealing, entering other homes, harming others, and sexual problems.

7. In general, responsible persons with applicants at higher mental levels were interested in rehabilitative training, whereas those with retardates at low mental levels were more concerned with the effects on the family of eliminating the retarded individual. For retardates with higher mental levels, the major accomplishments anticipated through institutionalization were academic education, vocational training, and elimination of uncontrollable behavior from the home. On the other

Current Trend

hand, families with an applicant at a lower mental level expected medical treatment, nursing care, habit training in self-care, development of speech, improvement of the mother's health, lessening of emotional stress, and reduction of effect on other children.

8. The source of recommendation for admission was related to the mental level of the applicant. There was a somewhat greater tendency for social agencies, psychologists, psychiatrists, juvenile courts, and school personnel to recommend institutionalization of high-level retardates. Family physicians, medical specialists, medical clinics, ministers, relatives, public health nurses, and friends tended to recommend institutionalization of low-level retardates. When the family itself made the decision, it more often had a retardate of low mental level.[19]

The findings of the Illinois Study are comparable in many ways to the factors influencing the institutionalization of mentally retarded individuals in New York City. In the New York study, Saenger found the following:

1. There is a greater tendency to institutionalize retardates at a low mental level than those at a high mental level. Although one out of nine trainable individuals (IQ 20–49) known to live in New York City is committed each year, only one out of ninety or so educable retarded (IQ above 50) is institutionalized. Matched samples of retardates in institutions and at home include about the same proportion of cases with physical handicaps.

2. Over half of the high-grade retarded children who are committed come from Puerto Rican and Negro families, while the prevalence of low-grade retardation resembles the economic and ethnic distribution of the population of New York City as a whole. Almost half of the known Puerto Rican imbecile children are committed, as compared to only one out of every four Negro, one of every ten Caucasian Catholic and Protestant, and one of every twenty Jewish children.

3. Retarded individuals with an IQ over 50 tend to be institutionalized because of behavior problems taking place outside the home. Sexual offenses almost always lead to institutionalization, especially in the case of girls. Problems of adjustment in the home rather than in the community are found mainly among the trainable retarded from middle-class homes. In these homes, trouble is restricted to the family setting, while among lower-class Negro and Puerto Rican families with trainable children, both home and community problems occur.

4. More institutionalized retardates have experienced a broken home. Although over 90 percent of the retardates in the community live with their natural parents, only 40 percent of the institutionalized retardates had been living with both parents prior to admission. The relationship between institutionalization and broken homes exists for both trainable (IQ 20–49) and educable (IQ 50 or over) persons. As might be expected, broken homes are found very frequently among Negroes and Puerto Ricans.

5. The socioeconomic level of institutionalized cases is lower than that of the families with a retarded individual in the community. Moreover, there is evidence of more parental inadequacy and emotional stress among families of institutionalized retardates.[20]

Farber, Jenné, and Toigo studied 268 families with a severely retarded child living at home to determine variables related to the willingness of the couple to institutionalize their retarded child. The study took place in Chicago in 1957–58. The major variables studied included socioeconomic status, marital integration of the couples, and emotional impact of the child upon the husband and wife. The following factors were associated with willingness to place the retarded child in a state institution:

1. *Socioeconomic Status*. The higher the socioeconomic status, the greater was the relative willingness of the husband as compared with the wife to institutionalize the retarded child. However, in high status families, the parents' willingness to place the child in an institution varied directly with the number of normal children in the family.[21] On the other hand, the lower the socioeconomic status, the greater was the relative willingness of mothers of retarded boys as compared with mothers of retarded girls to commit the child. As in the Saenger study, middle-class Jewish families were least willing to institutionalized their retarded children.

2. *Marital Integration*. The couple's degree of marital integration was associated with willingness to institutionalize only in the context of social organization variables, such as socioeconomic position and religion. In low socioeconomic status families, the greater the marital integration, the less were husbands willing to institutionalize their retarded children. In higher socioeconomic status families, marital integration was of little importance as a factor in the husband's willingness to commit the child.

3. *Personal Impact*. The emotional impact of the retarded child on the parents was found to be related to both husband's and wife's

willingness to institutionalize him. In addition, in those families characterized by low marital integration, the parents' willingness to institutionalize the retarded child was related to their dissatisfaction with their normal daughters. Apparently the normal daughters could not take over the parent-surrogate roles in caring for the retarded child in these families.[22]

The motivation for institutionalizing the retarded child is related to the age at which the child is committed. In a further analysis of the Farber-Jenné-Toigo data, Downey found that the better educated parents committed their children at a younger age. According to Downey, "Education of the parents is the crucial institutionalization factor for this not only determines *when* the child is placed but also *why* he is placed." The less educated parents are concerned with trouble in the neighborhood, vocational training, and academic schooling, while parents with a greater amount of education are more concerned with the child's potential effects on other family members, especially the normal siblings. Inasmuch as the age at which diagnosis is made is also related to degree of retardation, there is a close relationship between age at institutionalization, reasons for institutionalization, and severity of retardation. There is also a connection between these factors and the socioeconomic status of the parents, with the higher socioeconomic level parents tending to have their severely retarded children diagnosed at an earlier age and institutionalized earlier.[23]

Taken together, the Illinois and the New York City studies indicate that mental retardation alone is not a sufficient explanation for institutionalization. The mentally retarded individual must present some additional problems to either the family or the community which designate him as superfluous or threatening to social relationships. For the educable retardate, this trouble may take him into contact with official agencies, while for the trainable retardate, the difficulties may be restricted to the family itself. Status problems may impel the family to seek institutionalization; religion (especially Jewish) may deter parents from institutionalization. In any case, the parental requirements of residential institutions differ. In one instance, the parents anticipate rehabilitation for community living; while in the other they may seek the elimination of family problems and demand only custodial care by the institution.

Most families involved in institutionalizing their retarded child are in low-income, problem-beset sectors of the population, with an over-representation from minority groups. These are precisely the families who are helpless in influencing the staff of an institution to perform their tasks in an efficient manner. In addition, many of these families do not themselves take the initiative in having the child institutionalized. Instead, social welfare and legal agencies may be responsible. Under these circumstances, the families are not well-disposed toward the institution. Hence the factors that lead to institutionalization are not conducive to the emergence of congenial relationships between family and staff.

The Family and the Institution: Departure

Families differ widely in the extent to which they continue to display an interest in the child after institutionalization. The family may have the child home frequently on visits, they may write often to the institution asking for information about the child, and, finally, they may visit the institution often. On the other hand, the family may avoid contact with the institution. A study of families with children at the residential schools in Illinois revealed that occasionally the child was placed at birth and the mother was informed that the child had died; she was, therefore, not even aware of the retarded child's existence.

Downey studied factors related to the parents' continued interest in the child after institutionalization. The evidence of interest in the child included home visits, letters, parents' association activities, and family visits to the institution. Generally, the greater the amount of the parents' formal education, the less parental interest was manifested. Moreover, parents who placed older children demonstrated more interest than those who placed younger children (age seven or under). Presumably, the children who were placed at an older age were generally somewhat more intelligent (although all were classified as either trainable or almost educable retarded).[24]

The Downey study suggests that the family with high educational attainment tends to regard the child as "inhuman" and therefore no longer a member of the family with full status. The family with lower education, however, appears to consider the child as a family member who is living away from home. The low socioeconomic level child has more often than not been placed through the intervention of an official welfare or legal agency. Among lower-class families, children frequently live with relatives and away from their family of orientation for periods of time, sometimes in juvenile detention homes or with foster parents or relatives. The notion of a separation between family membership and residence is thus readily accepted by lower-class families.

The continuation of family interest in the institutionalized retarded child affects the probability of his returning home. Since families at high socioeconomic levels institutionalize their children for different reasons than do families at low socioeconomic levels, factors influencing the eventual release of the retarded child from the institution probably also differ by socioeconomic level of the family. Jane Mercer undertook a comparison between a group of residents at the Pacific State Hospital and a matched group of retardates who had been released from the hospital to their families.[25] The matching was done on year of birth, intelligence quotient, and year of admission; the families were not matched by socioeconomic level. A relatively smaller proportion of high socioeconomic retardates was released. (This finding is consistent with that of Downey on parental interest and with the studies of parental motivation in institutionalization.) For both the resident and released patients, the apparent intellectual level of the retarded persons from high status homes was below that for persons from lower socioeconomic levels. This lower level of intellectual functioning is evidenced in the Mercer report in two ways. First, the retardation was diagnosed prior to the age of seven much more frequently among the high status families. (Generally, the more severe the retardation, the earlier a diagnosis can be made.) Second, Mercer reported that the slow development of the child was more apparent to the high status parents than to the low status parents.

The results of the Mercer investigation lend themselves to a comparison between families of releasees and residents by socioeconomic level. Data for the families of *low* socioeconomic status reveal the following:

1. The released retardates apparently had a higher intellectual level of functioning than those retardates who were still in residence. Fifty-three percent of the residents had been diagnosed at six years of age or under, but only 36 percent of the released retardates had been diagnosed that early. The released retardates more often than the residents had been diagnosed at ages seven to fourteen (47 percent versus 23 percent). The released retardates also displayed diagnostic problems associated more often with educable than with trainable retardation.

2. Releasees more often than residents had been institutionalized through the efforts of official agencies, such as police, welfare, or

schools (72 percent as against 41 percent). The decision to institution-alize the child was more often in the hands of the families whose children remained residents than those who were released. Under-standably, those families whose children were institutionalized by an official agency were more insistent upon release of the retarded person.

3. Parents of the releasees were less willing to accept the official diagnosis of retardation as valid, and they were more optimistic that the retardates would eventually assume normal adult roles. One-third of the parents of the releasees (33 percent), as compared with 19 per-cent of the parents of the residents, did not think that their children were mentally retarded. While only 4 percent of the parents of the residents believed that their children would eventually assume normal adult roles, almost half (46 percent) of the parents of the releasees did so. It may be significant that although only a third of the parents did not think their children were retarded, almost half expressed optimism over the releasee's future. Apparently, some of the parents who either believed their children mentally retarded or were uncertain about the retardation also thought that their children would outgrow their condition. With this optimism, it is reasonable to expect parents of the eventual releasees to maintain a high degree of interest in the retardate and to continue regarding him as a family memeber.

The most pronounced finding in the Mercer study for *high* socio-economic status families was related to education of the mothers and siblings of the retardates. Consistent with Downey's findings, the parents of the residents had a higher initial socioeconomic status than that of the parents of the releasees. While 66 percent of the mothers of residents had completed or attended college, only 33 percent of the releasees' mothers had. These findings suggest that the mentally re-tarded child constitutes a greater threat to middle-class families.

In an analysis of the discharged patients at the Pacific State Hospital, Tarjan and his associates found that about two-thirds of those who had been admitted between the ages of fourteen through seventeen were discharged within four years after admission; about half of the retardates admitted at ages eighteen through twenty-four were discharged in the four-year period. In contrast, only about 10 percent of those admitted between birth and four years of age were discharged within four years, and only 20 percent of the children aged five through nine were released during that time.

Ages at admission and discharge tend to be related to the intelligence quotient of the retardate. In the Tarjan study, of those retardates with an IQ of 70 or over, about three-fourths had been discharged within four years following admission, and about 60 percent of the retardates with an IQ of 50–69 were released during that time. However, of those with an IQ of 0–19, only about 5 percent were released during the first four years in the hospital, and about 20 percent of retardates with an IQ of 0–29 were discharged. The lower the IQ, the lower is the median age of admission and the smaller are the chances of being discharged within four years after admission. The Tarjan study confirms the findings of the other studies on motivation in institutionalization and the differential turnover rates by intellectual level and age of the retardates.[26] Consistent with these results is the finding by Mercer that retardates with physical disabilities have a smaller chance of being discharged from institutions than retardates who do not present a burden of care.[27]

Windle has raised this question: What is the optimal age for discharge from an institution?[28] Reviewing studies on parole from residential institutions for the mentally retarded, Windle found no consistent relationship between age and outcome of parole. However, several studies of discharge from institutions report that the older the retardate at the time of release, the greater his chance of remaining in the community. A study by Whitney of releasees from the Elwyn Training School showed that only 2 percent of those discharged under the age of seventeen remained in the community, whereas 85 percent of those over the age of twenty-seven did so.[29] Tarjan *et al.* studied unauthorized absences from the Pacific State Hospital and found that these absences were more likely to last over one hundred days if the retardates were eighteen years of age or older. Obviously, in an unauthorized absence, there is little planning with regard to work or family relationships.[30] On the whole, retardates who go on unauthorized leaves (or escapes) are generally younger than retardates on other types of leave.[31]

In general, middle-class socioeconomic level parents with a severely mentally retarded child tend to institutionalize their child early in his life and then ignore his existence. The educable mentally retarded patients in institutions tend to come from families of low socioeconomic level, and these families often maintain an active interest in their child. The probability of discharge from the institution is greater for the educable child from a low socioeconomic level family than it is for the severely retarded child, who is generally from a middle-class home. One consequence of this situation is that middle-class families, who could be influential in the efficient operation of the institution, usually lack the interest to be active in pressure groups. The lower-class families lack both the motivation and resources to effect institutional change. They regard institutionalization as temporary, and they are incapable of effective concerted action. The parents of the retarded children, hence, cannot counteract political influences in the operation of public residential institutions.

Social Organization in Residential Institutions:
Encroachment and Defense

The ideal institution for the mentally retarded has been described as a completely authoritarian and isolated social system.[32] It would not have any turnover in personnel (either staff or inmates) except at crucial points in the lives of the inmates and staff members. The inmates would come to the institution upon birth and leave only through death. The staff members would spend their entire working careers at the institution, beginning with their first day out of training and ending with retirement. The institution would have no commerce with the outer world and would be governed by the executive officer of the institution, not by a committee or governmental department outside the institution. In other words, except for the outside necessities of giving birth to inmates or training of staff, the institution would be a self-sufficient society.

At the opposite extreme of the ideal institution would be one set up in the middle of a busy area, such as the waiting room at Grand Central Station in New York. Imagine the predicament of the superintendent who is instructed that he must maintain his organization and routine within the context of a busy railroad station and the milling throngs that pass through the station daily. Moreover, he is not supposed to use any identifying clothing or other marks to distinguish the inmates or the staff from the daily crowds. In addition, the institution is to be democratic, with all the rules determined by the various staff members and the inmates alike. In this situation, all of the commitments and pressures outside the institution permeate the norms and formal rules by which the staff and inmates operate.

The preservation of a residential institution for the mentally retarded under either of the two extremes described would be impossible. The necessity for recruitment of staff and inmates immediately opens the system to external influences. The staff and inmates come to the institution with a previous history of norms and values, and they generally continue contact with the outside world through their families, colleagues, or mass communications media. Institutional life may merely be an interlude for them; the inmates may return to the community afterwards, and the staff members may hold positions within the institution for a relatively short period in their life careers. Since the residential institution is not self-sufficient, food, clothing, books, and financial support must come from the outside. Most important, the governing body of a residential institution is almost always external. With all of these influences, the outside world is ever encroaching upon the institution. For example, the socioeconomic characteristics of retardates in institutions appear to affect the views of attendants. When Bartlett, Quay, and Wrightsman examined the attitudes of attendants toward retarded persons they found that many attendants thought most retarded persons would steal if they had the chance.[33]

On the other hand, if the institution is to be permitted to fulfill its purposes, the encroachment of the outside world must be limited. The residential institution established in the waiting room of a rail-road station presents a situation in which the external encroachment is unbounded. Without an isolated location, outsiders interfere with routines and order within the residential unit. Unless the participants can distinguish between staff, inmate, and outsider, they cannot regulate interaction within the institution. Most of all, unless commitments to persons and groups outside the institution can be subdued, the inmates and staff will tend to neglect the norms and consequent duties related to the institution itself.

The residential institution is continually faced with a struggle between indigenous and exogenous forces. The latter continually encroach upon the institutional domain, and, in defense, staff and inmates develop norms, formal rules, and customs and ceremonies to counteract the disruptive effects of the external world. Yet it must be recognized that the institution could not exist without these external forces; indeed, without some penetration by them, it could not socialize inmates to return to the outer world.

What are some of the exogenous factors that impinge upon life in the institution? They are the political climate; the ethnic and racial composition of the community; the degree of economic prosperity in the outside community; commitment to families by both inmates and staff; interest shown in the daily life of the institution by welfare agencies, parent organizations and religious groups; and the relationship between the particular institution and the educational establishments using its facilities. All of these affect the vulnerability of the residential institution to norms and values whose locus is outside.

These exogenous factors affect institutional life in various ways. Residential institutions often have high turnover in both staff and inmate populations. For example, since turnover in inmate population is related to the degree of mental retardation, those institutions with high proportions of educable rather than severely retarded individuals will be most vulnerable to external influences. In addition, the kind of influence the outside world has upon the institution depends upon the problems of that world. The institution with a high percentage of educable mentally retarded inmates will probably not have strongly organized parents' associations but will have to contend with lower-class families individually, and its inmates' vicissitudes will be those associated with lower-class existence. Finally, since age and sex are important determinants of social roles, the proportions of old versus young and male versus female inmates in the institutions will shape the kinds of difficulties that develop. Since age and sex are also related to the degree of mental retardation, the kinds of mentally retarded serviced in the institution will mold the institutional organization in certain ways. The following sections will examine some facets related to performance and turnover of staff and inmate population.

STAFF MEMBERS

This section is concerned with the role of the staff of public residential institutions not only within the institutions but as part of the labor force and professional groups. The norms and values of the workers in institutions reflect the social context in which their action occurs. Interaction of staff within the institutions is related to various factors, including: (a) partisan politics, (b) families of the inmates, (c) characteristics of the institution, (d) relationship to professional colleagues outside residential institutions, (e) the labor force of the community, and (f) the patient population. This section will focus on institutional characteristics, relations among colleagues, and the community labor force. Families and the patient population are dealt with elsewhere in this chapter.

Institutional Characteristics.   Cleland has attacked the position that small institutions for the mentally retarded are more efficient than large ones. He takes as a point of departure the suggestion Kirkbride made in 1855 that the optimal number of beds in a mental hospital should not exceed 250. Cleland suggests that there is no objective evidence to indicate that the size of the institution is related to the quality of care and treatment of the patients. He believes that the complexity of the variables that influence the effectiveness of programs and care mask the true significance of the size of the institution. First he suggests that, since institutions are social systems, not only the number of patients but the number of staff members as well should be considered in describing the population of an institution. Of the 124 state institutions for the mentally retarded listed in the 1962 directory of the American Association on Mental Deficiency, about 100 have over 500 beds. If all persons (including staff) were considered, Cleland suggests that almost all institutions on the list would have populations of over 500. A second factor he considers important is the rate of growth of the institutions. Those with a high rate of growth in patient-staff ratio, in utilization of physical facilities, and in complexity of organization face many tasks in organization. Cleland indicates that influence on patient care by such variables as quality and stability of the work force, communications channels, and location should be investigated. He points out that the attendants in institutions comprise over half of all personnel; because of their low level of education (estimated to be at the tenth grade), many difficulties arise in communication, delegation of responsibility, and discrepancies in values and treatment orientation between them and the professional staff.[34] Thus, the discrepancy between the staff's characteristics and the enormity of its tasks may be more important than the size of the institution in the effectiveness of treatment.

Relationships Among Colleagues. The professional standing of high-ranking institutional personnel affects the organization of staff and patients in residential institutions, where the allocation of resources is affected by the simultaneous pressure of overcrowding and understaffing. Especially significant in understaffing is the low prestige of psychiatrists, psychologists, and other professional persons working in state institutions.[35] For instance, the teacher in a state school has lower prestige than a public school teacher, which, naturally, affects the selection of state school teachers. According to Rettig and Pasamanick, like the psychiatrists employed in institutions, teachers in state schools place high value on the regularity and security their jobs affords and are relatively uninterested in professional recognition. Working with the mentally retarded does not affect job satisfaction. In fact, in the Pasamanick and Rettig study, the job satisfaction of state school teachers slightly exceeds that of the public school teachers.[36] Yet job satisfaction is not an adequate criterion of effectiveness as a teacher.

This lack of concern with recognition by their professional peers suggests that teachers and other professionals in state institutions tend to be "locals" rather than "cosmopolitans." A "local" professional evaluates his work from the viewpoint of the people with whom he maintains day-to-day contact; they are his reference group. The influence of state government on policies and administration would require the institution staff to be highly sensitive to the views of those in political power. The staff members, who must be attentive to their relationships with politically powerful persons inside and outside the institution, necessarily choose these groups as a reference for establishing their identity and evaluating their performance. The "cosmopolitan," on the other hand, is concerned with the evaluation of his performance by his professional peers no matter where they reside, and his primary identification is with his profession rather than with the institution. The cosmopolitan tends to focus upon research and evaluates his work in terms of its implications for his coprofessionals.

An explicit treatment ideology often provides a basis for mutual reinforcement of staff members to sustain a high level of performance.[37] This mutual reinforcement appears to operate effectively when professional, rather than hospital and political, reference groups are maintained. In contrast, local-oriented professionals may band together to restrict the amount of effort and time spent on duty. This limitation of productive activity can result from a covert understanding between the staff and the political authorities, who control personnel allocations in the institution formally and informally. Thus, the domination of the administration of residential institutions by political concerns has a profound bearing upon both the selection of professional staff and their subsequent performance.[38]

Community Labor Force.   Variables associated with the labor force in the community are especially pertinent for relatively unskilled occupations (such as attendants). The rate of turnover of attendants at state institutions for the mentally retarded depends upon various social and economic conditions in the institution and the community.

Butterfield, Barnett, and Bensberg studied the characteristics of twenty-six institutions in the southern United States. Their findings indicate that the annual rate of turnover of attendants is related positively to the ratio of professional persons (such as physicians, psychologists, and social workers) to the total number of residents and negatively to the existence of an attendant training program. Perhaps the amount of supervision by professional personnel motivates attendants to seek other positions; it may be that the professional-patient ratio is high in institutions with many severely retarded inmates who require much attention. Moreover, rates of attendant turnover are related to the socioeconomic characteristics of the county in which the institution is located. The larger the rate of unemployment in the county, the less the turnover of attendants; and the higher the population increase, the greater the turnover rate. Both of these characteristics are associated with the availability of jobs outside the institution. Being an attendant in an institution for the mentally retarded is apparently less attractive than working on the outside.[39] The ideal position for the attendant is one in which he is not visible to the professional personnel and his patients require little personal care. The combination of invisibility and an educable population may provide a congenial work setting for attendants, since both these elements are conducive to the formation of status systems which have been called "illegitimate opportunity structures," "elite delinquent structures," and "custodial hierarchical systems."[40]

In summary, the hiatus between the enormity of the tasks required and the characteristics of staff, the predilection of "local" rather than "cosmopolitan" professionals to work in residential institutions, and the reliance of institutions on marginal workers in the community for attendants and other relatively unskilled occupations—all these appear to be related to partisan political dominance over life in residential institutions. The accompanying understaffing and overcrowding locates much authority in the hands of the comparatively unskilled workers, permitting the workers to utilize the patient population for their own convenience. Since some workers themselves (such as attendants) tend to be drawn from surplus populations, their views are similar in many respects to those of the educable. Both their norms and their predicaments in handling overcrowded wards induce these workers to foster certain kinds of status systems and groupings among the patients. The character of the status organization and groups formed among the patients will be discussed in the following section.

LIVING IN THE INSTITUTION

Residential institutions for the mentally retarded exist for two purposes — the custody of the retardates and to prepare at least some of them to live in the community. Accordingly, two different staffs are generally maintained, and there are two different locations of activity. The custodial staff of an institution consists mainly of ward attendants, a nursing staff, and a housekeeping staff. The rehabilitation and welfare staff is composed of psychologists, teachers, and social workers. There is also generally a medical staff, and possibly a research staff whose contact with the patients is usually tangential and inconsequential. The custodial staff interacts with patients on the wards (or cottages) and at the work assignments in the institution. The psychologists, teachers, and social workers generally see patients in the office or the classroom. The patients come to recognize the custodial staff as holding more immediate authority over them; they see the rehabilitation staff as being there to assist them but as "outsiders" in the institution.

The immediate task of socialization of the retardates entering the institution lies in the hands of the custodial staff. As a rule, the ward attendants and nurses are responsible for the behavior of the retardates in their charge. One of the first problems of the custodial staff is to control the behavior of new patients. Accordingly, ward attendants and nurses frequently evaluate and identify their charges in terms of the length of institutionalization. Breaking the tie with the outside world is one of the institution's defenses against the encroachment of the norms and values of the external community upon institutional routines. There is usually a period, ranging from a few weeks to a few months, during which the retardates are not permitted to have visitors from the outside world. Nevertheless, the experience of the child before he is institutionalized affects his behavior on the ward.

Dentler and Mackler found that at first children whose mothers had fostered excessive dependence were more likely to exhibit high social initiative on the ward. These children, as well as those whose mothers stimulated verbalization, were able to conform to the rules of the ward and got into trouble less frequently than other children. The children who had been dependent upon their mothers seemed to behave as if the institution was to be a substitute home. However, the initial conformity seemed to decline as time went on. Later, children who were from less permissive homes learned to conform and were disciplined less frequently.

In their investigation, Dentler and Mackler noted that the ward attendants nominated the most able boys as work helpers but were themselves attracted to the smallest and least able children. The attendants thereby established an organization for the ward by rewarding the most able children for their work while fostering a continued dependence in the less able children.[41] In a study of ideology and personality of attendants in a mental hospital, Gilbert and Levinson found that they tended to be very high in authoritarianism and were oriented toward custodial rather than rehabilitative aspects of patient care.[42]

The importance of the variable of ability or intellectual functioning in status hierarchy in an institution is suggested by a study by Rosenberg, Spradlin, and Abel at the Parsons State Hospital, Kansas. They selected institutionalized retardates on the basis of high or low language ability scores and paired individuals for a series of sessions where they could interact. Each retardate was paired with another who had low ability for one series of sessions, then with one with high language ability for a second series. The quantity of verbalization in these sessions was found to be related to the comparative levels of ability of the pairs. Those retardates with low language ability spoke only to low-ability retardates, while those with high language ability spoke only to high-ability retardates. Under these conditions, there was little communication across language ability levels. On the ward this tendency would facilitate the development of cliques and social groupings comparable to social class hierarchies.[43]

The distinction between the more capable and the less capable tends to be formalized in the vocabulary of the inmates of the institutions. Marden and Farber studied determinants of social status among institutionalized mentally retarded boys on a ward at a state institution.[44] The boys in the ward they studied had a median age of almost sixteen years, a median age at admission of twelve years, a median IQ of 53, and had been in the institution a median of about four years. A preliminary study of the ward revealed that the boys labeled each other by the social classifications "high-brow" and "low-grade." These terms were used more often than others, and their meaning was understood by all the boys on the ward. The way in which the boys used these terms implied that "high-brow" was at the opposite pole of a status continuum from "low-grade," and that these terms were applicable to almost any activity on the part of a boy—working, homosexual activity, "bossing kids around," and so on.

The terms "high-brow" and "low-grade" stem from the system of nomenclature often used by staff members in state institutions. Under this system, the more severely retarded are classified as "low-grade," the less severely retarded as "high-grade." In most institutions in the United States, the term "low-grade" has become one of derision, even among the patients themselves. In the ward studied, the term "high-grade" was replaced by "high-brow," and its meaning was elaborated to include all favorable characteristics.

The boys on the ward made a further distinction between "working" boys and "class" boys. Working boys were those who held jobs in the institutional industries (the bakery, laundry, kitchen, hospital). Most of the working boys in this particular ward also attended the academic school in the institution. The class boys were those inmates who had been designated by the ward attendants to assist them in maintaining order among the other boys. They generally supervised the maintenance duties on the ward and sometimes administered punishment unofficially to nonconformists.

The fact that all class boys were assigned high-brow ratings by almost everyone on the ward indicates the importance attached to class boys. In general, being a working boy, having a high IQ (actual IQ scores were unknown to the inmates of the ward), and attendance at occupational therapy were also associated with high-brow status. Thus both the rehabilitative and custodial dimensions qualified inmates for high-brow status. However, there was a constant conflict on the ward between the working boys and the class boys. Frequently, the class boys would attempt to get the working boys to break rules so that their working privileges would be withdrawn, while the working boys would often defend low-grade inmates from the class boys.

All seventy boys on the ward in the Marden and Farber study deviated from the norms of the institution in many ways. The relationship between conformity to norms and ward status was complex. Interestingly, certain deviations were considered appropriate, while others were frowned upon as "low-grade." Particular characteristics appeared crucial for maintenance of a high-grade status. During the interviewing, the boys were asked to give their reasons for designating each of the other residents on the ward as high-brow or low-grade. The most frequent criterion used for status assignment was cleanliness or hygiene. The next category was rule-breaking behavior (for low-grades) or conformity to rules (for high-brows). These were followed by rehabilitativeness, display of power (or lack of power), behavior displays of privilege, intelligence, and sociability. Examples of reasons classified under these headings are presented below, though taken out of the context of private meanings on the ward, the appropriateness of the classification is not always apparent.

Some of the categories of reasons were reserved for high-brows or low-grades only. In other cases, if the respondent gave as a reason an item falling in a particular category, high-brow status could be predicted; but if the reverse was true, the category lacked predictive significance. The results on the reasons suggest four types of criteria for high-brow or low-grade classification:

1. *The mutually exclusive type*—hygiene, rehabilitation, and intelligence. By this criterion, virtually all the boys rated high were high-brows, and those rated low were low-grades. The reasons then constituted the most crucial variables with regard to ward status.

2. *The low category predictor* — power. In this type of criterion only low ratings are meaningful in predicting status. If the respondent said that the individual had power, he might or might not have classified that individual as a high-brow. However, if he indicated that the inmate lacked power, then he was almost certain to regard him as a low-grade.

3. *The high category predictor* — conformity and sociability. Here only high ratings are meaningful in predicting status. If the respondent said that the individual conformed or was sociable, he would probably regard him as a high-brow. But if the respondent indicated the opposite, he classified this individual as either high-brow or low-grade.

4. *The undifferentiating type*—display of privilege. In this type of criterion, only a high rating was given for any classification. The respondent considered the display of legitimate privilege as reflecting high-brow status. When he thought that the display was not legitimate, he considered this pretension as a basis for low-grade status.

This classification scheme suggests that the mutually exclusive categories constitute the basic criteria for status. The other categories then refer to activities characterized as "illegitimate" pretension of low-grades or as "legitimate" deviance of high-brows. When a boy who is essentially a low-grade according to the mutually exclusive categories tries to display power or privilege, his attempts are not accepted as legitimate by the other boys. However, if the boy who is classified as a high-brow according to the mutually exclusive categories deviates or acts in an anti-social manner which does not contradict his basic classification, this deviant or anti-social behavior is accepted as a legitimate deviance for a high-brow individual.[45]

Lack of power, which predicts only low-grade status, is primarily a variable oriented to behavior on the ward. Patients lacking power on the ward find it difficult to cope with the demands of the class boys, who consider themselves the elite of the ward. On the other hand, conformity and socialbility, which are high category predictors, characterize the working boys and other school boys more than the class boys. These categories, then, apparently refer to the rehabilitative dimension in the ward organization. Predictors of low status appear to reflect the custodial dimension; predictors of high status seem to express the rehabilitative dimension in institutional life. The low-grade individuals who lack power will apparently be in the custody of the institution for life, while the conforming and sociable individuals tend to find their way out of the institution.[46] The dual elite organization of the ward thus reflects the dual purposes of the institution.

Characterists of community status seem to be retained in the rehabilitative hierarchy in the institution. Good manners, socioeconomic characteristics, and race may be highly important in determining the positions of working boys or students in the social structure in the institution. Reversal of these characteristics may, however, occur in the custodial hierarchy with the glorification of the delinquent culture.

The delinquent culture is significant in the inmates' social organization. Edgerton and Sabagh suggest that, for educable mental retardates, the institution may represent an arena for self-aggrandizement rather than mortification. Outside the institution, the educable retardate may have been a peripheral member of a gang, a scapegoat, a butt of jokes. As one of the more intelligent inmates of the institution, he finds himself a leader and a person of many privileges. The low-grade retardates are clearly inferior to him, and the educable person recognizes that he himself is in the institution not because of a severe deformity but mainly because he had gotten into trouble either as a delinquent or as a troublemaker in school.[47]

Edgerton has written about an elite group at the Pacific State Hospital. The group he describes is similar in behavior to the class boys in the Marden and Farber study. The elite tend to have been delinquents prior to institutionalization and consider themselves as essentially normal. In the Marden and Farber study, one of the class boys remarked, "Why should I work my tail off on the outside when I can have anything I want here?" The elite in the Pacific State Hospital generally admit new members sponsored by one of their group. Ideally, one must be of appropriate age, lack physical handicaps, and demonstrate a knowledge of "hip" teenage speech, dress, behavior, and values. Possibly most important, he must demonstrate a fighting ability or toughness. (Here too, he is like the custodial-elite class boy in the Marden and Farber study.) Most often, these criteria can be met by Negroes or Mexican Americans. Girls are generally admitted by being girl friends of established elite male members. Being "hip" to current dances, newest and most popular music, style of dress and grooming, and "jive" talk characterizes the activities of the elite at the Pacific State Hospital described by Edgerton. Sexuality plays a large role in the elite group, though possibly there is much more discussion of sex than actual participation.

Edgerton indicates that the elite tend to oppose the authority of the staff, both covertly and overtly. Overt violations test the limits within which misbehavior will be tolerated. The elite members break regulations by design rather than haphazardly or impulsively.

The Marden and Farber study suggested that the custodial elite earns its keep by maintaining order among others, especially low-grade inmates. The basis for the elite group in the Edgerton study is similar to that for the class boys in the Marden and Farber investigation. Edgerton indicates that this group is necessary in that "employees who must manage these populations need help from the patients. Thus some patients must be recruited to perform tasks of work and supervision that employees cannot handle." He also indicates that "the employees have actively aided the rise of these patients to elite status by giving them preferred and suprvisory jobs . . . they can be used to 'police' wards due to their intelligence and fighting skills."[48]

Although Edgerton focuses upon the "hip" elite in the Pacific State Hospital, scattered through his report are indications of possible other elite groups of "squares." First of all, the elite group studied by Edgerton does not reserve the term "high-grade" for themselves. He indicates that the nonelite high-grades tend to buy "square" records. The "hip" elite group scorns "the high-grade who is obsequious before an employee." While the Edgerton study does not include high status patients who are more conforming and who reflect the rehabilitative dimension in social organization, their presence is probably an important element in sustaining the identity of the members of the delinquent-like elite.[49]

The incipient conflict between "hip" and "square" inmate hierarchies (or custodial versus rehabilitative elites) is also extended to the staff of residential institutions. It is significant that the custodial personnel in an institution are generally recruited from low socioeconomic levels and their jobs do not require a high level of training. Employees with these characteristics would be more prone to favor, identify with, and provide support for a "hip" elite who could help them supervise other inmates and maintain order. On the other hand, the rehabilitative staff consists of more highly trained individuals, often with graduate degrees, who more often come from middle-class backgrounds and are themselves "square." As might be expected, the rehabilitative staff support highly conforming inmates.

The role of the superintendent of the residential institution may be crucial in determining whether rehabilitative and research activities in the institution will take precedence over custodial duties. An investigation of probation officers by Ohlin, Piven, and Pappenfort indicates that regardless of their training, the officers tend to operate in terms of norms of the chief of their particular office unit. If the chief is punishment-oriented, the officers are punishment-oriented. If the chief is rehabilitation-oriented, so are the officers. The top administrator is more important than the officer's training (often as a social worker) in determining the officer's actions toward his probationers.[50]

Cleland and Peck reported that ward attendants at an institution for the mentally retarded tended to have a longer period of tenure when they were highly authoritarian.[51] Possibly, the administration in this institution favored an authoritarian perspective on the part of ward attendants and so offered a congenial atmosphere for those who conformed to this viewpoint. Since there is generally both a more frequent turnover in rehabilitation staff than in custodial staff and a reliance on the custodial staff for the "dirty work" of the institution, the custodial staff frequently hold major positions of power, and inmate elites associated with a custodial staff are encouraged.[52] Where the administration supports the custodial staff, authoritarianism will probably pervade the institution, and the custodial inmate elite will have much power.

The rehabilitative staff of an institution represents the encroachment of the outer world. These personnel must deal with outsiders, and they are oriented to the demands of the outside world on the institution. Yet the custodial staff must defend itself against demands by the rehabilitative staff in order to maintain the order and hygiene necessary for sustaining the inmate community. They can guard against the encroachment of the external world by maintaining a "hip" elite, which itself is rebelling against the conventional norms and values of society. Perhaps for this reason Edgerton found an elite group that glorified delinquent culture and Marden and Farber observed class boys who themselves were deviants in many ways. Thus it does not appear to be an accident that custodial elites tend to be "hip" and delinquent-oriented, while rehabilitative elites tend to be conventional and conforming.[53]

Cloward has suggested that residential institutions, such as prisons, have two kinds of opportunity structures representing the legitimate and illegitimate status hierarchies. The illegitimate opportunity structure is supported by the staff covertly to retain order and to avoid conflict with the inmates.[54] Toigo has applied Cloward's concepts of legitimate and illegitimate opportunity structures in a study of a training school for delinquent girls. His results reveal that some cottages are characterized by a delinquent orientation, whereas others conform more to the official norms of the institution. The delinquent-oriented cottages are organized on the basis of illegitimate opportunity structures; the conforming cottages, on the basis of legitimate means.[55]

Berk has compared the informal organization of prisoners in three prisons ranked on a continuum ranging from a strong treatment orientation to a strong custodial orientation. His criteria for determining treatment orientation are (a) the presence of a full-time counselor or treatment personnel; (b) the existence of a rehabilitative program; (c) the implementation of educational, vocational, or other rehabilitative programs. He has found the following:

> The functioning of informal leaders was . . . directly linked to the functions performed by the inmate subsystem, and, as a consequence, the informal leaders' main task in the custodial prison was one of exercising control over the behavior of other inmates. In order to effectively implement this end, the informal leadership employed the same techniques as the formal organization and developed a highly consolidated and centralized power structure and, like the formal organization, it also relied on coercion and force, rather than on consensus or cooperation to insure conformity.

In contrast, the informal leaders in the treatment institution, because the treatment goal allowed for a broader range of inmate adaptation, performed a variety of functions depending on the particular needs of the inmate and functioned more as coordinators and integrators of behavior rather than as controllers, as they did in the custodial prison. Not only did the informal leaders play very different roles in the two types of prison, but techniques of leadership differed as well, since the inmate subsystem in the treatment institution tended to be based more upon consensus and cooperation than was true of the custodial prison.[56]

In the more treatment-oriented prisons in Berk's investigation, the informal leadership structure was less centralized, and more inmates emerged as top leaders. The leaders in the custodial institution were less well-liked by others. Berk's findings are consistent with the distinction between the rehabilitative and custodial social structure found by Edgerton and by Marden and Farber in institutions for the mentally retarded. The custodial elite in Edgerton's study was in fact a highly cohesive group dependent upon coercion for maintaining its position in the inmate society. The Marden and Farber study pointed to the coexistence of a rehabilitative elite who were not as cohesive a group but were generally well-liked by the other inmates. Together, these findings portray the dual nature of social organization among inmates in residental institutions.

 SUMMARY

The dominant conception of an ideal residential institution has not changed for over a century. Since the founding of the first institution in the United States in 1848, social reformers have defined an ideal institution as one that is small in size and dedicated to the rehabilitation of the mentally retarded. From the beginning, also, public residential institutions for the mentally retarded have been subjected to political pressures, and political considerations are among the foremost in the creation and execution of policies regarding treatment and care. In the past, the relatives of the institutionalized retarded have been the politically impotent—they have tended to be poor, problem-beset members of the surplus population themselves. Only a few recently constructed research-oriented institutions associated with universities have been relatively free from political interfernece.

The vulnerability of residential institutions to political considerations has affected the social organization of residential institutions in many ways. Their locations tend to be chosen for political expediency rather than for efficient service to the retarded population. Often the institution has a dual authority system, with both the superintendent and an agent of the political party in power giving directives to the employees. There are probably political considerations in matters of purchasing, construction work, and especially in providing priorities in the admission of patients. The dominance of political considerations in the administration of institutions affects also the selection and efficiency of staff members. Generally, partly because of political party intrusions into administrative matters, the professionals in institutions are "locals" and not "cosmopolitans." Their professional status is low, and they tend to be isolated from their professional peers. Attendants can be retained only when the economic level of the county in which the institution is situated is low and competing jobs are scarce. In addition, almost every institution considers itself as understaffed and overcrowded.

The character of the inmate or patient population also affects the social organization of institutions. Less than 5 percent of the mentally retarded live in specially provided public and private residential institutions. During periods of economic depression, the rates for admission of the mildly retarded generally rise more than do those for the severely retarded. In recent years, the rates for the admission of the severely retarded have increased markedly, much more than might be warranted by economic consideration alone. The growth of the number of severely retarded persons in institutions may have resulted from the increased activity of parents' groups, greater survival rates of the severely retarded, and increased birthrates among middle-class populations.

Mental retardation alone does not account for admission to residential institutions. Persons admitted to residential institutions tend to be characterized by physical disabilities, little prior schooling even at older ages, low socioeconomic level of the families, high rates of family instability, many behavior problems and a high rate of delinquency, membership in minority groups, the presence of health and emotional problems in the family, and much contact by the families with social welfare and legal governmental agencies.

Lower-class and middle-class families differ in maintaining contact with the retardate in the institution. Middle-class families have a considerably lower rate of contact with their institutionalized member, while lower-class families maintain continual contact and expect to reabsorb the child. The continued relationship between the lower-class families and their institutionalized member serves to maintain the retardate's identity much as it was prior to his entrance into the institution. Since the retarded member generally participated in delinquent activities and was considered a behavior problem, his pre-institutional norms and view of the world would be sustained during the period of his institutionalization.

The professional staff of the institution is oriented toward the rehabilitation of the retarded. Its effectiveness, however, is limited by the professionals' lack of commitment to the expectations and standards of a "cosmopolitan" professional reference group. Instead, since the professional staff consists of "locals," the custodial staff of the institution gains considerably in power. As a result, two status hierarchies develop among the inmates. One hierarchy is oriented toward the rehabilitation staff, and inmates identified with this hierarchy conform to the conventional standards of the community. But the custodial staff (who tend to be drawn from lower-class families themselves), in order to maintain control and to minimize the amount of necessary work, nurture the formation of a custodial status hierarchy. The elite in this custodial hierarchy generally consists of delinquents, who, by virtue of their relatively high mental ability and deviant orientation, are skilled in maintaining control over other inmates. The custodial elite generally come from lower-class homes where family interest in them has been maintained, and they too may be released eventually. The norms and values of the custodial elite thereby perpetuate a private culture among both inmates and retardates in the community, which increases the probability that these retardates and their children will remain as part of the organizational surplus population in society. Although the political influence exerted upon institutional staff and policies by state government may seem remote from sustaining a culture of outcasts, the evidence suggests that there is indeed a connection between the two.

   GENERAL DISCUSSION

This chapter may have overemphasized the role of partisan politics in the operation of residential institutions for the mentally retarded. Perhaps even when partisan politics is absent, other factors in the social structure of institutions are sufficiently potent to foster the development of dual systems of organization. Some of these factors may include (a) differential communication and identity between rehabilitative and custodial staff; (b) educational and socioeconomic differences between rehabilitative and custodial personnel; (c) size and variation in social, physical, and mental characteristics of the inmate population; (d) turnover in all segments of the inmate population and staff; and (e) extent of supervision or collaboration between the rehabilitative and custodial staff. A task of future investigations will be to determine the extent to which indigenous factors (like those listed above), as compared with the influence of partisan politics or the socioeconomic characteristics of the community, affect the social structure of residential institutions.

NOTES

[1] Samuel Gridley Howe, "A Letter to the Governor of Massachusetts, Upon His Veto of a Bill, Providing for an Increase of State Beneficiaries at the School for Idiotic Children" (Boston: Ticknor and Field, 1857).

[2] President's Panel on Mental Retardation, *A Proposed Program for National Action to Combat Mental Retardation* (Washington, D.C.: U.S. Government Printing Office, October, 1962), p. 134.

[3] Howe, *op. cit.*

[4] Lewis Anthony Dexter, "On the Politics and Sociology of Stupidity in Our Society," *Social Problems,* 9 (Winter, 1962), pp. 221–228.

[5] Samuel A. Kirk, Merle B. Karnes, and Winifred D. Kirk, *You and Your Retarded Child* (New York: Macmillan, 1955), pp. 141–156. The community center proposal will be described in some detail in the Epilogue to this book.

[6] Howe, *op. cit.*

[7] *Ibid.* Howe was one of the three commissioners appointed by the legislature in 1846 to investigate conditions of the mentally deficient in Massachusetts.

[8] *Ibid.*

[9] Anselm Strauss and Melvin Sabshin, "Large State Mental Hospitals," *Archives of General Psychiatry,* 5 (December, 1961), pp. 565–577. Quotations from pages 570–571.

[10] See Louis H. Orzack, "Role Implications of Change in a New Organization." paper presented at Fifth World Congress of Sociology, International Sociological Association, Washington, D.C., September, 1962.

[11] Gunnar Dybwad, *Challenges in Mental Retardation* (New York: Columbia University Press, 1964), p. 117.

[12] C. E. Meyers, E. G. Sitkei, and C. A. Watts, "Attitudes Toward Special Education and the Handicapped in Two Community Groups," *American Journal of Mental Deficiency,* 71 (July, 1966), pp. 78–84.

[13] President's Panel on Mental Retardation, *op. cit.,* p. 131.

[14] Herbert Goldstein, "Social Aspects of Mental Deficiency," Ed.D. dissertation, University of Illinois, 1957, p. 116.

[15] Max Culver, "Intergenerational Social Mobility Among Families with a Severely Mentally Retarded Child," unpublished Ph.D. dissertation, University of Illinois, 1967.

16 Richard A. Cloward, "Social Class and Private Social Agencies," *Proceedings of the Annual Meeting of the Council on Social Work Education*, 1963, p. 132; August B. Hollingshead and Frederick C. Redlich, *Social Class and Mental Illness* (New York: Wiley, 1958); Saul Harrison, John F. McDermott, Paul T. Wilson, and Jules Schrager, "Social Class and Mental Illness in Children," *Archives of General Psychiatry*, 13 (November, 1965), pp. 411–417.

17 In their analysis of factors in the institutionalization of retardates from the waiting list for admission to Pacific State Hospital in California, Sabagh, Eyman, and Cogburn found that patients from families with relatively high incomes tended to be admitted more speedily than those from low-income families. Moreover, in a regression equation that included behavioral and psychological variables, family income was the most important factor in accounting for speed of institutionalization. (Georges Sabagh, Richard K. Eyman, and Donald N. Cogburn, "Speed of Hospitalization: A Study of a Preadmission Waiting List Cohort in a Hospital for the Retarded," *Social Problems*, 14 [Fall, 1966], pp. 119–128.)

18 See Chapter 6, "Mental Retardation: A Problem in Social Reform."

19 Illinois Department of Public Health, "The Waiting List, A Study of the Mentally Retarded," A Report to the Interdepartmental Committee on Mental Retardation, December, 1965.

20 Gerhart Saenger, *Factors Influencing the Institutionalization of Mentally Retarded Individuals in New York City*, A Report to the New York State Interdepartmental Health Resources Board, January, 1960.

21 In their analysis of children on a waiting list for the Pacific State Hospital in California, Sabagh, Eyman, and Cogburn found that "patients who have at least one living sibling at home may be admitted more swiftly than those with no living siblings." Sabagh, Eyman, and Cogburn, *op. cit.*, p. 122.

22 Bernard Farber, William C. Jenné, and Romolo Toigo, "Family Crisis and the Decision to Institutionalize the Retarded Child," *Council for Exceptional Children, NEA, Research Monograph*, Series A, Number 1, 1960.

23 Kenneth J. Downey, "Parents' Reasons for Institutionalizing Severely Mentally Retarded Children," *Journal of Health and Human Behavior*, 6 (Fall, 1965), pp. 163–169.

24 Kenneth J. Downey, "Parental Interest in the Institutionalized, Severely Mentally Retarded Child," *Social Problems*, 11 (Fall, 1963), pp. 185–193.

25 Jane Mercer, "Social System Perspective and Clinical Perspective: Frames of Reference for Understanding Career Patterns of Persons Labeled as Mentally Retarded," *Social Problems*, 13 (Summer, 1965), pp: 18–34.

26 George Tarjan *et al.*, "The Natural History of Mental Deficiency in a State Hospital," *A.M.A. Journal of Diseases of Children*, 96 (July, 1958), pp. 64–70.

27 Jane R. Mercer, "Patterns of Family Crisis Related to Reacceptance of the Retardate," *American Journal of Mental Deficiency*, 71 (July, 1966), pp. 19–32.

28 Charles Windle, "Prognosis of Mental Subnormals," *Monograph Supplement to American Journal of Mental Deficiency*, 66 (March, 1962), No. 5.

29 E. A. Whitney, "A Statistical Study of Children Admitted and Discharged from Elwyn," *American Journal of Mental Deficiency*, 53 (1948), pp. 182–186. Extent of retardation seems to be a factor in optimal age. Brown, Windle, and Stewart studied severely retarded individuals who had been placed in a family care program. Retardates under fifteen years of age more often than older patients remained in placement for at least two years. (S. J. Brown, C. Windle, and E. Stewart, "Statistics on a Family Care Program," *American Journal of Mental Deficiency*, 64 (1959), pp. 535–542.

30 George Tarjan et. al., "Effectiveness of Hospital Release Programs," *American Journal of Mental Deficiency*, 64 (1960), pp. 609–617.

31 Charles Windle and Harvey F. Dingman, "The Front and Back Doors of a Hospital for Mental Defectives," *Training School Bulletin*, 56 (1959), pp. 8–14.

32 F. L. Wells, "The State School as a Social System," *Journal of Psychology*, 5 (1938), pp. 119–124.

33 C. J. Bartlett, Lorene C. Quay, and L. S. Wrightsman, Jr., "A Comparison of Two Methods of Attitude Measurement: Likert-Type and Forced-Choice," *Educational and Psychological Measurement*, 20 (1960), pp. 699–704.

34 Charles C. Cleland, "Evidence on the Relationship Between Size and Institutional Effectiveness: A Review and Analysis," *American Journal of Mental Deficiency*, 70 (November, 1965), pp. 423–431. See also J. J. Parnicky and Richard C. Zigler, "Attendant Training—A National Survey," *Mental Retardation*, 2 (1964), pp. 76–82.

35 Benjamin Pasamanick, Salomon Rettig, and Frank Jacobson, "A Comparative Study of Status, Job Satisfaction, and Factors Making for Job Satisfaction of State Employed and Private Practicing Psychiatrists," paper presented at annual meeting of American Psychiatric Association, N.D.

36 Salomon Rettig and Benjamin Pasamanick, "A Comparative Analysis of the Status and Job Satisfaction of State School and Public School Teachers." Mimeographed.

37 Rose Laub Coser, "Alienation and the Social Structure: Case Analysis of a Hospital," in Eliot Friedson, ed., *The Hospital in Modern Society* (New York: Free Press, 1963), pp. 231–265.

38 See Peter M. Blau and W. Richard Scott, *Formal Organizations* (San Francisco: Chandler Publishing Company, 1962), pp. 64–67; and Alvin W. Gouldner, "Cosmopolitans and Locals," *Administrative Science Quarterly*, 2 (1957–1958), pp. 281–306 and 444–480.

39 Earl C. Butterfield, Charles D. Barnett, and Gerard J. Bensberg, "Some Objective Characteristics of Institutions for the Mentally Retarded: Implications for Attendant Turnover Rate," *American Journal of Mental Deficiency*, 70 (March, 1966), pp. 786–794.

40 See the following section, pp. 208–216. Some institutions, such as Porterville in California, place much emphasis upon discouraging preferential treatment to patients. Attendants and the ward nursing personnel are apparently rewarded for discouraging the formation of "juvenile delinquent groups" and "the more delinquently oriented patient tends to be eliminated from the Porterville . . . waiting list." See James J. Shelton, John C. Schoenherr, and George E. North, "Lack of a Patient Elite: Ethnography in a Hospital for the Mentally Retarded," *American Journal of Mental Deficiency*, 70 (November, 1965), pp. 389–392.

41 Robert A. Dentler and Bernard Mackler, "The Socialization of Retarded Children in an Institution," *Journal of Health and Human Behavior*, 2 (Winter, 1961), pp. 243–252.

42 Doris C. Gilbert and Daniel Levinson, "Ideology, Personality, and Institutional Policy in the Mental Hospital," *Journal of Abnormal and Social Psychology*, 53 (1956), pp. 263–271.

43 S. Rosenberg, J. E. Spradlin, and S. M. Abel, "Interaction among Retarded Children as a Function of Their Relative Language Skills," *Journal of Abnormal and Social Psychology*, 63 (1961), pp. 402–410.

44 Philip W. Marden and Bernard Farber, "High-Brow Versus Low-Grade Status Among Institutionalized Mentally Retarded Boys," *Social Problems*, 8 (Spring, 1961), pp. 300–312.

45 *Ibid.*, p. 311.

[46] The studies by Zigler indicate that retarded "children coming from relatively good homes evidenced a much greater increase in their motivation for social reinforcers than did children coming from more socially deprived homes." Edward Zigler, "Motivational Determinants in the Performance of Retarded Children," *American Journal of Orthopsychiatry*, 36 (October, 1966), p. 851.

[47] See Robert B. Edgerton and Georges Sabagh, "From Mortification to Aggrandizement: Changing Self-Conception in the Careers of the Mentally Retarded," *Psychiatry*, 25 (1962), pp. 263–272.

[48] Robert B. Edgerton, "A Patient Elite: Ethnography in a Hospital for the Mentally Retarded," *American Journal of Mental Deficiency*, 68 (November, 1963), p. 383.

[49] The focus on the elite retardates does not imply the lack of any organization among the severely retarded. For example, see Craig MacAndrew and Robert Edgerton, "On the Possibility of Friendship," *American Journal of Mental Deficiency*, 70 (January, 1966), pp. 612–621.

[50] Lloyd Ohlin, Herman Piven, and Donnell M. Pappenfort, "Major Dilemmas of the Social Worker in Probation and Parole," *National Probation and Parole Association Journal*, 2 (1956), pp. 211–225.

[51] Charles C. Cleland and Robert F. Peck, "Psychological Determinants of Tenure in Institutional Personnel," *American Journal of Mental Deficiency*, 63 (1959), pp. 876–888.

[52] Thomas J. Scheff, "Control over Policy by Attendants in a Mental Hospital," *Journal of Health and Human Behavior*, 2 (1961), pp. 93–105.

[53] The distinction between the delinquent and rehabilitative social structures in an institution may extend to such diverse activities as homosexuality or dating. Cf. Robert B. Edgerton and Harvey F. Dingman, "Good Reasons for Bad Supervision: 'Dating' in a Hospital for the Mentally Retarded," *Psychiatric Quarterly Supplement*, 1964, Part 2 pp. 1–13.

[54] R. A. Cloward, "Social Control in the Prison," *Theoretical Studies in Social Organization of the Prison* (New York: Social Science Research Council, 1960), Pamphlet 15.

[55] Romolo Toigo, "Illegitimate and Legitimate Cultures in a Training School for Girls," *Proceedings of the Rip Van Winkle Clinic*, 3 (Summer, 1962), pp. 3–29. Quote on pages 24–25.

[56] Bernard B. Berk, "Organizational Goals and Inmate Organization," *American Journal of Sociology*, 71 (March, 1966), pp. 532–533.

9. 🌿

Community Relationships

Many evaluation studies have utilized profiles to describe the functioning of individuals and groups. A test of psycholinguistics, for example, may indicate that an individual can "encode" and "decode" well but that a deficiency in the use of language lies in the association processes. A test of psychological functioning may indicate that there is a large discrepancy between an individual's ability to remember numbers, apply reasoning, and use words, on the one hand, and his spatial perception, on the other. These profiles indicate disabilities that prevent individuals from acting "normally." Thus a blind person is normal in many other respects; a deaf person would be normal if only he could hear; a crippled person would be normal if only he could repair his limbs; a mentally ill individual would be normal if only he could heal his sick mind. Similarly, the "outsider" who is a jazz musician or a criminal may be quite conventional in most aspects of his life with regard to age, sex habits, family life, educational background, and moral values. The marked stigmata in an individual's social profile require some means of adjustment to minimize their effect on his interaction with others and consequently on his life career.

For mentally retarded persons, the fact of mental retardation itself is not the major departure from normal life in most instances. The severely mentally retarded individual generally suffers from physical deformities, inability to communicate adequately, and severe limitations on activity. The educable retarded individual generally has faced economic privation, unstable social relationships in the family, and other forms of social handicap that make him unacceptable to most normal individuals. In neither case is mental retardation *the* stigma that projects itself into an otherwise normal situation. For these reasons, mental retardation is not an isolated kind of problem with unique stigmata; it intrudes into numerous kinds of social and medical problems.[1]

If mentally retarded persons have a variety of social and medical deficits, labeling a child as mentally retarded probably will not have drastic consequences by itself. The position taken in this book is that this labeling is a ritual for legitimating the child's inclusion in the surplus population. Because of a variety of other problems, the child would eventually be part of that population anyway. The ritual of labeling seems necessary in American society because some explanation must be given as to why in a society stressing equal opportunity this particular child is doomed to failure. Hence, in the view taken in this book, labeling is regarded by the official agencies of the society as a justification for the medical and social failures of the incompetent child.

This chapter deals first with the marginality of the educable mentally retarded. It describes the occupational life of the mildly retarded and the growth of special education programs. The chapter then discusses the school and community relationships of the severely mentally retarded.

Growth of Educational Programs for the Educable Mentally Retarded

Although the modern movement toward the education of the mentally retarded began with Itard and the Wild Boy of Aveyron, the diffusion of programs for retarded children living at home was sporadic until the beginning of the twentieth century. Special classes for the retarded underwent an extensive development in Saxony in the 1860s. In England, the first special school was founded in Leicester in 1892. The first sustained American special class for mentally deficient children was established in 1896 in Providence, Rhode Island. Other classes were initiated, but hopes for them were too optimistic, and preparation was poor. In Cleveland, Ohio:

About 14 of the most serious cases of imbecility in the most congested quarters of the city were gathered together and a superior, conscientious teacher placed in charge. The good folk responsible for this inauguration were united in their belief that the pupils would soon become as normal children, once they were properly taught. The teacher heroically attacked the problem, but before the close of the school year, all were aware that their experiment was doomed to failure. At the close of the term, the class was disbanded—the imbeciles returned to their homes, probably not much the worse for the "schooling," but the poor teacher suffered a mental collapse which necessitated a sojourn at our capitol State Hospital.[2]

By 1911, however, there were public school classes for mentally deficient children in ninety-nine American cities.[3] From 1900 to 1930, there was a steady increase in the number of special classes in public schools in the United States. For example, in 1922, there were 23,000 children enrolled in public school classes for the mentally retarded. During the economic depression of the 1930s, special class programs declined. After World War II, there was again an increase in the number of these classes. In 1948, about 87,000 mentally retarded children were enrolled in special classes; ten years later, the number of children enrolled had risen to about 213,000.[4] Since then the rise has been even sharper. By 1963, about 390,000 mentally retarded children were in public-school special classes.[5] There are now classes not only in preschools and elementary schools but in the high schools as well. In Illinois alone, in 1963 there were about 380 special classes for educable mentally retarded children outside the city of Chicago.[6]

Why did the number of educational programs for the educable mentally retarded grow rapidly in the years 1900 to 1930, and then again after World War II? The first period of rapid growth corresponds to the period of high immigration rates and the presence of a large segment of foreign-born and rural-born population in the cities. Significantly, the major cities, especially on the East Coast, were among the leaders in developing classes for the mentally retarded. In these cities there was a large segment of low-socioeconomic-status foreign and rural migrants.

During the 1900 to 1930 era, the conception of the mentally retarded as "neuropaths" was prevalent; they were believed to be the end product of generations of degenerate living. It was thought that, by emphasizing manual, concrete work for them, instead of academic, abstract subjects, the retarded could be trained to be useful in society. Through "decent" living, not only might further degeneracy be impeded but the genetic stock might actually be improved. Thus it was not accidental that people like Goddard, who popularized the theory of genetic degeneracy through his work on the Kallikaks, were active in the special education movement during the first quarter of the twentieth century.

Following World War II, the emphasis upon achievement in education was stimulated by the technological advances of the late 1940s and the 1950s. Automation made greater demands on literacy, and technical understanding required reliable and stable individuals to operate and maintain complex machinery. The demand for unskilled and semiskilled workers declined. During this time, some special educators began to define the cutting point for mental retardation at IQ 80 or higher rather than at the traditional 70 or 75. The increase in intellectual demand thereby produced a corresponding need for removing the mentally retarded from the regular classrooms (where they might impede the progress of others) and for providing them with training appropriate to their apparent capacities.

While both eras of expansion of special education facilities represented attempts to reform the retarded population, the retardates selected for these classes were chosen because they were failures, not because of their incompetence. Moreover, failure implied not merely the inability to perform intellectual tasks, but to behave appropriately in the classroom, as well. Here again, being mentally retarded was a contributing but not a crucial factor affecting the retardates' lives.

Educational Programs and Labeling
the Mildly Mentally Retarded

Not all children who have been diagnosed as mentally retarded are in special classes. In some school systems, mildly retarded children are "socially promoted" until they reach an age when they can withdraw from school legally. In other systems, they are retained in lower grades year after year. Often, however, educable retarded children may be able to perform well enough in the regular classes so that they do not seem out of place there. With increasing age, however, the discrepancy between normal and retarded children increases.

This section discusses the consequences of labeling children as educable mentally retarded. It deals with (a) the general problem of accuracy in labeling, (b) labeling the child in the regular classroom, (c) labeling the child through special-class placement, and (d) the effects of labeling on the child's life outside of school.

ACCURACY IN LABELING

The use of labels by personnel of agencies dealing with the handicapped has been investigated by Krause. In his study of factors in the duration of residence in mental hospitals, Krause developed a series of propositions for investigation. These propositions pertain to the extent to which disabilities of individuals conform to those defined legally or in terms of treatment categories. There are some handicapped individuals whose disability undoubtedly fits into the legal or treatment categories; these are the "normal cases." There are others whose disabilities are harder to classify; they are marginal cases. The labels actually refer only to "normal cases."[7]

The propositions formulated by Krause can be reworded to apply to labeling in mental retardation:

1. The more labels used in an agency, the more precise and valid they will be. Presumably the multiplicity of labels reflects the number of effective treatment programs.
2. The greater the number of marginal patients, the fewer labels will be applied. Accordingly, the preciseness and validity of the labels will be impaired.
3. The power of the patients to choose agencies or to continue treatment is directly related to the preciseness and validity of the labels applied in the agency. Patients from low socioeconomic level families generally have little power to choose agencies and, therefore, fall into the marginal category disproportionately.
4. The more scientific the body of knowledge utilized by professionals in dealing with patients, the more valid and precise are the labels. In mental retardation, since the etiology in most cases (especially among educable retardates) is unknown, often labels must be inaccurate and invalid.[8]

Perhaps there is relationship between a marginality of cases and the definition of retardation as "deviance." The mental retardation label should be viewed in the context of other labels applied to individuals in regard to socioeconomic, ethnic, racial, sexual, personality, and aesthetic attributes. The stereotypical educable retardate is probably a poverty-stricken, ugly, coarse, repulsive, Negro or white hillbilly male. Inconsistency between labels, like the status inconsistency described by Lenski and others, operates to make an individual case a marginal one.[9] Investigation is needed to determine how, in either daily interaction or professional disposition, this label inconsistency is handled. Possibly, the more that labels other than "retardation" enter into decisions, the greater emphasis is given to the definition of mental retardation as a form of deviance.

LABELING IN REGULAR CLASSROOMS

Several studies have indicated that retarded children in the regular classes tend to be derogated and generally disliked, if not ignored, by other children. However, the basis for this rejection is not their stupidity but their lack of attention to social amenities. They are disliked because they are dirty, loud, belligerent, aggressive, and "behavior problems." Their stupidity is merely a contributing factor in defining their position in the classroom.

Johnson undertook a sociometric study of educable mentally retarded children in regular classes in grades one through five in two communities without special classes. There were thirty-nine children with IQs of 69 or below. These children were generally isolates and/ or were rejected by their classmates because of reprehensible behavior traits.[10]

Because these attitudes might have reflected the backwardness of the school system in which the study was made, Johnson and Kirk repeated this study in a school system with a more "progressive" reputation. The results were similar; the retarded children in the regular classes were found to be isolated or rejected despite the teachers' efforts to encourage other children to include the retardates in their activities. A later study by Baldwin in a different school system showed comparable results.[11]

LABELING THROUGH SPECIAL CLASS PLACEMENT

Ordinarily, when retarded children are placed in special classes, the decision is made not solely on the basis of tested intellectual ability, but because they disrupt classroom routines and interfere with the other pupils. "The child who is difficult to handle, the child who is learning nothing from his exposure to a regular classroom, the child who has remained in the same grade for several years, and the brain-injured child of intelligent parents who seek special placement for him —these children are more likely to be singled out for placement in a special class."[12] In most communities, special classes are generally filled to their legal limit, and usually the younger, relatively brighter and more competent children must wait for admission.

Because of this greater probability of selecting problem children for special class placement, comparisons between the consequences of special class versus regular class placement are difficult to discern. Ordinarily, there are no major differences in achievement between the regular and special class children, and there is some indication that the educable mentally retarded children in regular classes are, in fact, superior in academic achievement. For example, Mullen and Itkin found that retardates in a regular class gained more in arithmetic than the special class children did. However, the differences may result from the selection of children for special classes precisely because of problem behavior.[13]

Goldstein and his associates undertook a study to determine how the school's labeling and treatment of a child as mentally retarded affected his life when there had been no prior experience of failure academically. They administered intelligence tests to six-year-old children entering school for the first time in three counties in central Illinois. Of the approximately 120 children who scored below 85 on both the Primary Mental Abilities and the Stanford-Binet tests, half were placed in a newly organized special education program; the others were permitted to continue in the regular classes. At the end of four years, the two groups were compared. During the course of the study, the IQs of some of the children rose. Separate analyses were made for children with terminal IQs of 81 or above and for those with IQs of 80 or below. The results of the analyses were as follows:

1. For the children with higher IQs, the comparison group (the children in the regular classes) attained somewhat higher academic achievement scores in reading, arithmetic, and basic social information.
2. Among children with lower IQs (80 or below), the special class children excelled in all three academic areas under investigation.

The results of the analysis of academic achievement data suggest that the special class is beneficial to children whose IQs are 80 and below but not an effective educational setting for children who are usually classified as borderline or slow learners. The study is especially significant in that it included children who later functioned intellectually in the normal range but were initially classified as mentally retarded. These children suffered slightly in academic achievement by being placed in the special classes. However, being classified as mentally retarded did not appreciably revise their life chances. In some ways, it may have improved their ability to get along in the world in that the special classes were smaller and the children were not under as much pressure to attain academic excellence.[14]

LABELING AND RELATIONSHIPS OUTSIDE OF SCHOOL

Various kinds of social relationships can be subsumed under non-school interaction. This section will treat the following topics with regard to the effects of labeling a child as educable mentally retarded: (a) family, (b) interaction with friends and neighbors, (c) community relationships, and (d) the retardates' view of their world.

Family   Few studies have been undertaken to determine the consequences for family relationships of the educable retarded label. In an investigation reported by Goldstein, Moss, and Jordan, mothers were asked to compare their children with other children on school learning, quickness in "catching on," ability to do numbers, and in reading by themselves. Mothers of children in special classes tended to see their children in a less derogatory manner than mothers with retarded children in regular classes.[15]

As part of the same investigation, Meyerowitz compared children who had been placed in a special class with (a) those who were permitted to remain in the regular grades and (b) a group of normal children. All of the children were six years of age and had just entered school a few months previous to the investigation. He compared their mothers with mothers of severely retarded children.[16] The questions used in this study consisted of a unidimensional scale to test the demands of the child on the mother. The mother was asked to indicate the extent to which (a) the particular child needs patience and understanding, (b) he is hard to handle, (c) the parent feels worn out from taking care of the child, and (d) the parent's life revolves around the child. Meyerowitz found that the demands felt by the mothers of the educable children were intermediate between those of the parents of severely retarded and normal children. The mothers of the educable children in special classes perceived their child as making somewhat greater demands than mothers whose mildly retarded children had been permitted to remain in regular classes. Yet the difference between these two groups was not as great as that between either of them and the mothers of the severely retarded on the one hand and the normal children's mothers on the other. The Meyerowitz study suggests that, although the label of "mentally retarded" has some effect, the child's behavior is the major determinant of his interaction with his mother and her perception of him.[17]

Meyerowitz also reported that two years later there was little difference between regular and special class groups in parents' perceptions of their children's abilities. Children in the regular class were more often seen by their parents as "below average" in academic abilities (25 percent versus about 17 percent).[18]

Friends and Neighbors   Research indicates that the consequences of the mentally retarded label for interaction with friends and neighbors are superficial. In a neighborhood sociometric study, Meyerowitz found that retarded children in the regular class tended to interact to a slightly greater degree with normal children than did educable children in a special class but that neither retarded group was overtly rejected by the other children in the neighborhood. The tendency for regular-class retarded children to interact more with other neighborhood children reflects the continued contact with them in the school, since the special-class children were taken on buses to other locations. Thus the effect on children who are labeled as mentally retarded is not necessarily derogatory but may be the result of differential opportunities for interaction.[19]

The consequences of being labeled mentally retarded for social relationships outside of school are also indicated in a study of educable mentally retarded high school boys in Illinois by Fuchigami.[20] Unlike the classroom, where children are thrown together through more or less formal selection procedures, out-of-school friendships are voluntary. The scapegoating of retarded individuals in school may not carry over to the neighborhood. Fuchigami's study involved interviews with 111 educable retarded boys between the ages of sixteen and eighteen who were in special classes in high schools. His analysis revealed the following:

1. The boys generally reported more participation in neighborhood activities than in social activities connected with school.
2. The boys seemed to have two sets of friends—one in school and the other in the neighborhood. They reported more friends who

were of normal intelligence in the neighborhood than in school. Most friends were boys.

3. Those respondents with IQ scores over 60 generally participated in more social activities both in school and in the neighborhood than did boys with lower IQs. The retardates with IQs over 60 also reported more friends of normal intelligence.

4. Those respondents who went to a school not attended by others in their neighborhood especially tended to have educable retarded friends in school but friends of normal intelligence in the neighborhood. Those who attended the same school as others in their neighborhood, however, tended to have friends of normal intelligence both inside and outside of school.

5. Dating was related to the level of intelligence, but only a small proportion of retarded boys at any level of IQ attended school dances or athletic events with a date. Fewer than 10 percent of the respondents included girls as their best friends in or out of school. Boys from higher income levels tended to date more often than boys in the low income group. Here again, the multiple social handicapping of retarded individuals is apparent.

The Fuchigami study suggests that the labeling of the retarded has more relevance for the social interaction of educable boys in school than outside of school. Among boys who have been labeled as retarded, the level of intelligence does affect patterns of friendship and courtship. The findings are further complicated by the debilitating effects of low income on participation in school activities and dating. Yet the educable boys from low income families reported more friends of normal intelligence outside of school than the boys in the high income group did. In same-sex relationships among low income groups, mental retardation apparently is not a significant label.

Community and School Relationships   Although the presence of special education services in the community may result in the labeling of a large proportion of children as mentally retarded, the consequences of special class attendance do not seem so severe as those of institutionalization. Institutionalization removes the individual from possible contact with friends of normal intelligence and takes him out of conventional society.

Henderson studied admissions to institutions during a ten-year period. He found that more boys than girls were admitted, and the number of admissions increased steadily from age six to sixteen. The average IQ of the group admitted to the institutions was lower than that of children typically accepted in special classes in public schools. The large communities tended to have a higher rate of commitment of educable mentally retarded children than the smaller communities. In some counties special classes had been established during the first part of the ten-year period. Henderson's analysis revealed that these counties showed a *decrease* in admission rate from the first to the last half of the ten-year period studied, while counties of comparable population size, but without special classes, showed a slight increase in rate during that time. Inasmuch as educable retarded children tend to be institutionalized for delinquency and dependency, his study suggests that the presence of special education classes cuts down on the deviant behavior of retarded children.[21]

Like institutions, special classes for the educable mentally retarded often contain many children who, aside from learning problems, are troublesome or delinquent. Carriker compared retarded adults who had been in special classes in Omaha and Lincoln, Nebraska, with retarded persons who remained in regular classes. He found that the special class retardates more often had lived in homes for dependent children and had juvenile court records. As adults, however, there were few differences between the two groups. In both groups, about half of the men and most of the women were married, 50 percent had court records as adults, and 60 to 70 percent were entirely self-sufficient financially. Carriker suggested that the special class may have compensated for earlier social deficits.[22]

An investigation by Porter and Milazzo compared retarded adults who had previously attended special classes with retardates whose school experience had been restricted to regular classes. There was little difference in home and family conditions for the two groups. The special-class individuals, however, showed a more adequate community adjustment. While none of the special-class retardates had ever been arrested, a third of the regular-class adults had been in police custody at some time. Most of the special-class individuals reported that they attend church regularly, but only a minority of the regular-class retardates were church attenders. The greatest differences were related to employment. Seventy-five percent of the special-class retardates but only 17 percent of the regular-class individuals were employed fulltime. Two-thirds of the regular-class retardates had never been employed; all of the special-class individuals had held jobs.[23] The Porter and Milazzo findings are thus consistent with the

Henderson and Carriker studies in indicating that special classes for educable retarded children seem to decrease the amount of deviant behavior exhibited by the retardates and serve to minimize the potential effects of being retarded in contemporary society.

The Retardates' View of Their World   If labeling has a significant effect on the socialization of the educable mentally retarded, their view of the world can be expected to reflect this influence. Accordingly, studies of differences in perceptions by retarded and intellectually normal individuals might reveal this influence. In Richardson's investigation, he assumed that each child has a fundamental core of categories which he uses with great consistency even when there is considerable variation in persons described, in the settings in which the persons are described, and in the actual behavior. The kinds of experiences the children faced were believed to determine the nature of these cores of descriptive categories. Comparing children of low intelligence (IQ roughly 70–85) with children of high intelligence (IQ above 115), Richardson found that the children with low intelligence tended to refer to the views of others and to statements about obligations and conventional norms more frequently. He found also that retarded children tended to use terms relating to aggressiveness more often (being mean, being mad at someone, teasing, or causing trouble). The extent to which Richardson's findings were a result of the peculiar experience of children who have difficulty in understanding or comprehending social reality, or whether these differences occurred because of differential experiences due to being labeled as "mentally retarded," cannot be determined.[24]

Richardson and his associates also investigated reactions to physical disabilities. They found that children who are mentally retarded (IQ below 100) ranked preferences in terms of types of physical disabilities differently from those children who are not retarded. However, a group of institutionalized retarded children provided a set of rank order preferences different from those of mentally retarded children living in the community. Because the retarded residing in institutions are constantly exposed to a variety of physical disabilities, the difference between the two retarded groups may represent only this situation. In fact, the institutionalized mentally retarded children were more similar in their rank order of preferences to a group of children residing in a psychiatric institution than they were to the mental retardates living in the community.[25]

The findings of the various investigations suggest that there is no clear-cut behavioral stigma by which mentally retarded persons (especially at the educable level) can be readily identified. The cues for identity in ordinary social situations are those which are also found among other forms of deviance or social degradation. These tendencies suggest a lack of consensus in defining when a person is mentally retarded, especially at low socioeconomic levels. For example, one study compared teachers' nominations of fifth-to-eighth-grade students as possibly mentally retarded (IQ under 85) with actual scores on a Stanford-Binet test. The data indicated that, unlike other teachers, those in an "ethnic" school with mainly Negro and Mexican-American children failed to nominate the majority of the children found by the test to be mentally retarded.[26] This lack of consensus prevents mental retardation from becoming a primary determinant of the educable retardate's life chances. Instead, various elements of degradation intrude into the social relationships of persons who also happen to be retarded.

Probably, unless institutionalization occurs, the label (or the fact) of mild mental retardation itself is not the primary determinant of the future course of the child's life. Instead, in combination with relationships with others in the school, home, and neighborhood, the retardation may intensify existing problems in social relations. It may provide an additional reason for scapegoating, an additional handicap in dating and recreation, or a greater certainty of continued low economic position. Yet, if the child remains in the community, being educably mentally handicapped may not be the greatest obstacle interfering with his life chances.

Occupations of the Educable Mentally Retarded

This section describes, first, the social context that provides meaning to occupations and, second, the ability of the educable retarded population to obtain and hold jobs.

Social Context of Occupations

One of the characteristics of populations in the low socioeconomic levels is their diverse and unsteady occupational histories. Various sociologists have made a distinction between determinate and indeterminate career patterns. In a determinate career pattern, the person starts at the bottom in an occupation, and, by observable degrees, he moves from position to position within that occupation until he arrives at a point he deems "success." The university teacher who begins at the rank of instructor and is then promoted through full professorship represents one example. Another is the physician who achieves success through obtaining a more lucrative practice as time goes on or who is promoted through the ranks in a research hospital. The indeterminate career pattern, however, shows an individual taking a variety of types of employment throughout his lifetime. One year he may be a used-car salesman, the next a construction worker, the third year a store clerk, then an automobile salesman again, and afterwards perhaps a real-estate salesman.[27]

The interpretation is that the indeterminate career is fraught with uncertainty and anxiety. The individual is always in danger of being fired, either through his own incompetence, through failures in interpersonal relationships, through business slumps, or through technological change. The implication is that if the lower-class individual could stay on a single job and maintain a single skill he would do so. This point of view therefore implicitly regards the lower-class individual who shifts from occupation to occupation as being inferior to the individual who stays with a particular occupation. This perspective elevates specialization in occupation into an ethic.

But lower socioeconomic populations, as organizationally surplus, may take a different point of view. The primary task of individuals, according to lower-class perspective, is to survive. The uncertainty of any single occupation makes it desirable to be proficient in a number of occupations. Having once worked in a particular occupation, the individual can then claim this experience in seeking future employment. The aim in an occupational career under these conditions is not to achieve greater specialization in a particular occupation but to learn a variety of skills that might increase employability. Without specialized skills, an individual may find paths to upward social mobility closed. At the same time, however, he finds a variety of generally unskilled or semiskilled jobs open to him because of his diversity of experience.

Diversity as opposed to specialization as a mode of occupational socialization has a variety of consequences. First of all, the individual must regard his work and his avocations in terms of the marketable experience that they will provide. Second, he inevitably sees himself as manipulated by the whims of the labor market and his employers. Accordingly, economic considerations such as wages, job security, and fringe benefits achieve greater importance in choosing one's "life's work" than personal interest, compatibility of the work with his personality, and special qualifications.[28] Third, he develops a distaste for those individuals who rely upon specialization in particular occupations which carry them through their entire careers. His opinion is that these individuals do not have diverse kinds of work experience as insurance against economic adversity. A "real man" can do anything.

The lower-class perspective can be observed in other contexts. The residents of a northwestern community, Port Haven, provide an example of the population whose work careers are based upon diversity rather than specialization. During his lifetime (or perhaps concurrently) a man may engage in numerous income-producing activities of different kinds. There is an emphasis in Port Haven upon a man's being self-sufficient.

> This was a frontier area only recently and in the experience and memory of people living today. The pioneer family had to be self-sufficient in many things in order to survive. The pioneer was of necessity a jack-of-all-trades. . . . If a multiplicity of occupations was necessary for survival, the pioneers made a virtue of necessity. The man who was self-sufficient in the many activities necessary for survival under frontier conditions was well thought of. While in other parts of the country the tendency was to greater specialization and dependence on a single source of occupation, here pride lay in being able to do the many things necessary for self-sufficiency. This attitude was strengthened by every depression and occupational misfortune that occurred over the years.
>
> In many ways the situation is the same today. The pattern of multiple, part-time occupations is well-established in the area, contrasting with that of more urbanized, industrialized, older parts of the country. . . . Port Haveners value steady employment and assured income above job specialization.[29]

The consequences of role failure may vary by social class. The contrast between specialization of career by the middle class and generalization of work potential by the lower class suggests an interpretation of differential perceptions of mental retardation. The middle-class emphasis upon the presupposition of competence implies that role failure is an evidence of deviance. To protect themselves against role failure, individuals are expected to specialize in their educations and careers. The mentally retarded, according to the middle-class perspective, cannot, through specialized training, insure himself against role failure. Therefore, in his certain failure in educational and career specialization, the retardate is regarded as a deviant, different qualitatively from others. In contrast, at low socioeconomic levels, although competence is valued, there is no presupposition of its presence, and people do not react to the possibility of role failure by specialized training. Instead, the creation of work generalists implies that the difference between the normal and the retarded is one of degree of competence.

As a consequence of the difference in meaning of retardation in middle-class and lower-class segments of the population, the label of mental retardation should have profound effects on reactions to mental retardation in these population segments. For middle-class persons, the label of retardation and a work career as a generalist probably follow a course associated with deviance. Degradation ceremonies involving the "mortification of the self" should produce intense reactions in middle-class retardates.[30] Among groups valuing specialization, the retardate is an "outsider." On the other hand, the lower-class retardate may face fewer problems, especially since he works and lives with other lower-class persons. His stupidity will not set him apart as a generalist living in a group valuing occupational specialization.

JOB-HOLDING

Compared with persons of normal intelligence, the mildly retarded are marginal members of the labor force. However, for over thirty-five years studies on occupational adjustment have shown repeatedly that elements other than level of intellectual functioning are responsible for job success. In summarizing literature on the employability of mentally retarded adults, Kolstoe and Shafter list such factors as personal conduct, social relations, and specific vocational skills.[31] These skills are, of course, an asset for anyone seeking employment. In specifying these items, Kolstoe and Shafter have indicated that job requirements for mentally retarded individuals are essentially no different from those for others. Inasmuch as retarded individuals work at only unskilled and semiskilled jobs, it is little wonder that the main problems occur in interpersonal areas rather than in the tasks themselves.

To determine the reasons for failure of releasees from institutions,

Tarjan and his associates studied three categories of retardates from Pacific State Hospital in California consisting of patients placed on vocational leave, home leave, and family care, respectively. Each patient was followed for a four-year period after discharge. The social worker in charge of each case reported the reasons for failure. Those releasees who failed on vocational leave did so because of inadequate work performance, problems in interpersonal relations, or voluntary return to the hospital for unspecified reasons. Patients on home leave generally failed because of antisocial behavior. Those on family care leave failed because of home and community environment, poor health, or intolerable behavior. The major causes again refer to interpersonal difficulties and inability to comprehend the nature of the interpersonal relations.[32]

Comparing employed and unemployed mentally retarded males, Kolstoe found that the employed group was rated higher on cheerfulness, cooperation, respect for superiors, ability to mind one's own business, being on time, showing initiative, and work efficiency.[33] Walker and Shauffler also found through a study of about 900 educable retarded persons known to the Cleveland social agencies that emotional factors, training, and environmental conditions were more important than mental level in determining the adequacy of social adjustment.[34] Albert Shafter developed a rating instrument for predicting success or failure of releasees from an institution for the retarded. Factors relating to social relations rather than to performance of an occupational task had the highest predictive values.[35] Similarly, in a study by Cohen, various problems interfered with the job. These included difficulty with the employer, occasional pilfering, sexual problems, altering checks, and inability to account for days away from work. Often the retardate did not get along with his parents and siblings.[36] Still, when the mentally retarded who were able to retain their jobs for thirty days or longer were compared with a group matched by age and IQ who could not hold a job, the job-holders had a higher level of reasoning ability.[37]

Under the impetus of the national interest in promoting the welfare of the mentally retarded, much emphasis has been given to vocational rehabilitation programs. To evaluate the effectiveness of these programs, the U.S. Vocational Rehabilitation Administration undertook a study of the socioeconomic characterists of the rehabilitated mentally retarded as compared with the nonretarded in the years 1958 and 1963. Since most progress had been made after 1960, the 1958–1963 comparison was intended to indicate the effectiveness of the new programs. The data included all records of individual states and participating agencies in the federal-state program of vocational rehabilitation. In 1963, about 5,900 persons with orthopedic handicaps, epilepsy, or severe mental illness were reported in these records as having mental retardation as a secondary disability.

The mentally retarded served by the vocational rehabilitation agencies differed from the nonretarded persons in age, sex, race, and personal mobility. Because an effort was made to reach the retarded who were still in school, the nonretarded rehabilitants were older than those with mental retardation as a primary disability. The median ages in 1963 were nineteen for the retarded and thirty-five for the nonretarded. Seventy percent of the retarded were under twenty years of age as compared with only 17 percent of the nonretarded. The trend had shifted considerably since 1958, when only 58 percent of the retarded were under twenty. However, sex differences in proportions of retarded and nonretarded rehabilitants were slight. As for race, a somewhat greater proportion of the retarded than the nonretarded were Caucasian in 1963 (87 versus 80 percent). There was a slight increase in the proportion of Negro retardates rehabilitated from 1958 to 1963 (7 to 11 percent).

The effectiveness of the vocational rehabilitation program in finding work is suggested by changes in unemployment rates. Prior to rehabilitation, 7 percent of the retarded were employed in 1963; only 4 percent were working in the competitive labor market. In contrast, 28 percent of the nonretarded were employed prior to rehabilitation, with 17 percent competitively employed. After participation in the program, there was little difference between the retarded and nonretarded in the percentages employed in the competitive labor market. Seventy-eight percent of the retarded, as compared with 75 percent of the nonretarded, were working in the competitive labor markets after rehabilitation. Yet the rate of employment after rehabilitation for the retarded had not shifted from 1958 to 1963.

The patterns in the kinds of jobs obtained had not changed significantly in the five-year period. In both 1958 and 1963, about three-fourths of the mentally retarded were placed in service, semi-skilled, or unskilled occupations. Roughly 10 percent were placed in white-collar jobs, especially clerical and sales positions, and fewer than 10 percent in agriculture and skilled positions. However, the proportion placed in skilled positions increased from 4.3 in 1958 to 7.5 percent in 1963. In contrast to these findings on the retarded rehabilitants, the nonretarded persons in the rehabilitation program tended to be placed to a greater extent in white-collar positions (about 30 percent) and skilled positions (14.4 percent), with fewer than 50 percent in service, semiskilled, or unskilled occupations. The patterns for those persons with mental retardation as a secondary disability were generally comparable to the findings for the retarded whose mental disability was their major disabling condition.[38]

In general, the characteristics of mentally retarded clients rehabilitated by state vocational rehabilitation agencies are similar to those presented in other studies of socioeconomic attributes of the mentally retarded. Persons who are mentally retarded seem destined to remain at low socioeconomic levels in jobs with high rates of turnover.[39] Since these are marginal positions they are especially vulnerable to the vicissitudes of economic prosperity and depression. Unfortunately, the VRA study was unable to determine the length of tenure of the jobs held by retarded and nonretarded rehabilitants in the investigation. Attributes other than level of intellectual function may affect job tenure.

A major clue regarding the employability of the educable mentally retarded may be found in the study of Krishef and Hall on reasons for leaving jobs. Krishef and Hall studied 177 adult retardates in Hennepin County, Minnesota, about the year 1953. The largest single basis for leaving previous employment was a cutback in the work force.[40] In contrast, the high employment rate found by Charles in his follow-up of the Baller sample occurred during the war years. Prior to World War II, many retarded persons in the sample had been receiving relief; but, with the labor shortage during the war, employment became more regular.

The Krishef and Hall and the VRA investigations support the contention that the educable mentally retarded are generally marginal workers and their employment depends for the most part on the demands of the labor market. Inasmuch as the mentally retarded individual has very little potential for high achievement, he can expect little in the way of rewards from society. Only when the demands for full employment of the potential work force are sustained can the mentally retarded population anticipate a willing reception of its limited talents in factory, service, or agricultural occupations.

Given the value of diverse work experiences among lower-class populations, a question can be raised as to what constitutes vocational rehabilitation. Is training in a sheltered workshop or in a particular job sufficient experience for a lower-class retardate? If vocational rehabilitation is to be considered as an education preparing an individual for a work career, it too should reflect the diversity sought in work experiences. There has been no investigation involving the work careers of mentally retarded individuals who have received training in diverse work experiences. The consequences of such training for the interpersonal relationships of the mentally retarded also deserve study.

Generally, the findings of investigations on factors influencing the ability of educable mentally retarded persons to hold jobs are difficult to evaluate. One reason is that the work setting is not included as a variable for study. Few if any studies of the employability of the mentally retarded report the size of the work group, the amount of interaction between workers necessary for performing the job, and the status of the retardate in the work group. A second source of difficulty in the evaluation of these studies is their failure to take into account the various labels that define the socioeconomic status of the retardate. His racial or ethnic characterizations may be as important in job failure as his lack of ability. A third problem in assessing these studies is the lack of information about his relationship with his family or social worker. Possibly the retardate with many extra-occupational emotional and intellectual resources can maintain adequate social relationships on the job.

It may be true that the educable mentally retarded fail on the job because they cannot develop an image of modern society or of social relations sophisticated enough to enable them to operate effectively in their work setting. On the other hand, characteristics related only incidentally to mental retardation may be the crucial factors in job-holding. The continued presence of the educable mentally retarded as a segment of the economic organizationally surplus population suggests that both their combination of deviant labels and their incompetence are important in maintaining the existing social structure.

Social Mobility of the Mildly Mentally Retarded

This book has stressed the minimal life chances of the mentally retarded; here it will review specific studies on social mobility. The extent of social mobility of the mildly retarded and, afterwards, factors in social mobility will be discussed.

EXTENT OF SOCIAL MOBILITY

Very few people hope to find themselves in unskilled or semi-skilled jobs at the height of their working lives.[41] They aspire to professional and skilled occupations in reporting their preferences, if not in their actions. In the Delaware study by Jastak and his associates, the aspirations of both retarded and nonretarded respondents were similar; only 3 percent of the retarded and none of the nonretarded aspired to unskilled occupations. On the other hand, about 50 percent of the retarded as compared with 73 percent of the nonretarded hoped to obtain professional or skilled occupations. In contrast to their aspirations, about 40 percent of the employed retarded held unskilled jobs, whereas only 10 percent of the nonretarded were working in such occupations. Additionally, none of the retarded (but 45 percent of the nonretarded) were in skilled, clerical-sales, managerial, or professional occupations.[42]

This discrepancy between aspiration and actual occupation can be viewed in terms of social mobility. When Jastak and his associates investigated why people left their previous jobs, they found that over half the retarded (52 percent) but only 38 percent of the nonretarded were either fired or dissatisfied with working conditions. On the other hand, only 17 percent of the retarded, but 41 percent of the nonretarded, left their last jobs to obtain better employment. These findings are consistent with those on social mobility as compared with father's occupation. The Delaware study showed that in 71 percent of the cases the retarded held occupations of lower status than their fathers' (as compared with 20 percent downward mobility among the nonretarded). Only 7 percent of the retarded were upwardly mobile intergenerationally as compared with 31 percent of the nonretarded. The same mobility pattern is apparent in the change from first full-time job to current job held. Thirty-six percent of the retarded, but only 21 percent of the nonretarded, were downwardly mobile in the comparison of their current jobs with their first full-time jobs. On the other hand, just 2 percent of the retarded as compared with 43 percent of the nonretarded were upwardly mobile in this respect. These findings clearly showed the general downward social mobility of the mentally retarded population.[43]

Other studies report comparable results. Investigating the employment history of 177 retarded individuals in Hennepin County, Minnesota, Krishef and Hall found that 60 percent left their previous employment because of dissatisfaction, inability to handle the job, inability to develop proper work habits, or insufficient skill. Only 16 percent left for better jobs.[44] The discrepancy between aspiration and probable attainment is also indicated by employers' attitudes on hiring the mentally retarded. In an investigation regarding the receptivity of employers in this direction in Frankfort, Kentucky, Hartlage found that 85 percent of the employers believed that mentally retarded persons would be less valuable workers than nonretardates; 10 percent felt there would be no differences; and only 5 percent regarded the mentally retarded as more valuable than the nonretarded. The major concerns of the employers were the inability of the retarded to adjust to new situations and to work without close supervision. On the other hand, the employers also felt that the retarded would have a lower absentee rate. In spite of any positive views, however, employers did not view the employment of retardates as economically feasible in the long run.[45]

FACTORS IN SOCIAL MOBILITY

Two kinds of factors in the social mobility of the mildly retarded are depicted in this section. First, the sources of aspirations will be described, then the influence of social structure on social mobility of the retarded.

Sources of Aspirations.   The occupational aspirations of the educable mentally retarded tend to be formed in the home rather than in school. Erdman studied the vocational aspirations and expectations of ninety-eight Caucasian educable retarded high-school boys in six Wisconsin cities. The boys ranged from sixteen through eighteen years of age and from 44 to 80 in IQ. Ninety-five percent of them came from families where the father was in a skilled, semiskilled, or unskilled occupation. Almost half of the boys expected to do the same kind of work their farthers did. Of these, about one-third gave as a reason that the occupation was stimulating; these boys were mostly children of parents at the skilled or semiprofessional level. The 49 percent who did not expect to do the same kind of work as their fathers generally indicated that they either lacked the intellectual requirements for the work or did not care for the working conditions associated with the job. Most boys who complained about the working conditions were the children of semiskilled or unskilled fathers. About half of the children of fathers in these latter jobs aspired to jobs of higher socioeconomic levels than their fathers. Yet, although

58 percent of the fathers were in semiskilled or unskilled occupations, 63 percent of the boys chose occupations at these levels. There was thus a slight tendency for the retarded boys to expect to be downwardly mobile in socioeconomic levels.[46]

The vocational aspirations of the boys in the Erdman study were often defined by their parents. About 80 percent of the boys discussed their choice of a vocation at home with their parents. In contrast, only 34 percent had discussed their vocational careers at school with teachers or counselors. However, when boys reported that their fathers had expressed a specific choice for them, the fathers' expectation was generally one of a skilled occupation, whereas the boy's choice was a semiskilled or unskilled job.

Other studies have also found that the home provides an important reference point in determining occupations of children of normal intelligence. First, children often rely on their parents for guidance counseling. Ryden found that almost 90 percent of the students in his study depended chiefly on their parents for vocational guidance. Reciprocally, about three-fourths of the parents regarded active participation in their child's vocational choice as part of the parental role. Almost a third of the parents already had selected a career for their child before the child had completed his sophomore year in high school.[47] Other studies have shown similar tendencies. For example, Peters found that parents were the most important influence in vocational choice as compared with friends, professional acquaintances, or other relatives.[48]

A second kind of home influence on vocational choice is the father's occupation as a specific reference point. The child can then determine whether he wishes to follow his father in his occupation or to aspire to an occupation with other working conditions, training requirements, or compensation. Tendencies for sons to aspire to their father's occupations depend heavily upon the socioeconomic characteristics of the group studied. The Erdman study indicated that, in general, the higher the socioeconomic level of the father, the greater the tendency to select an occupation similar to his.[49]

Studies of occupational choice suggest that families often may impart feelings of relative deprivation when educable mentally retarded children go forth to earn a living themselves. Since retarded individuals usually enter the labor market at unskilled or, at most, semiskilled occupations and remain at this level the rest of their lives, they cannot avoid noticing the departures of fellow-workers for better jobs, promotions given to others with less seniority, and being laid off during cut-backs at slack periods. They may even realize that they do not have the intellectual capacity to gain privileges of promotion, job security, or better positions. This awareness of intellectual inadequacy may merely exaggerate for the mildly retarded the hopelessness of their employment and family situations.

Social Structure and Social Mobility.   Changes in social structure also influence the probability of the retarded's social mobility. An interesting consequence of automation of industry, government agencies, and educational institutions has been pointed out by Faunce: as automation proceeds in society, the division of labor will become less diversified rather than more so. This homogenization of the work force may increase its sense of professional identity and the similarity of its perspective of society.[50] However, this situation may also intensify existing tendencies toward (a) specialization, (b) an emphasis on high technical standards in the labor force, (c) limitations on the accessibility of the poorly educated surplus population to slots in the major institutions of the society, and (d) an increasing popularity of those theories of individual ability and social process which are repressive to such deviants as the mentally retarded. As a consequence, the view of mildly retarded persons as deviants rather than incompetents may become more popular. This relationship between automation and the perspective of retardation as deviance should be studied.

Modern society is faced with a dilemma concerning the mentally retarded. On the one hand, it seeks to integrate them into the ongoing currents of social life; on the other, it refuses to abandon its emphasis on achievement in social and economic status. Dexter has suggested that the tyranny of schooling is such that all persons are expected to excel in academic subjects, and the retarded individual is thereby doomed to failure.[51] The emphasis on academic subjects, however, is itself connected with the changes that have taken place in the social structure since the mid-nineteenth century. These changes include an increase in tertiary occupations (especially professional and white-collar categories) and are not merely the whims of school administrators. In a society where lower-class occupational generalists of normal intelligence can maintain their social position only with difficulty, retardates are almost certain to be downwardly mobile. Only a full-employment policy by government can sustain occupational generalists and enable the educable retarded to lose their stigmatized identity in adulthood.

Conclusions Regarding Community Relationships
of the Mildly Retarded

In the early twentieth century, the mentally retarded were often viewed as a somewhat subhuman species. Henry Goddard commented:

> A child once feeble-minded is never made normal. A very, very small percentage of them can be trained so that they may be able to eke out a miserable existence, perhaps supporting themselves; but it is probably cruel to require even that of them. It would be much kinder and more humane to give them the opportunity to live in a social environment like a colony, where the harder problems of life do not come up to them, but where they can work and do as much as they are capable of doing, and can therefore live comfortably and happy.[52]

Goddard recommended that mentally deficient children be placed in separate schools, which could then develop into residential institutions, ultimately removing the mentally deficient from the society.

There now seems to be little question that the educable mentally retarded are capable of self-support in unskilled or semiskilled occupations.[53] Depending on economic conditions and the availability of unskilled work, roughly 60 to 90 percent of the educable mentally retarded seeking work can find jobs. In the Delaware study by Jastak, for example, the rate of unemployment for the retarded was 8 percent, as compared with 3 percent for the nonretarded. The dissatisfaction that emerges in the work situation may not be solely a function of the retardation itself. Chances are that the retarded individual has grown up in a home characterized by instability and insufficiency in resources. This factor alone would affect the ability of the retardate to get along with his fellow-workers and employers. Perhaps equally important is the fact that the educable mentally retarded person grows up in a society that emphasizes achievement. The retarded person, having been molded by forces comparable to those influencing the nonretarded, finds himself unable to get ahead. Moreover, chances are that he is beset by health and familial problems in a world he does not understand. All these factors increase the probability that the educable retarded will remain as a surplus in social organization. Only as he becomes an economic necessity in the occupational world can the mentally retarded individual escape his "surplus" status.

Community Relationships of the
Severely Mentally Retarded

Various kinds of services have developed in recent years for the mentally retarded population. Because the greatest pressure has been from organized middle-class groups rather than lower-class parents, most of the services have dealt with treatment of the severely retarded. Many family service agencies have provided guidance programs, household assistance, or temporary institutionalization of the child. In these programs, the National Association for Retarded Children has attempted to act as spokesman. The result has been an emphasis on medically relevant services. Dybwad writes:

> The key problem confronting parents of mentally retarded children is the need for competent diagnostic services. Rather than find a solution through increasing the resources of existing child guidance clinics under psychiatric auspices, the basic NARC legislative program suggested that funds be made available to the U.S. Children's Bureau for development of pediatric clinic facilities as part of the maternal and child health programs supported by the Bureau in all the states. By 1959, Bureau funds had assisted in the establishment of fifty such clinics in forty-four states, and more than thirty community retardation clinics were operating with support from other sources.[54]

Many services to the mentally retarded emphasize their existence as a surplus population. Two federal programs alone (the Public Assistance Program of Aid to the Permanently and Totally Disabled and the Social Security Program of Old-Age, Survivors, and Disability Insurance) paid out in 1963 "almost one hundred million dollars in federal funds to mentally retarded adults (as against only thirty million dollars for all service programs together)".[55] These funds do not include the assistance provided by such programs as Aid to Dependent Children, which also supports "a considerable number of both mentally retarded adults and mentally retarded children." Dybwad has reported that in 1960 and 1961 about 70 percent of all persons eligible for childhood Disability Benefits "were found to be unable to engage in any substantial gainful activity owing to mental retardation. . . . The total number of mentally retarded persons receiving these benefits [in 1963] exceeds one hundred thousand. Mental retardation, therefore, accounts for more than two-thirds of all disability cases under this part of the program. All other types of physical and mental disabilities added together account for less than one-third of the case load."[56]

THE SEVERELY RETARDED IN THE COMMUNITY

The severely retarded population cannot participate in normal family and work activities regardless of the social situation. For the severely retarded trainable child in the community, the major portion of activities generally centers in the home. This restriction to family life is related to the fact that the severely retarded are incapable of communicating effectively with others. Research in institutions has indicated that the children engage in much stereotypical, repetitive behavior in relation to other persons and physical objects, and in showing marked preferences for specific locations on the ward.[57]

Spreen has estimated that all the mentally retarded with an IQ below 20, about 90 percent of the retardates in the 21 to 50 IQ ranges, and a little less than half of the mildly retarded have language disorders. Several studies have found a lag in language development of retardates in sentence length and complexity, discrimination of speech sounds, and the percentage of nouns used. Mentally retarded individuals living in institutions show poorer language development than those living at home. But, since the mentally retarded in institutions often come from a different population than those residing at home, the effect of the institutionalization is not clear.[58]

In an eighteen-month study of the conversational style of ten retarded children aged 7.6 to 12.75 years of age and with an IQ range of 25 to 45, Sampson determined that the average vocabulary was about 1900 words per child. During 250 interviews, Sampson attempted to "stimulate as much speech as possible in a natural manner." He was able to enlarge the children's vocabularies by 102 to 484 words. Although most sentences were of one- or two-word utterances, there were also some complete three- and four-word sentences representative of adult speech style.[59]

The difficulties with language in severely mentally retarded children necessarily interfere with the accrual of the appropriate social categories and their corresponding norms and values prevalent in society. Because of this deficiency, such persons cannot possibly participate as responsible individuals in the urbanized world and its complex social arrangements.

EDUCATIONAL PROGRAMS FOR THE SEVERELY RETARDED

Following World War II, many upper-income, highly educated parents became active in sponsoring community schools for trainable, severely mentally retarded children. Perhaps the increase in birth rate following World War II produced a sufficiently large number of severely retarded children among middle-class families to demand that facilities be provided for the education of these children. Since then, pressure has been sustained for the maintenance of day schools and special classes for severely mentally retarded children. The training programs for these children have focused upon self-care, music, art, minimal literacy, and vocabulary training.

When day schools were established for trainable mentally retarded children in the early 1950s, several attempts were made to assess the changes wrought to the child and his family. One of the parents' most frequent reactions was that the school gave them "peace of mind." Most of these studies found that during the first year the children showed some improvement in their intellectual functioning, but this rate of improvement was not sustained in the following years. Although the parents expressed hope during the first year that the child would be able to perform academic work, they were disappointed in the succeeding year.[60]

What happens to trainable children who are exposed to day-school programs? Several investigations have followed up children who had been admitted to special classes for the trainable mentally retarded. Lorenz studied a group of sixty-six children eighteen years after their admission to a special class. Forty-seven percent of them had been institutionalized. However, factors other than retardation were responsible for the institutionalization in that more boys than girls were in institutions, and the institutionalized retardates tended to have come from lower socioeconomic levels.[61]

Delp and Lorenz followed seventy-five adults who had attended classes in a special occupational center in St. Paul, Minnesota. At the time of the follow-up, the median IQ for the group was 36. One-third of the group (twenty-five individuals) were now in institutions, and nine had died. Of the forty-one retardates living in the community, only five men had regular full-time or part-time jobs, while five others did odd jobs.[62]

Gerhart Saenger studied 520 severely retarded adults, randomly selected from 2,600 former pupils in classes for the trainable in New York City between 1929 and 1955. Most of the retardates in the Saenger sample had an IQ between 40 and 50 and thus were at the upper level of the trainable classification. The information on their post-school life was obtained through interviews with parents. At the time of the study, two-thirds of the pupils were still living in the community, 26 percent had been institutionalized, and 8 percent had died. More than half of those living at home had only limited inter-action with other family members. Slightly over half of the retardates were able to help around the house regularly, and almost 90 percent could take care of their own physical needs completely. However, almost two-thirds were unable to leave the immediate neighborhood, less than 10 percent showed an interest in the opposite sex, and about one-fourth were employed at the time of the study. Of those unem-ployed, just 9 percent had worked previously. Although more men than women had been institutionalized, the adjustment of the women was generally less satisfactory than that of the men.[63]

Tisdall traced children who had been enrolled in the twenty-two pilot project classes in public schools for the trainable mentally re-tarded in Illinois between 1953 and 1955. The follow-up occurred approximately five years after the 126 children had first been enrolled. Twelve percent of the children were in institutions at the time of the follow-up; most of them were reported as having been disruptive influences on their families. Twenty-five percent of the children were still living at home but were now receiving no formal training. Half of these children had reached the upper age limit for public school classes, and the remainder had either left the special classes because their mentality was too low or they had been withdrawn by their parents, or were excluded because of behavioral problems. Another 24 per-cent of the children were still attending special classes and generally constituted the younger children with higher IQs. The remainder of the children were either enrolled in parent-sponsored classes because they had reached the upper age limit for the public school (18 per-cent), were in sheltered workshops (7 percent), had moved to another community (7 percent), had transferred to classes for the educable mentally handicapped (4 percent), or had died (2.4 percent). Hence the alternatives for most trainable children were either to continue in day classes or to remain in the home when school attendance was not feasible.[64]

The orientation of most programs dealing with the severely mentally retarded is to make them as normal as possible. In spite of the fact that very few of the severely retarded (imbecile or trainable classification) will ever be financially independent, sheltered workshops provide them with an opportunity to act as if they were part of the labor force. Inasmuch as these sheltered workshops are long-term arrangements, they operate as inefficient factories which specialize in tasks that cannot be done cheaply by machines and do not require much skill. Usually, the sheltered workshops perform such duties as pasting labels, packing items in kits, assembling loose-leaf booklets for sales personnel, and other types of repetitive and uncomplicated work.

The sheltered workshop is a relatively new institution that permits the retarded individual to remain at home with his family of orientation yet not be underfoot all day. In accordance with the Protestant ethic, the retardate is engaged in serious work rather than in frivolities. The sheltered workshop program is thus consistent with the general American and Western European value system, which itself derogates mental retardation. The fact that it is a relatively new program suggests that instead of moving in the direction whereby the mentally retarded would not be considered as surplus, there is, if anything, more emphasis upon achievement and work.

The sheltered workshop movement began after World War II and did not expand into large proportions until the following decade. According to Dybwad:

> When Vocational Rehabilitation was first firmly established in this country with the passage in 1920 of the National Civilian Vocational Rehabilitation Act, the mentally retarded were not included among those with disabilities that could be served. At that time, the "Colony" idea, as developed by Rome State School in New York, was by and large the only program pinpointed at rehabilitation. In 1943, Public Law 113, known as the Barden-LaFollette Amendments, for the first time specifically included mental retardation, and also widened the concept of rehabilitation. Finally, in 1954, Congress passed Public Law 565 which greatly increased not only the available funds but also the uses to which this money could be placed, and from that year date the numerous special rehabilitation projects for the mentally retarded that are now in existence [in 1960]. (A Sheltered Workshop Directory issued recently by the National Association for Re-

tarded Children lists one-hundred such establishments throughout the country.)[65]

SUMMARY

This chapter has treated the mildly and severely retarded separately because of the differences of their roles in the community. The mildly retarded generally live at low socioeconomic levels in the society, while the severely retarded are not so strongly selected by socioeconomic level. This difference alone has important implications for their role in society. In modern society, the ethic at higher socioeconomic levels is to become proficient at specialized tasks in the division of labor. At low socioeconomic levels, the ideal is the occupational generalist, the person who can perform adequately at any job to insure survival. The lower-class individual thus seeks a variety of work experiences in contrast to the highly specialized educational training prized at the upper socioeconomic levels.

There is little doubt that the educable mentally retarded, as a marginally incompetent group, can be trained to perform adequately at an unskilled or semiskilled position. However, the educable retardates (especially those without special-class training) often have difficulty in holding a job. Factors in job instability include deviant behavior at work, delinquency away from the job, inadequate work performance, problems in interpersonal relations, and frustrations through a lack of upward social mobility. Although both lower socioeconomic class retardates and nonretardates frequently begin at unskilled, low-paying positions, as the years pass the retardates find themselves working at the same (or lower) level of skill and pay while their nonretarded colleagues have better jobs and broader work experience. As one retarded person who had worked in the community for several years indicated, "Why should I bust my neck for a buck an hour when I've got it made here [in the institution]?" Federal programs, as well as those sponsored by the National Association for Retarded Children, are impeded, first, by the fact that the retarded are inept and perform only marginally in the community. The retarded cannot achieve status as occupational generalists. Second, they are impeded by the ethnic and other deviant characteristics which seem to work to their detriment.

The severely mentally retarded are, by definition, life-long dependent persons. Classes for the trainable mentally handicapped and sheltered workshops can ease some of the personal strain in caring for the severely retarded, but neither can perceptibly alleviate the burden.

GENERAL DISCUSSION

This chapter has dealt with the community life of the mentally retarded. Sarason and Gladwin take the position that the ability to develop social and occupational skills adequate for a "normal" life in the community does not require the same kind of intellectual competence necessary for school achievement. Therefore, although a score on IQ tests may predict a child's potential school achievement effectively, Sarason and Gladwin believe that it is inappropriate to apply the same criterion to judge his competence in adult life.[66]

The findings in this chapter, however, indicate that the social and academic competencies in the educational institution are comparable to those required in occupations and community relationships. The view held in this book is that educational, political, and economic institutions constitute a core of integrating mechanisms in modern society and that the coordination of activities in this core is made possible by the existence of a "public culture." Successful participation in these social institutions requires that individuals be socialized in the language, values, norms, and perspectives of the "public culture." Unless this kind of socialization occurs, the life chances of the individuals are very limited. Regardless of that basis, the mentally retarded are grossly undersocialized in characteristics reflecting the public culture.

If life chances depend upon the extent of socialization in aspects of the public culture, the education of the mildly retarded as well should be aimed in this direction. The few studies of graduates of special education programs that have been cited suggest that the rules of the public culture can be incorporated into a curriculum for the educable retarded. These curricula generally make explicit those rules and assumptions which most people learn more informally.[67] One of the latent consequences of special education may be to facilitate learning how to "pass" as nonretarded in adulthood. Although these special programs cannot solve the fundamental problems of reducing organizationally surplus populations, they seem to increase the life chances of some retarded individuals.

With regard to severely retarded persons, an area of investigation that is potentially of major significance concerns the minimum intellectual conditions for the development and persistence of a social system. The question of the functional prerequisites of a society has been raised. By observing severely retarded individuals, perhaps we can determine marginal kinds of social interaction and functioning of social systems emerging with minimal language and conceptual ability.[68] In this respect, studies of groups of mongoloids or persons with generalized definable intellectual deficiences can be undertaken. These investigations may provide numerous insights into effects of incompetence on social relationships of the mentally retarded.

NOTES

[1] Cf. the concept of "cumulative deficit," by Martin Deutsch, in "The Role of Social Class in Language Development and Cognition," *American Journal of Orthopsychiatry*, 35 (January, 1965), pp. 86–87.

[2] Charlotte Steinbeck, "Report of the Special Class Department," Cleveland, Ohio, 1918. Cited in Herbert Goldstein, "Social Aspects of Mental Deficiency," unpublished Ed.D. dissertation, University of Illinois, 1957. Historical summary on special classes from Goldstein and Eugene E. Doll, "A Historical Survey of Research and Management of Mental Retardation in the United States," in E. Philip Trapp and Philip Himelstein, eds., *Readings on the Exceptional Child* (New York: Appleton-Century-Crofts, 1962), pp. 38–40.

[3] *Provisions for Exceptional Children*, U.S. Bureau of Education, Bulletin Number 14, U.S. Government Printing Office, 1911.

[4] Samuel A. Kirk, *Educating Exceptional Children* (Boston: Houghton Mifflin, 1962), p. 23; and Halbert B. Robinson and Nancy M. Robinson, *The Mentally Retarded Child, A Psychological Approach* (New York: McGraw-Hill, 1965), p. 460.

[5] Romaine P. Mackie, "Spotlighting Advances in Special Education," *Exceptional Children*, 32 (October, 1965), pp. 77–81.

[6] Robert Fuchigami, "An Investigation of the Extent of Integration and Some Related Factors Affecting the Social Relationships of Educable Mentally Handicapped Children in Illinois," unpublished Ed.D. dissertation, 1964, p. 10.

[7] Elliott A. Krause, *Factors Related to Length of Mental Hospital Stay*, Community Mental Health Monograph Series, Massachusetts Department of Mental Health. Cited in Marvin B. Sussman, ed., *Sociology and Rehabilitation* (Washington, D.C.: American Sociological Association, N.D.), pp. 43–44, 142–144.

[8] The remaining propositions pertain more to the agencies than to the interaction between patient and professional. *Ibid.*, pp. 142–144.

[9] Gerhard Lenski, "Status Crystallization: A Non-Vertical Dimension of Social Status," *American Sociological Review*, 19 (1954), pp. 405–413; Gerhard Lenski, "Social Participation and Status Crystallization," *American Sociological Review*, 21 (1956), pp. 458–464; K. Dennis Kelly and William J. Chambliss,

"Status Consistency and Political Attitudes," *American Sociological Review*, 31 (1966), pp. 375–382.

10 G. O. Johnson, "A Study of the Social Position of Mentally Handicapped Children in the Regular Grades," *American Journal of Mental Deficiency*, 55 (1950), pp. 60–89.

11 G. O. Johnson and S. A. Kirk, "Are Mentally Handicapped Children Segregated in the Regular Grades?" *Exceptional Children*, 17 (1950), pp. 65–68. Willie K. Baldwin, "The Social Position of the Educable Mentally Retarded in the Regular Grades in the Public Schools," *Exceptional Children*, 25 (1958), pp. 106–108.

12 Robinson and Robinson, *op. cit.*, p. 465.

13 Frances A. Mullen and William Itkin, *Achievement and Adjustment of Educable Mentally Handicapped Children*, U.S. Office of Education Cooperative Research Program, Project No. SAE 6529, Chicago Board of Education, 1961.

14 Herbert Goldstein, James W. Moss, and Laura J. Jordan, *The Efficacy of Special Class Training on the Development of Mentally Retarded Children*, U.S. Office of Education, Cooperative Research Project Number 619 (Urbana, Illinois: Institute for Research on Exceptional Children, 1965).

15 *Ibid.* Family aspects of investigation directed by J. H. Meyerowitz.

16 The data for mothers of severely retarded children were taken from Bernard Farber, William C. Jenné, and Romolo Toigo, "Family Crisis and the Decision to Institutionalize the Retarded Child," *Council for Exceptional Children, NEA Research Monographs*, Series A, #1, 1960.

17 Joseph H. Meyerowitz, "Maternal Involvement and Educational Retardation," *Journal of Marriage and the Family*, 28 (February, 1966), pp. 89–91

18 Joseph Meyerowitz, "Parental Awareness of Retardation," *American Journal of Mental Deficiency*, 71 (January, 1967), p. 641.

19 Reported in Goldstein, Moss, and Jordan, *op. cit.*

20 Fuchigami, *op. cit.*

21 Robert A. Henderson, "Factors in Commitment of Educable Mentally Handicapped Children to Illinois State Schools," unpublished Ed.D. dissertation, University of Illinois, 1957.

22 William R. Carriker, *A Comparison of Post-School Adjustments of Regular and Special Class Retarded Individuals Served in Lincoln and Omaha, Nebraska, Public Schools*, Report to U.S. Office of Education, HEW, 1957 (Contract Number SAE-6445).

23 Rutherford B. Porter and Tony C. Milazzo, "A Comparison of Mentally Retarded Adults Who Attended a Special Class with Those Who Attended Regular School Classes," *Exceptional Children*, 24 (May, 1958), pp. 410–412.

24 Stephen A. Richardson, in Bernard Farber, ed., *Directions of Future Sociological Research in Mental Retardation*, Report of Conference Sponsored by National Association for Retarded Children, 1960.

25 Norman Goodman, Stephen A. Richardson, Sanford M. Dornbusch, and Albert H. Hastorf, "Variant Reactions to Physical Disabilities," *American Sociological Review*, 28 (June, 1963), pp. 429–435.

26 Sister Rose Amata McCartin, Harvey F. Dingman, Edward Meyers, and Jane R. Mercer, "Identification and Disposition of the Mentally Handicapped in the Parochial School System," *American Journal of Mental Deficiency*, 71 (September, 1966), pp. 201–206. See also S. Olshansky and J. Schonfield, "Parental Perceptions of the Mental Status of Graduates of Special Classes," *Mental Retardation*, 3 (1965), pp. 5, 16–20.

27 Raymond W. Mack, "Occupational Determinateness: A Problem and

Hypotheses in Role Theory," *Social Forces*, 35 (October, 1956), pp. 20–25; Harold L. Wilensky, "Orderly Careers and Social Participation: The Impact of Work History on Social Integration in the Middle Mass," *American Sociological Review*, 26 (1961), pp. 521–539; Joseph R. Gusfield, "Occupational Roles and Forms of Enterprise," *American Journal of Sociology*, 66 (May, 1961), pp. 571–580.

28 Herbert H. Hyman, "The Value Systems of Different Classes: A Social Psychological Contribution to the Analysis of Stratification," in Reinhard Bendix and Seymour Martin Lipset, eds., *Class, Status and Power* (New York: Free Press, 1953), pp. 432–433.

29 Angelo Anastasio, *Port Haven, A Changing Northwestern Community*, Pullman, Washington, Washington Agricultural Experiment Station, Washington State University, May, 1960 (Bulletin 616), pp. 23–24.

30 See Harold Garfinkel, "Conditions of Successful Degradation," *American Journal of Sociology*, 61 (1955), pp. 420–424.

31 Oliver P. Kolstoe and Albert J. Shafter, "Employability Prediction for Mentally Retarded Adults: A Methodological Note," *American Journal of Mental Deficiency*, 66 (1961), pp. 287–289.

32 George Tarjan, Harvey F. Dingman, Richard Eyman, and Sheldon J. Brown, "Effectiveness of Hospital Release Programs," *American Journal of Mental Deficiency*, 64 (January, 1959), pp. 609–617.

33 Oliver P. Kolstoe, "An Examination of Some Characteristics Which Discriminate Between Employed and Not Employed Mentally Retarded Males," *American Journal of Mental Deficiency*, 66 (1961), pp. 472–482.

34 Helen M. Walker and Mary C. Shauffler, *The Social Adjustment of the Feeble-Minded: A Group Thesis Study* (Cleveland: Western Reserve University Press, 1930).

35 Albert J. Shafter, "A Method of Predicting Placement Outcome for Institutionalized Mental Defectives," *Midwest Sociologist*, 17 (1955), pp. 35–39. See also Albert J. Shafter, "Criteria for Selecting Institutionalized Mental Defectives for Vocational Placement," *American Journal of Mental Deficiency*, 61 (1957), pp. 599–616.

36 Julius S. Cohen, "An Analysis of Vocational Failures of Mental Retardates Placed in the Community After a Period of Institutionalization," *American Journal of Mental Deficiency*, 65 (1960), pp. 371–375.

37 Albert M. Barrett, Ruth Relos, and Jack Eisele, "Vocational Success and Attitudes of Mentally Retarded Toward Work and Money," *American Journal of Mental Deficiency*, 70 (1965), pp. 102–107.

38 Vocational Rehabilitation Administration, Division of Statistics and Study, *Selected Characteristics of the Mentally Retarded Clients Rehabilitated by State Vocational Rehabilitation Agencies in Fiscal Years 1958 and 1963* (Washington, D.C.: Government Printing Office, April, 1964).

39 See Allen Dobroff, "Economic Adjustment of 121 Adults Formerly Students in Classes for the Mental Retardates," in Lotar V. Stahlecker, ed., *Occupational Information for the Mentally Retarded* (Springfield, Ill.: Thomas, 1967), pp. 754–755. About two-thirds of the retardates reported three or more employers in the period from 1941–1953. In this period only 13 percent had received promotions to journeyman, leader, foreman, supervisor, or higher civil service rank.

40 Curtis H. Krishef and Manford A. Hall, "Employment of the Mentally Retarded in Hennepin County, Minnesota," *American Journal of Mental Deficiency*, 60 (1955), pp. 182–189.

41 Ralph Turner, *The Social Context of Ambition* (San Francisco: Chandler 1964), p. 36.

258 *Treatment of the Retarded in Contemporary Society*

Jastak, MacPhee, and Whiteman, *op. cit.*

For general discussion of the relationship between level of intelligence and social mobility, see Seymour Martin Lipset and Reinhard Bendix, *Social Mobility in Industrial Society* (Berkeley: University of California Press, 1959), pp. 227–236.

Krishef and Hall, *op. cit.*

Lawrence C. Hartlage, "Factors Affecting Employer Receptivity Toward the Mentally Retarded," *American Journal of Mental Deficiency,* 70 (1965), pp. 108–113.

Robert L. Erdman, "Vocational Choices of Adolescent Mentally Retarded Boys," doctoral dissertation, University of Illinois, 1957.

A. H. Ryden, "Including Parents in Counseling," *Occupations,* 29 (May, 1951), pp. 587–590.

Edwin Peters, "Factors Which Contribute to Youth's Vocational Choices," *Journal of Applied Psychology,* 25 (August, 1951), pp. 428–430.

See also Lipset and Bendix, *op. cit.,* pp. 182–199.

William A. Faunce, "Automation and the Division of Labor," *Social Problems,* 13 (Fall, 1965), pp. 149–160.

Lewis Anthony Dexter, *The Tyranny of Schooling* (New York: Basic Books, 1964).

Henry H. Goddard, *School Training of Defective Children* (New York: World Book Company, 1923), p. xviii.

See Stahlecker, *op. cit.,* pp. 201–406.

Gunnar Dybwad, *Challenges in Mental Retardation* (New York: Columbia University Press, 1964), pp. 9–10.

Ibid., p. 185.

Ibid., p. 187.

Gershon Berkson, "Stereotyped Movements of Mental Defectives: Ward Behavior and Its Relation to an Experimental Task," *American Journal of Mental Deficiency,* 69 (1964), pp. 253–264.

Otfried Spreen, "Language of Functions in Mental Retardation: A Review. I. Language Development, Types of Retardation, and Intelligence," *American Journal of Mental Deficiency,* 69 (1965), pp. 482–494.

O. C. Sampson, "The Conversational Style of a Group of Severely Subnormal Children," *Journal of Mental Subnormality,* 10 (1964), pp. 89–100.

Reports on study projects for trainable mentally handicapped children in Illinois, 1954 and 1956; J. V. Hottel, *An Evaluation of Tennessee's Day Class Program for Severely Mentally Retarded Children,* Nashville, George Peabody College for Teachers, 1958; Leo F. Cain and Samuel Levine, *A Study of the Effects of Community and Institutional School Classes for Trainable Mentally Retarded Children,* U.S. Office of Education, Cooperative Research Project Number SAE 8257 (San Francisco: San Francisco State College, 1961).

Marcella H. Lorenz, "Follow-up Studies of the Severely Retarded," *A Study of Public School Children with Severe Mental Retardation,* edited by M. C. Reynolds, J. R. Kiland, and R. E. Ellis (St. Paul, Minnesota: Statistical Division, State Department of Education, 1953).

H. A. Delp, "Follow-up of Eighty-four Public School Special Class Pupils with IQ's Below 50," *American Journal of Mental Deficiency,* 58 (1953), pp. 175–182.

Gerhart Saenger, *The Adjustment of Severely Retarded Adults in the Community* (Albany, New York: Interdepartmental Health Resources Board, 1957).

William J. Tisdall, "A Follow-up Study of Trainable Mentally Handicapped Children in Illinois," *American Journal of Mental Deficiency*, 65 (July, 1960), pp. 11–16.

[65] Dybwad, *op. cit.*, p. 156.

[66] Richard L. Masland, Seymour B. Sarason, and Thomas Gladwin, *Mental Subnormality* (New York: Basic Books, 1958), pp. 305–306.

[67] For example, see Barbara Edmonson, Ethel M. Leach, and Henry Leland, *Perceptual Training for Social Behavior: A Pre-Vocational Unit for Retarded Youth* (Kansas City, Kansas: University of Kansas Medical Center, Children's Rehabilitation Unit, 1965), dittoed.

[68] See the diary of a mongoloid taught to read and write, May V. Seagoe, *Yesterday Was Tuesday, All Day and All Night* (Boston: Little, Brown, 1964).

10.

Epilogue: Past and Future

This epilogue will summarize briefly the social context and consequences of mental retardation, and it will indicate kinds of programming that can be undertaken to handle social problems related to retardation. To present a coherent exposition, the epilogue will not focus on the insufficiency of research evidence but will speculate instead on the world of the retarded as revealed in previous investigations. Gaps in social research pertaining to the mentally retarded have been discussed throughout the book.

Social Context and Social Consequences of Mental Retardation

This book has suggested that the mentally retarded constitute a segment of a superfluous population. That is, the major institutions of society could continue to operate as before if all of the mentally retarded individuals in society were removed to another planet. The position of the mentally retarded seems to be based both on their incompetence and on their being labeled as such. Yet neither the actual incompetence nor the label can explain the persistence of the mentally retarded as a designated class of people in society. In modern society mental retardation is only one of a series of phenomena that may inhibit the life chances of any individual. The inhibiting effect is especially pronounced in mild mental retardation when a combination of social characteristics converge.

260

Mental retardation has been regarded by some persons as deviant behavior and by others as incompetence. Deviant behavior implies an aberrant role and set of values associated with the stigmatized label. Those who view the mentally retarded as deviants have tried to show a relationship between retardation and other deviant behavior. Those who see the retarded as incompetent have treated mental retardation in terms of the unique problems it presents. They consider the difficulties faced by retardates as stemming mainly from actual incompetence. The perspective of the retarded as surplus population suggests that both the deviance and the incompetence views of the retarded population's role in society are insufficient, and that a more adequate explanation should incorporate both positions.

The fact that the mentally retarded constitute only a small minority (roughly 3 percent) of the population and are organizationally surplus prevents them from exerting a major influence upon society. Moreover, the prevalence of mental retardation among adolescent boys who tend to remain in slums and rural areas and who, later in life, have low fertility rates and high death rates prevents the mentally retarded from constituting a major social problem. It is mainly through their contribution to the more general surplus population that the mildly mentally retarded threaten the social structure.

The isolation of population segments from the dominant public culture facilitates the development of mental retardation and reinforces the position of retardates as outcasts in society. Secluded from the major institutions of the public culture, persons who genetically or physiologically might otherwise be capable may fail (a) to develop norms related to highly cooperative behavior and inhibition of aggressive behavior, (b) to incorporate the vocabulary and grammar of the language of the public culture, (c) to emphasize rationality rather than fun or other expressive behavior, and (d) to be highly motivated toward social mobility. The competitive nature of the institutions of the public culture in modern industrial society insures the existence of superfluous populations and, consequently, the perpetuation of private cultures associated with these surplus populations.

The major steps taken to handle problems of mental retardation have been generally inadequate or inappropriate. Nineteenth-century social movements pertaining to mental retardation were associated with other contemporary political and social problems; for the most part, the late nineteenth- and early twentieth-century reformers had little personal connection with the mentally retarded and subordinated programs dealing with mental retardation to other concerns.

After World War II, the parents' group movement became a major force in matters of social reform with regard to the mentally retarded. This group, however, was made up of parents of severely mentally retarded children. The parents were mainly middle-class and upper-middle-class individuals who were interested in special-class training and medical services for the severely retarded. Their interests only tangentially pertained to the educable, mildly retarded population. As a result, current social movements have affected the severely retarded almost exclusively.

The effects of the severely retarded child on the family have been felt mainly in the middle class, since for these families especially the retarded child is a stigma and is damaging to their life chances. The personal impact is strong for both parents and siblings of the retarded child. Upward social mobility is inhibited, and emotional problems are abundant. In this group, major social problems pertain to the normal family members rather than to the severely retarded child himself.

The family life of the mildly retarded population presents a different picture from that of the severely retarded group. Families of orientation of educable retardates display environments that are unstable and stultifying; the families of procreation tend to duplicate their parental families. Perhaps most significant, they often seem inadequate as parents. However, since many retardates marry persons of normal intelligence, the effect of mental incompetence on family relationships cannot be properly gauged merely by correlating mental incompetence with the presence of family problems.

Residential institutions also provide an insufficient amelioration of problems associated with mental retardation. First, fewer than 5 percent of the mentally retarded are in institutions. Second, historically the public institutions for the mentally retarded have been dominated by political concerns, which have apparently influenced the selection of personnel, admission of patients, location of institutions, confusion of lines of authority within the institutions, and the inhibition of effective treatment programs. Even more important, political influences have indirectly fostered the development of deviant subcultures among the patients in the institutions and have interfered with their adjustment to the institution and to postinstitutional existence.

Studies of the community relationships of the mentally retarded indicate further how the problems of mild mental retardation are intimately associated with other social problems, including poverty, adjustment of migrants, slum life, broken families, and legal difficulties. Various studies also suggest how the plight of the mentally retarded is delicately connected with the prosperity of the society. When times are good, the mentally retarded adults "pass" economically and in their family life. With economic depression, the mentally retarded are among the first to be laid off, and other problems ensue. The effectiveness of programs in special education and social welfare is closely related to social conditions in the community.

To summarize, the dilemma of modern society with regard to the mentally retarded is as follows: Many social conditions and genetic factors prevent the development of adequate intellectual functioning. Yet, to maximize efficiency, the organization of modern society demands a surplus population in order that its selection procedures may work. The techniques that modern society has developed for dealing with the mentally retarded have been insufficient — possibly because society is motivated to maintaining them as a surplus population.

Programming

The solution implied in the above summary is that surplus populations should be integrated into the major institutions of the society through amelioration, which would remove the diverse limitations on life chances simultaneously. Several kinds of therapeutic and preventive action can be undertaken. The four kinds of programs suggested below follow in a broad sense the functional tasks of social systems as described by Parsons.[1] The first level has to do with the effective use of resources to increase the adaptation of mentally retarded individuals. The second level of programming concerns the attainment of goals through the restructuring of the immediate family milieu. This type of programming does not change the institutional arrangement in society but merely increases the efficiency of goal attainment of groups in which mentally retarded or potentially mentally retarded persons belong. The third level of programming involves a rearrangement of the institutions in the society and the manner by which these institutions are integrated. The fourth kind of programming goes even further: it demands a change in the value system of the society. It is comprehensive in that it not only deals with particular sets of the population but with the entire structure of relationships in society. These four levels of programming are discussed below.

EFFECTIVE USE OF RESOURCES

The first level of programming involves the utilization and allocation (and often the diffusion) of resources. It is concerned with increasing the efficiency of institutional arrangements dealing with socialization and personal development. The various institutions include preschools for populations in which the probability of mental retardation is high, as well as prenatal clinics, improvements in special education curricula, and sheltered workshops.

The recent increase in resources affecting the education of the mentally retarded is evidenced by the widespread diffusion of special classes. Perhaps just as important is the continual reduction of mentally retarded pupils per teacher. In 1948, there were 87,000 children in special classes served by about 5,000 teachers, or a ratio of 17.4 pupils per teacher. In 1963, the number of retarded children in public-school special classes rose to 390,000, while the number of teachers was 25,000, or a ratio of 15.6 children per special-class teacher.[2] Thus a major consequence of the increased allocation of funds in special education is a decrease in the size of classes for mentally retarded children.

In such states as California, which expanded rapidly in the postwar years, the enrollment of children in classes for the educable mentally retarded quadrupled in the 1948–1958 decade. There were only 7,500 pupils in special classes for the educable retarded in 1948–1949, but by 1958–1959 the number had jumped to 29,900. Enrollment in special classes for the educable retarded in California has continued to rise. By 1963–1964, there were 48,000 educable pupils enrolled. By far the greatest diffusion of special classes for the educable retarded in California in the 1954–1964 decade occurred in the spread of high school practice for the educable mentally retarded. In 1954–1955, there were only 3,000 pupils enrolled in high school classes for the educable. By 1963–1964 there were 11,000.[3]

The growth in special classes for trainable mentally retarded children is comparable to that for the educable mentally retarded. In California, where there were only 33 classes for trainable children in 1952–1953, the number had risen to 546 in 1965–1966.

The diffusion of educational programs for the mentally retarded has resulted in part from the enactment of laws in the various states to attain the educational goals that are currently in vogue. This goal is "free education for all children."[4] The President's Panel on Mental Retardation has noted that "many state institutions guarantee each child the right to basic educational opportunities at public expense. These mandates do not specifically exclude children because of physical or mental handicapping conditions."[5]

GOAL ATTAINMENT: THE FAMILY

A second level of programming pertains to the families of individuals who are retarded or potentially retarded. The hope here is that, by providing an adequate social and cultural milieu, the society can integrate the individual into the public culture. Adult education in child-rearing, providing the parents with marital counseling and occupational therapy, casework intervention in family and kinship relations, providing a housekeeper or temporary institutionalization constitute the kinds of services connected with this program for remediation and care. Of course, remediation through influencing goal attainment in families with severely retarded children would differ from that in families with educable, mildly retarded members.

The ordinary goals of family life tend to be impeded by the presence of a severely mentally retarded child. The research on family relationships reviewed earlier in this book indicates the presence of emotional problems for parents and siblings, as well as interference with their upward social mobility. Both the parents' group movement and social welfare agencies have been concerned with the retarded child's effect on the family. Most often this concern has been with the creation of problems in mental health. However, one of the major goals in family life in the United States is "giving the children a start in life." Family counseling might then concern itself with the effects of the retarded child upon the father's occupational advancement and the siblings' educational plans. Not all the effects of the retarded child would be in the direction of interfering with social mobility; conceivably he might spur some families on to greater efforts. The father may immerse himself in his work in order to avoid family problems, the parents may expect greater academic achievement by the normal children, and they may decide to avoid having additional children.

With regard to educable retarded persons, other kinds of reforms have been suggested to enable families to attain their goals. These reforms have included the institution of an annual minimum income, occupational and academic training for low-income parents, assistance by welfare agencies in job-getting and keeping, and the development of programs to keep married couples and children together. One of the frequent proposals involves the strengthening of the role of males in the lower-class family, generally directed toward Negro families. The rationale is that the presence of powerful and stable male figures in the family will provide role models for children, a stable and adequate income, a basis for upward social mobility, and an opportunity for extensive interaction in a nuclear family based on affection and security. Generally, the intention is that by strengthening family relationships, and especially the role of the father as an "instrumental leader," the family members can be integrated more easily into the major economic, political, and educational institutions of the society.[6]

REVISION OF INSTITUTIONAL ARRANGEMENTS

The third level of programming is concerned with the integration of institutions in society. Sometimes this revision is accomplished by creating new institutions. New programs for the severely retarded might include public guardianship and community centers for the aged, adolescent, or infant retarded. This remediation is intended to take place not only through an educational program but also through the development of norms and other institutional devices which provide a life interest in or solve some of the basic problems pertaining to severe mental retardation.

The community center for the severely mentally retarded proposed by Kirk, Karnes, and Kirk provides an example of the institutional arrangements that can be introduced. As proposed, the center would have several units, each one associated with an outside agency. The units would include residential arrangements, a day school, consultation, and a sheltered workshop.

The residential unit would serve several purposes. First, it could provide a half-way house for individuals moving from a state hospital or residential institution to a home in the community. It could ease the adjustment of the individual as he enters the job market and tries to reestablish social relationships in the community. The residential unit could also serve individuals waiting for placement in a state hospital, thereby reducing the pressure in the home and easing the retarded individual's adjustment to hospitalization. A third function of the residential unit would be to provide temporary residence in case of family emergency.

The day-school unit of the community center for the mentally retarded would serve both those children living at home and those in the residential unit. It would have connections with both state hospital systems and the local schools. The school programs would be geared to the needs of trainable or severely mentally retarded children.

The consultation unit would offer families with retarded individuals information and advice pertaining to hospitalization, welfare services, diagnostic and medical services, and childrearing. This unit would act both as a referral agency and as a counseling unit.

The sheltered workshop unit in the Kirk, Karnes, and Kirk community center would provide an economically productive life for older trainable retarded individuals living at home. It should also have a vocational guidance program for graduates of classes for the educable mentally retarded. Kirk, Karnes, and Kirk include as part of the sheltered workshop unit a recreational center. Possibly this center would provide the most important functions for the retarded individuals. In addition to the arts and crafts activities usually associated with a recreational center, it might also provide the mentally retarded individuals with a variety of experiences regarding dating, the organization of social events such as dances or plays, and a sense of community.[7]

Changes in the integration of institutions which might affect the life chances of the mildly retarded are many and complex. These reforms concern modifications in social institutions, so that role failure in one institution does not imply failure in another. Sarason and Gladwin have suggested that the individual who has been labeled as mentally retarded in school may later attain some success in occupation and marriage.[8] However, Duncan's research indicates that the school acts as an intervening condition in relating the family (as the locus of retarded intellectual development) to occupational achievement. The situation is complicated further by the existence of ethnic background as a prior condition to the family. In attempting to eliminate the correlations between those phenomena which inhibit life chances, it would be necessary to break down the mutual influences among ethnic group membership, family organization, schooling, and occupation.[9] The reforms implied in revising the effects of the integration of social institutions on the life chances of persons actually or potentially labeled mentally retarded pertain to the guarantee of civil rights, broadly conceived.

The interaction between ethnic group membership, family organization, schooling, and occupation has been modified in recent years. The effect of ethnic group membership on assortive mating has been undergoing change both legally and in practice. Whereas, prior to the 1954 Supreme Court decision, a majority of the states forbade marriage between Negroes (and other nonwhites) and Caucasians, by 1967 all statutes prohibiting inter-racial marriage were either repealed or declared unconstitutional. In practice, the fading of ethnic group boundaries (among Caucasians) in their ability to define a field of eligible potential mates has been more rapid than the erasure of racial boundaries. Generally, research on assortive mating indicates that the trend in the United States is toward the "universal availability" of persons as potential marriage partners.[10] The relationship between ethnic group membership and schooling is also being modified. The recent efforts in preschool programs, compensatory education, programs for actual and potential school dropouts, and postschool training have as their main goals reducing the effects of the private cultures of Negroes, Puerto Ricans, southern Caucasians of rural origin, and other slum ethnic groups. Similarly, the entire organization of the Catholic educational system in the United States is being revised to stimulate schooling among Roman Catholics. At the same time, fair employment acts and nondiscrimination policies are aimed at reducing the relationship between ethnic group membership and occupation. This anti-ethnic revolution has as its end the incorporation of numerous populations with well-developed private cultures into the public culture.

The same reforms that are reducing the effects of ethnic group membership in social participation also minimize the disabling influences of family disorganization on schooling and occupational life. If compensatory education is successful, it will eliminate the current correlations between such variables as educational achievement and the presence of the father in the home, the amount of communication between parents and children, or the presence of literary materials in the home.

Yet, even if these programs are successful, the social functions of the surplus population will persist in maintaining (a) the rational, competitive system for selecting personnel; (b) the ameliorative industries; and (c) social classes. This analysis suggests that although a revision of the integration of social institutions may change the composition of the organizationally surplus population, the role played by this population ensures the continued existence of "the other America."[11]

CHANGES IN VALUES

The fourth level of program development requires a basic change in the values of the society. This change is predicated on the proposition that personal growth, rather than institutional efficiency, should be the major criterion for participation in the social, political, economic, and educational institutions in society. This program would be a comprehensive strategy to incorporate the surplus population into the major institutions and public cultural patterns in the society; to be effective, it requires a profound modification of the social structure.

The relationship between the value system and the treatment of surplus populations is suggested by Oscar Lewis' discussion of the culture of poverty. Lewis notes that the culture of poverty is an adaptation of the lumpenproletariat to their hopeless condition. People with a culture of poverty have strong feelings of marginality and helplessness, as well as of dependence and inferiority; Lewis associates this culture with capitalistic society. The elimination of the culture of poverty consequently requires a change in the political and economic structure of society. Lewis writes:

> On the basis of my limited experience in one socialist country—Cuba—and on the basis of my reading, I am inclined to believe that the culture of poverty does not exist in socialist countries. I first went to Cuba in 1947 as a visiting professor for the State Department. At that time I began a study of a sugar plantation in Melena del Sur and of a slum in Havana. After the Castro Revolution I made my second trip to Cuba as a correspondent for a major magazine, and I revisited the same slum and some of the same families. The physical aspect of the slum had changed very little, except for a beautiful new nursery school. It was clear that the people were still desperately poor, but I found much less of the despair, apathy, and hopelessness which were so diagnostic of urban slums in the culture of poverty. They expressed great confidence in their leaders and hoped for a better life in the future. The slum itself was now highly organized, with block committees, educational committees, party committees. The people had a new sense of power and importance. They were armed and given a doctrine which glorified the lower class as the hope of humanity.[12]

Lewis does not imply that socialism is the only alternative to the retention of the lumpenproletariat under capitalism. He indicates that in societies based on caste or corporate kinship groups poverty does not have the degrading effects found in modern capitalist societies. Similarly, the Jews of Eastern Europe, although they were poverty-stricken, did not exhibit the major characteristics of the culture of poverty. Their tradition of literacy and learning, the tight organization of the community, and their sense of threat from outsiders precluded the development of the characteristics of the cultures of poverty described by Lewis.

Lewis' exposition points out a fundamental conflict between a system based on competitive values and attempts to integrate surplus populations in the major social institutions. The ambivalence in the treatment of the mentally retarded seems to be inherent in the structure of modern industrial society. The change in the value system would not only affect the handling of the mentally retarded but might contribute markedly to the prevention of retardation. It should be noted that the prevalence figures of mental retardation in Scandinavian countries and in the USSR are lower than those in the United States. Dunn and Kirk raise the question: "Could this be due to less cultural deprivation, more tax-supported medical services, and a lower rate of prematurity?"[13]

Naturally, the value-modification solution with regard to surplus populations is the most difficult to accomplish. The program most immediate and most amenable to manipulation is, however, the least successful. Just how serious we are in wanting to solve social problems relating to surplus populations (in particular the mentally retarded) will determine exactly how much effort and sacrifice we are willing to undergo in order to revise modern society.

NOTES

[1] Talcott Parsons, "An Outline of the Social System," in Talcott Parsons, Edward Shils, Kaspar D. Naegele, and Jesse R. Pitts, eds., *Theories of Society* (New York: Free Press, 1961), pp. 30–79.

[2] Computed from data in Romaine P. Mackie, "Spotlighting Advances in Special Education," *Exceptional Children,* 32 (October, 1965), pp. 77–81; and U.S. Office of Education, *Statistics of Special Education for Exceptional Children: Biennial Survey of Education in the United States, 1952–1954* (Washington, D.C.: Department of Health, Education and Welfare, 1954).

[3] California Department of Education, *Programs for the Educable Mentally Retarded in California Public Schools* (Sacramento: Superintendent of Public Instruction, March, 1965).

[4] California Department of Education, *Programs for the Trainable Mentally*

Retarded in California Public Schools (Sacramento: Superintendent of Public Instruction, 1966), p. 3.

[5] President's Panel on Mental Retardation, *Report of Task Force on Law,* Washington, D.C., 1963, p. 10.

[6] See, for example, Daniel P. Moynihan, "Employment, Income, and the Negro Family," *Daedalus,* 94 (Fall, 1965), pp. 745–770; Martin Deutsch, "Minority Group and Class Status as Related to Social and Personality Factors in Scholastic Achievement," *The Society for Applied Anthropology,* Monograph #2, 1960; Michael Lewis, "Competence and the American Racial Dichotomy: A Study in the Dynamics of Victimization," unpublished doctoral dissertation, Princeton University, 1967.

[7] Samuel A. Kirk, Merle B. Karnes, and Winifred B. Kirk, *You and Your Retarded Child* (New York: Macmillan, 1955).

[8] Richard Masland, Seymour Sarason, and Thomas Gladwin, *Mental Subnormality* (New York: Basic Books, 1958), pp. 303–304. At present, there are no empirical data to indicate the conditions under which this occupational and marital success may occur.

[9] Otis Dudley Duncan, "Discrimination Against Negroes," *Annals of the American Academy of Political and Social Science,* 371 (May, 1967), pp. 85–103. See also O. D. Duncan, "Intelligence and Achievement: Further Calculations," unpublished papers, April and July, 1966.

[10] See Bernard Farber, *Family: Organization and Interaction* (San Francisco: Chandler, 1964), pp. 103–184.

[11] Cf. Michael Young, *The Rise of the Meritocracy, 1870–2033* (London: Thames and Hudson, 1958). (Penguin Books, 1961.)

[12] Oscar Lewis, *La Vida* (New York: Random House, 1966), p. xlix.

[13] Lloyd M. Dunn and Samuel A. Kirk, "Impressions of Soviet Psycho-Educational Service and Research in Mental Retardation," *Exceptional Children,* 29 (March, 1963), p. 301.

INDEX OF NAMES

INDEX OF SUBJECTS